AF305027

Demystifying Madrasah And Deobandi Islam

LEGACY AND HISTORY OF DARUL ULOOM DEOBAND

Asad Mirza

Vitasta

Published by

Renu Kaul Verma

Vitasta Publishing Pvt Ltd

4348/4C, Ansari Road, Daryaganj

New Delhi - 110 002

info@vitastapublishing.com

ISBN: 978-81-19670-76-5

© Asad Mirza

First Edition 2024

MRP ₹595

Editor: Dr A.D. Gnanagurunathan
Typeset & Cover Design by Rohit Gautam
Printed by Vikas Computer and Printers, New Delhi

*Dedicated to the everlasting memory of Shāh Waliullah Dehlavi,
Maulana Muhammad Qasim Nanautavi, Maulana Rashid
Aḥmad, Maulana Husain Ahmad Madani*

and

*My Grandfather, Hafiz Abdul Aziz Mirza
And Maternal Grandfather, Shah Mushir Uddin Usmani Nadwi*

Contents

Acknowledgments

I am highly indebted to Maulana Wahiduddin Khan (Late), Maulana Abu Qasim Nomani, Maulana Arshad Madani, Maulana Asrarul Haq Qasmi (Late), Maulana Mahmood Madani, Maulana Syed Rabey Hasani Nadwi (Late), Maulana Saeed-ur Rehman Azmi, Prof Akhtar-ul Wasey, Maulana Rashid Kandhalwi, Maulana Kahlid Saifullah Rahmani, Ajay Upadhyay, John Butt, Prof Ebrahim Moosa, Maulana Sufiyan Qasmi, Maulana Nadeemul Wajedi, Dr Waris Mazhari and Dr Faheem Akhtar Nadvi, all of whom accepted my request for an interview and enlightened me on different aspects and history of Darul Uloom, Deoband, in lengthy and insightful sessions between 2015 to 2022.

Prologue

During the last 15 years or so I have visited *Darul Uloom*, Deoband, numerous times. Based on my personal interaction with the faculty and students there and the leaders of *Jamiat Ulema-i Hind* in New Delhi, I have always wondered about the incorrect reporting on *Darul Uloom* or any incident involving a *madrasah* being referred as a *Deobandi Madrasah*. It set me pondering over the underlying reason and its prevalence, particularly in the West, and this is one of the foremost reasons for writing this book.

The book also tries to bring out the history and ideology of Shah Waliullah, which influenced philosophically the pioneer *Ulema* of Deoband to a large extent. The chapters have been designed to integrate and contextualise the contemporary political and cultural situation of Islam in India, while placing them in a historical perspective.

This book tries to bring out the unique character of *Darul Uloom*, its founders, the dominant Muslim thought of those times i.e. *Fikr-e Waliullahi*, contribution of its founders to the national freedom struggle, how *Darul Uloom* shaped up in the subcontinent after the Independence of India. The spread of *Darul Uloom* in different counties, how the Western media viewed it through a misleading prism and declared it to be the spring of terrorism worldwide.

In the last 20 years or perhaps since the concept of clash of civilisations occupied the mental space of our rulers and administrators, reams have been devoted to the question as to what is a *madrasah*. But, unfortunately no one has tried to analyse the main perception of a *madrasah* in true Islamic sense, or even if they had tried to, the result was half-baked. Now, since the West was more concerned about the Taliban and its links with *Deobandis*, an effort should have been made to research, analyse and then offer some interpretation of what a true *Deobandi Madrasah* is. Perhaps, as most of the writers were from the West, they were unsuccessful in incorporating the basic ethos or mental make-up of someone living in the Indian subcontinent. Moreover, many had inaccurate frameworks to study them. The fundamental issue, when dealing with *Deobandi madaris* (plural of madrasah), is that one has to analyse the situation prevailing in India before the power was in Muslim hands and thereafter. The *Deobandi* leaders were born and brought up in Indian ethos and culture and their thoughts were shaped by true Islamic tenets. They were able to synthesise the two with the prevailing situation and came out to lay the foundation of an institution, premised on the Islamic principles but also taught about coexistence and tolerance, even when these words were not part of the common vocabulary. My effort through this book is to draw out those salient features of this great institution.

It has been my privilege to enjoy a good relationship with the leading *Ulema* of *Darul Uloom* and *Jamiat* such as Maulana Asad Madani and his son Maulana Mahmood Madani and other leaders of *Darul Uloom*. Perhaps, this close relationship with them was due to the influence of my paternal and maternal grandfathers and their blessings. My grandfather Hafiz Abdul Aziz Mirza Amrohvi was an alumnus of *Darul Uloom,* Amroha, and a very close confidante of the Late Maulana Abrarul Haq Saheb of Hardoi, while my maternal grandfather Shah Mushir Uddin Usmani (descendent of Bandagi Miyan RA of Amethi, Lucknow) received his *Fazilat* degree from *Nadwa-tul Ulema*, Lucknow, as a student of the revered Hazrat Maulana Syed Abul Hasan Ali Hasani Nadwi RA. It was perhaps a result of their blessings that I was granted easy access to the leading scholars of Muslim thought in India and the warm welcome and cooperation, which I received from them, compelled me to undertake this book, a project which started in 2018 and finished in 2023.

I wish that after reading this book, the readers will realise the real essence of *Darul Uloom* and its leaders and project it in a more positive and real manner.

Asad Mirza
asad.mirza.nd@hotmail.com

Darul Uloom, Deoband
An Introduction

The town of Deoband, about 40 kms before Saharanpur, used to be a dusty, sleepy town like many others in western Uttar Pradesh, surrounded by lush green sugarcane fields and mango orchards.

Travel to Deoband by road used to be a back breaking journey touching four to five hours, even though it is only 177 kms away from the national capital New Delhi. However, liberalisation and the focus on highway development has brought winds of change, both to the city and the world famous institute situated there. The city has become nearer to Delhi, thanks to the upgradation of a state highway, and now boasts of a new flyover, arching over the city.

Earlier, *tonga* (horse driven carriage) or cycle rickshaws used to be the main modes of transport in the town, but now the narrow lanes are crowded by e-rickshaws, full of passengers clad in white *kurta-payjama* and skull caps, and flowing black *burqas*, from the slits of which you can even spot a jeans clad leg, and *maulvis* in their trimmed or flowing beards and *sherwanis* hurtling around town on motorcycles or scooters.

In the city, near the *Darul Uloom's* campus you will find institutes inviting you to join spoken English or computer courses, shops selling religious books maintain their inventory and sales on a computer, and ATM machines of different banks greet you at every nook and corner of the campus and the city. An impression is conveyed that the city and the institute have moved along with the times.

Darul Uloom, meaning the 'house of learning' is based in this tiny city called Deoband. It is in consonance with the Indian tradition of identifying institutes or objects or even persons with a link to their city of origin, being made part of their name like Moradabadi utensils, which are made in Moradabad, poet Firakh Gorakhpuri who was born in Gorakhpur. The people and institutes of Deoband like the *Darul Uloom* came to be known as *Deobandi*, a term which has been accepted and recognised globally, and has become synonymous with *Darul Uloom* and its graduates, academics and philosophy. Though officially, most of the graduates of the *Darul Uloom* use 'Qasmi' as their surname, to denote that they have studied at *Darul Uloom*.

The founders of *Darul Uloom* or the people associated with establishing the *Darul Uloom* movement are identified as the *Deobandi* leaders, who see themselves as followers of an academic tradition, based on orthodox Sunni Islam. Though the institution's name established at Deoband was *Darul Uloom*, but in practical parlance, the institute, the thoughts of its teachers and leaders are usually referred to as *Deobandi*. Similarly, throughout the book *Deobandi* is used to denote the institution, the people associated with it and the thought or *Fikr* of the institute.

The word *Darul Uloom* is applied to that teaching institution where higher education of all rational and traditional sciences is imparted and a body of expert teachers may be present to complete the students' education. Thus, the words *Darul Uloom, Deobandi* or *Deoband* and university are synonymous. *Darul Uloom* grew out of the Islamic academic tradition of medieval Persia, Arabia and Mughal India, and it considers its visionary forefather to be Shah Waliullah Dehlavi, the celebrated Indian Islamic scholar and thinker of the 18th century.

Nowadays, referring to these graduates as *Deobandi* has also become prevalent. This usage has also led to describing anyone associated with *Darul Uloom's* philosophy or activities as a *Deobandi*, which to a large extent is a misnomer.

The Princeton Encyclopedia of Islamic Political Thought[1] describes the *Deobandi* movement as that which emerged from religious schools and institutions, devoted to the purist religious tradition associated with *Darul Uloom*, an Islamic school. *Darul Uloom* while considered traditional and orthodox today, originally represented a modern approach, emulating British colleges with its fixed curriculum, salaried teachers, regular class schedules, and hostel facilities. Its founders wanted to continue the tradition of Shah Waliullah, who had sought to cleanse South Asian Islam of local customs. In their view, British rule had undermined Islamic religious laws and learning in India.

Deoband became not just the name of an institution but of a particular orientation towards religious knowledge and the method of its transmission, and came to signify commitment to a particular legal methodology and style of institutionalised spirituality. As Prof Barbara Metcalf puts it,

The *Ulema* and their schools were *Deobandi*. Increasingly, the name of Deoband came to represent a distinct style, a *maslak*, of Indian Islam.[2] *Ulema* were, and continue to be, defined as *Deobandi* because of their association with *Darul Uloom*, Deoband, having studied in the school, one of its affiliated *madrasah*, or any *madrasah* modeled after it, and because of their commitment to traditionalism, and in particular the legal and spiritual orientation fostered at the institution.

Spannaus (2018) in his paper *Darul Uloom Deoband and South Asian Islam* opines that *Deobandi* Islam is a significant religious movement in South Asia and globally, and it exists both as a network of institutions – Islamic schools – and as a religious orientation. The two cannot be easily separated; Deoband began as a single school devoted to a particular understanding of correct Islamic practice and knowledge, which forms the *Deobandi maslak* (path/philosophy), distinct from other Indian Muslim groups.[3]

Masooda Bano is of the view that within South Asia, as well as among the South Asian Muslim diaspora in the West, Deoband represents the most influential Islamic scholarly tradition. In Pakistan, India and Bangladesh, which together host close to 500 million Muslims, the largest number of *madrasahs* belongs to the *Deobandi* school of thought.[4]

In the aftermath of the first war of Independence in 1857, the *Deobandi* school of Islam was founded in the later half of the nineteenth century. It was part of a series of revivalist movements that were sweeping British India. After the 1857 revolt against the British colonialists, Muslims in British India were the primary targets of the ensuing British crackdown, as the revolt was fought under the titular leadership of the Mughal emperor. As part of the crackdown, the British occupied religious sites and institutes in Delhi, the capital of the Mughal Empire for several centuries. Muslim clerics in Delhi enjoyed the patronage of the Mughals, but this changed once the British occupied the city. The last Mughal emperor was exiled to Rangoon, Burma, and the British occupied the mosques in Delhi. Consequently, many *Ulema* (religious clerics, plural of *Alim – an Islamic scholar*) had to migrate to various locations, such as the northern Indian town of Deoband, to preserve their religious life and culture.

Foundation of Darul Uloom

In 1866, *Darul Uloom* was founded in the town of Deoband as one of the first major seminaries to impart education in theology of Sunni Islam. In addition to being close to other Muslim cultural centres in northern India, the founders of *Darul Uloom* believed that the decision to establish the seminary had divine sanction.

Elucidating the factors responsible for the establishment of *Darul Uloom*, leading Islamic scholar and commentator, Maulana Asrarul Haq Qasmi, former MP Lok Sabha and founder of All India Talimi-wa Milli Foundation said:

'Before 1857 the situation in the country started deteriorating vastly and even the attacks on *madaris* started mainly in western UP. Secondly, an attempt to impose an alien culture also started. In this background a team of *Ulema* gathered, and guided by the teachings of Shah Waliullah started a new movement and *Darul Uloom* is the result of transformation of Shah's thoughts and teachings. Perhaps, he was also the first Islamic theologian who introduced the concept of tolerance and willed that every Muslim could follow his own *Maslak* (school of *Shariah*) but work unitedly against the enemy, which for his time was a revolutionary thought.'

The reference to tolerance here, in Maulana Asrarul's statement means that an effort was made to evolve a system of imparting *Sunni* Islamic theological studies which should not antagonise other sub-sects or communities within the Islamic fold and also to form an association with or collaborate with other religions in the country to forge an alliance against the colonial rulers.

'So when *Darul Uloom* was established, its first task was to introduce and educate people about Islam, and ensure that the Muslims themselves should study Holy *Qur`an* and *Hadeeth* in depth, so they could explain the religion through reasoning and inference (istidlal) to others. The foremost aim of establishing the *Darul Uloom* was to provide guidance, to the wider populace of India. The founders of *Darul Uloom* aimed at establishing a centre of excellence, which would guide the lay Muslims on religious issues besides providing them a way forward to integrate with other communities in the country. The *Darul Uloom's* founders were aware that with crumbling of the Muslim state structure, there was a need to establish a big centre of learning which could guide the smaller institutions and the followers. Thirdly, due to their astute understanding of the political conditions of the day, they wanted to establish a centre, which will be able to bring different communities in India together, to fight against the colonial rulers,' added Maulana Asrarul.

Mohammed Baber (1943) in his article *Role of Ulema-e-Deoband in the Independence Movement* wrote:

'Despite having a "traditional" approach to the Islamic Sciences, the *Darul Uloom* was a very modern institution.

It was run by professional and paid staff, students were admitted for fixed periods of study, examinations were held at the end of the year, and certificates presented upon graduating and financial contributions came from the public, instead of relying on government grants or patrons.'[5]

Maulana Asrar was also of the view that the Indian *Ulema* worked shoulder to shoulder with other religionists to free India from the colonial rule. That is the reason why *Sheikh-ul Hind* Maulana Mahmood Hasan supported Gandhian philosophy and not the revolutionary ideals of Netaji Subhash Chandra Bose. So the *Ulema* did not choose violence even during the freedom struggle, this was and is a unique style of *Darul Uloom's* leaders.

The British Government had crushed majority of the rebellion and resistance to its colonial rule across India. Therefore, the *Ulema* gathered at Deoband and created a safe haven for those who were still committed to preserving Islam and resisting the British occupation. Once they gathered and organised, they began to develop a plan not only to build a resistance, but also preserve and spread Islamic teachings in the subcontinent.

Khursheed Alam Dawood Qasmi (2012) in his article *Role of Darul Uloom Deoband in India's Freedom Struggle* wrote that *Sheikh-ul Hind* Maulana Mahmood Hasan issued a *Fatwa* making it the duty of all Indian Muslims to support Mahatma Gandhi (1869-1948) and the Indian National Congress, and participate in their non-cooperation and mass civil disobedience movements through non-violence. Maulana died on 30 November 1920, wishing to get martyrdom for India's freedom. Though *Sheikh-ul Hind* was no more, he left a good number of students, who followed the footprint of their elders or leaders and worked tirelessly for the freedom of India.[6]

The *Deobandi* movement became the most popular school of Islamic thought not just in India but in the subcontinent too e.g. among Pashtuns living on both sides of the Durand Line. Many prominent Pashtun community leaders established *Deobandi* seminaries in these areas. Khan Abdul Ghaffar Khan, a prominent Pashtun leader, was instrumental in establishing several schools based on *Deobandi* curriculum in the Pashtun belt.[7]

A point to note here is that given Deoband's official position of not engaging in politics, the *Ulema* of Deoband founded the *Jamiat Ulema-e-Hind* (JUH) in 1919, a socio-cultural organisation of Indian Muslims. JUH also represented the Muslims in the political arena and was a key ally of the Indian National Congress during the freedom struggle of the country.[8]

The training of *Ulema* and the study pattern at *Darul Uloom* was modelled on a variety of British institutions whose effectiveness had been witnessed by the *Ulema*. The founders of *Darul Uloom* knew such institutions well. Many of them were in government service previously, including three former Deputy Inspectors of the Education Department. Some had even studied at schools such as the Dilli College, and all of them confronted the influential missionary societies. While serving at these institutions, they learnt their methods and chose to compete with them on an equivalent footing. Two characteristics of the new institution – *Darul Uloom* were particularly striking: the participation of people with no kin ties amongst the administrators of the new institute and the system of popular financing.[9]

John Mohammed Butt, a British citizen, converted to Islam in the 1970s while living amongst Pashtuns in the border areas of Afghanistan. He has worked with BBC as a journalist earlier and currently runs a small radio station in Afghanistan. He says, that the decision to establish *Darul Uloom* in the late 1800s was based on two approaches adopted to deal with the Britishers after the rout of Indian nationalists in 1857. The first was the Deoband approach, which resigned to the fact that they cannot defeat the British, and by establishing a fortress of classic Islamic knowledge, they could at least save their religion, which the British were unlikely to encroach. The other was Aligarh, and although they reached a similar conclusion regarding their inability to overthrow the British, they decided to embrace modern and Islamic sciences in a modern milieu. Both of them were valid.

John is of the view that founders of *Darul Uloom* considered themselves the inheritors of Shah Waliullah's tradition.

Founding Principles of the Darul Uloom

The core principles which guided the *Ulema* of *Darul Uloom* were:

1. *Tawheed* (the indivisible oneness or concept of monotheism in Islam i.e. Allah is one)
2. *Sunnah* (sayings and practices of the Prophet Mohammad (PBUH-peace be upon him))
3. *Ittibaa'us Sahaabah wa Hubbuhum* (following and loving the Prophet's companions)
4. *Taqleedul Madhaahib fil Fiqh* (following a juristic school of thought)

5. *Jihad fi Sabeel-illah* (the combat or the spiritual struggle within oneself for Allah's appeasement or against sin to appease Allah)

If a survey is done of the academic, religious, communal and political history of the past one hundred and fifty-three years in the subcontinent, it will be clear how the eminent *Ulema* of the *Darul Uloom*, Deoband, have discharged the most important obligation of preserving the Holy Book (The *Qur`an*) and the *Sunnah* (precedents set by the Prophet-PBUH). The glorious services they have rendered in this regard are undoubtedly *sui generis*.

Darul Uloom was perhaps the first institution, which successfully established Islamic *madaris* through the cooperation and contributions of the common Muslims.

From the last decade of the thirteenth century *Hijri* (Muslim calendar), the *Darul Uloom*, Deoband, has been a cradle of Islamic arts and sciences and Islamic education and culture; it has held the position of the greatest Islamic educational centre in the country.

As such, whenever a problem arose in the country and the Muslims felt any difficulty, they automatically looked towards the *Darul Uloom*, Deoband. From its academic lap have risen such great *Ulema, Sheikhs* and men of accomplishments by whose academic and spiritual grace, no doubt, the whole of Asia continues to benefit.

The *Ulema* of Deoband have been honouring the duty of academic and religious guidance to the Muslims of the subcontinent for more than a century-and-a-half.

In older *madaris*, before the *Darul Uloom* came into existence, like the famous *Farangi Mahal* in Lucknow, family members taught students in their own homes or in a corner of a mosque. There was no central library, no course required for each student, no series of examinations. A student would seek out a teacher and receive a *sanad* (a certificate/degree), listing the books he had read and then move on to another teacher or return home. The *Ulema* who taught students in such a setting depended primarily on revenue from their royal endowments and on the largesse of princes whose courts they graced and for whom they trained government servants. Such During the Mughal Empire, such *Ulema* were part of the larger structure of a Muslim state.[10]

In context to the factors, which contributed to the *Darul Uloom's* establishment, Barbara D Metcalf (1980) in *Islamic revival in British India: Deoband*, wrote:

> 'For most of the *Ulema* the goal of their work was how to create, in any sphere available, a community both observant of detailed religious law and, to the extent possible, committed to a spiritual life as well. To do so was, in general terms, to return to the tradition of "the tongue and the pen" espoused by Shah Abdul Aziz. The *Ulema* in Muslim history have tended to oscillate between participation in the state and the exercise of independently based local leadership. The North Indian *Ulema* in choosing the latter style, thus adopted a well-known strategy with historical precedent. Again echoing precedent, they made the *madrasah* the institutional basis of their work. Yet the new *madaris* were distinctive in their basis of support, their organisational style, and their goals. Their pattern was soon to be set by a school founded by Rasheed Ahmad, Mohammad Qasim and others in 1866 in a town called Deoband.'[11]

Maulana Wahiduddin Khan opined,

'The spiritual founder of *Darul Uloom* was Shah Waliullah and the practical founder was Maulana Mohammad Qasim Nanautavi. I think that during those days, for youngsters of illustrious families, their first option to study was *Darul Uloom*, which ultimately led to a fine crop of young educated and influential leaders graduating from *Darul Uloom*.'

Barbara Metcalfe further writes:

The *madrasah* began modestly in the old *Chattah Masjid* under a spreading pomegranate tree that still stands. The first teacher and the first pupil, in a coincidence deemed auspicious, were both named Mahmud: Mulla Mahmud, the teacher, and Mahmood Hasan, the pupil, who was later to become the school's most famous teacher. Despite the timeless atmosphere surrounding this cherished vignette of its inauguration, the school was unlike earlier *madaris*. Its founders, emulating the British bureaucratic style for educational institutions, in fact eschewed the informal pattern of education that the scene under the pomegranate conjures. The school was conceived as a distinct institution, not relegated to a wing of a mosque or a home and dependent on the parent institution. As soon as possible, it acquired classrooms and a central library. A professional staff ran it, and its students were admitted for a fixed course of study and required to take examinations for which prizes were awarded at a yearly convocation. Gradually, an informal system of affiliated colleges emerged. Many of the colleges were ultimately staffed by the school's own graduates, and their students were examined by visiting *Deobandis*. Financially, the school was wholly dependent on public contributions, mostly in the form of annual pledges, not on fixed holdings of *Waqf* or pious endowments contributed by noble patrons. The school was, in fact, so unusual that the annual printed report, itself an innovation, made continuing efforts to explain the organisation of the novel system.'[12]

In the world of Islam, particularly in the Muslim countries of Asia, the *Darul Uloom*, Deoband, currently occupies the position of a great centre of learning and gnosis. No other religious institution can challenge its religious eminence, educational culture and simple Islamic living. The graduates of Deoband have fanned out to many countries of the world and are rendering useful Islamic services; in fact these very graduates constitute the real history and are the wealth of the *Darul Uloom*, Deoband. By virtue of their education and accomplishments, these gentlemen command great positions. The glorious service they have rendered for the survival, strengthening and maintaining of Islamic knowledge and religious life in India is unparalleled. Sayyid Mohammad Al-Hasani (1963), the author of *Sirat-e Maulana Sayyid Mohammad Ali Monghyri*, writes:

'No sensible and just man can deny this reality that valuable help has been rendered to the maintenance, survival and stability of Islamic life in India by the graduates of the *Darul Uloom*, Deoband, fanning out to each and every corner of India, they have protected the pristine religion and kept it safe from innovation, interpolation and misconstruction (*ta'vil*); and whatever true Islamic beliefs, religious sciences, respect for the men of religion and true spiritualism that are seen in the country today, it (Deoband) has no doubt had a conspicuous and basic contribution to it.'[13]

Accomplishments of Darul Uloom

- Muslim Identity – Even before the end of Mughal rule, the Muslim identity had been eroding in India. Over time, Muslims had become influenced over time by the customs and culture of other religions around them; the British presence only worsened this situation. To counter this, a grassroots effort was initiated to revitalise and preserve the Islamic identity and necessary religious practices among the common populace.

- Islamic Education – Up until the British colonisation of the Indian subcontinent, Islamic education at both the basic and advanced levels was conducted in the classical model of seeking knowledge. After having dealt with an organised effort against not only Islamic education but also against the Islamic identity itself, coupled with the already deteriorating condition of the Muslims, the *Ulema* decided to organise and restructure the institutions and standard of Islamic education. Thus, the initiation of the *Darul Uloom* and the adoption of the *Dars-e Nizami* curriculum.

- Politics of the Subcontinent – Two phases:

  First Phase: During British colonialism – The *Ulema* participated in the nationalist movement led by the Congress party to oust the British from the subcontinent, and also floated platforms like *Jamiat Ulema-i-Hind* (JUH) in 1919 to be an active part of the political discourse of that time. (Detailed description of *Darul Uloom's* role in the freedom struggle of India given in Chapter 6) Second Phase: After Partition – After partition, the *Deobandi Ulema* have remained politically active in the subcontinent in their respective countries like Pakistan,

Afghanistan, and Bangladesh etc. They strive to give the Muslims a voice in their country's politics and represent Islamic interests in the law making and governing of their country. In India, though they have been active at a slightly lesser scale but have always been at the vanguard to safeguard Muslim interest or position on various issues of the community.

- Repudiating Deviant Sects – The *Deobandi* scholars have also been vigilant in refuting deviant sects and erroneous thoughts within Islam.

- Modern thought and *Hadeeth* rejection – It began with the erroneous interpretation of *Ahadeeth* (plural of *Hadeeth*) and criticism of *Sahabah* (companions of the Holy Prophet - PBUH), which developed into 'reason over obedience' thinking and eventually took the form of all-out *Hadeeth* rejection. But the *Ulema* of Deoband have been able to uphold the sanctity of *Ahadeeth* and its correct place in understanding various issues, which beset the Muslim community from time to time.

The *Deobandi* movement and particularly the *Darul Uloom* system were established to provide structure in areas of education and politics for the Muslims of the subcontinent. The emphasis was placed on *Hanafi Fiqh* (School of Islamic Law) because it was the *Fiqh* of the majority. Strict adherence to *Fiqh* was encouraged to create religious discipline in people who had been corrupted for centuries, as mentioned above, and who were now prey to new unorthodox ideologies. In addition, the memorisation of the Holy *Qur`an* has remained an integral part of the educational curriculum in *Deobandi* institutions.

The structure and simplicity of the educational system is that the *Darul Uloom* is based upon a remarkable and potent combination. It has been proven for over a century-and-a-half that it can produce efficient results. Likewise, it can be recreated anywhere, at any time with wondrous results.

The *Deobandi* thought in India, which in the West is often related to *Wahabism*, is a rather strange mix of not being puritanical or fanatical in a comprehensive sense as demanded by Abdul Wahab. Nor do they (*Deobandis*) go all out in favour of various activities of *Shirk* (the sin of practicing idolatry) and *Bidah* (innovation in religious matters), as espoused by the *Barelawi* Sect. Rather, *Deobandi* thought has been influenced by the Indian ethos and culture, while imbibing its plurality, and yet maintaining the pristine form of Islam. Thus, due to its Indian model, it has been seen favourably by extreme ideologies and syncretism. And the manner in which it has grown over the years and affected and guided millions of Muslims in India and across the world is an acknowledgement of its uniqueness and universality.

The same rationale could be attributed to the fact that in recent years, in spite of extremist Islamic ideologies being espoused by various scholars and organisations, the ordinary Indian Muslim has not fallen prey to their negative influences. We find only a miniscule percentage of Indian Muslims being radicalised, as compared to other countries, and even those who have been radicalised, do not have a base founded on *Deobandi* ideals or have any association with the institute. Besides, some of them have been able to quickly see through the real designs and activities of their new leaders and have abandoned the path of radicalism or extremism.

The Constitution of the Darul Uloom and Its Eight Principles

At the time when the *Darul Uloom* at Deoband, was established, the old *madaris* in India had become almost extinct, and the condition of surviving the ravages of time was bleak. Under these circumstances, Maulana Nanautavi and his fellow *Ulema* sensed the imminent danger for the Muslim community. They knew only too well that nations have attained their rightful status solely through knowledge. So, without depending upon the government of the day, they founded the *Darul Uloom*, Deoband, with public contributions and co-operation. One of the principles that *Hujjat-ul-Islam* Maulana Muhammad Qasim Nanautavi proposed for the *Darul Uloom* and other religious *madaris* was that the *Darul Uloom* should be run trusting in Allah and with public contributions for which the masses alone should be relied upon.

In this constitution, Maulana Nanautavi has shown that the following eight principles should be the fundamentals for the establishment of seminaries, known as *Usool-e-Hashtaghana*[14]:

(1) The first fundamental is that the functionaries of the *madrasah*, as far as possible, should always heed the augmentation of the donations for the institute. 'Make an effort and also persuade others to do the same'.

(2) The well-wishers of the *madrasah*, as far as they can, should endeavour for continuous supply of food to the students rather, than increasing the number of students.

(3) The counsellors of the *madrasah* should always bear in mind that the *madrasah* should acquire excellence, and no one should be unyielding. Opinions and counter-opinions were encouraged, but all decisions were to be made by consensus, upholding the institute's well-being and need, not that of any individual.

(4) It is necessary that all teachers be of the same *Mashrab* (thought or humour), and neither presumptuous like the other religious divines of the time nor insult each other. By this Maulana Nanautavi meant that all teachers should subscribe to the common *maslak* (A system of religious belief and worship, all *Deobandis* are referred to as believers in *Deobandi maslak* following *Hanafi* Islam) of *Darul Uloom* and there should be no rivalry or conflict amongst them on fundamental issues.

(5) The fixed syllabus already prescribed or to be prescribed later through some other deliberation, should always be completed; otherwise the *madrasah* will, firstly, not have good strength, and even if it does get good strength, it will be useless, as it may produce unworthy *Ulema*.

(6) So long as there are no regular means of income for the *madrasah*, it will go on like this, if it pleases Allah, provided we pin our faith in Him. This principle was coined in the belief that if there is an assured income for the institute, then the administrators may stop striving for funds from common people. And, if it so happens then it may also result in the institute becoming a centre of politics, subscribing to and upholding the views of the largest donor, which would be completely detrimental to the future of the institute. In short, a destitution of sorts should always be kept in mind.

(7) The participation of the government of the day, as also that of the affluent appears to be very harmful.

(8) The donation of such people who can afford as much as they can and do not expect fame from it seems to cause more prosperity (*Barakah*). On the whole, the donor's good faith appears to be the provision for greater durability.

Maulana Muhammad Tayyab Sahib has apothegmatically

elucidated these eight principles, which have been published in a separate pamphlet entitled *Azadi-e-Hind ka Eik Khamosh Rahnuma*[15]. In the first, second, sixth, seventh, and eighth clauses of this constitution, public donation has been specifically suggested as the substitute for endowments, and at the same time it has also been stressed that it is necessary to abstain from assured sources of income as otherwise hope and fear which are the real cause of appealing to Allah will be lost.

Prof W Cantwell Smith, Director of the Department of Islamic Studies, McGill University, Montreal, Canada, in his book, *Modern Islam in India* wrote, 'Next to the Al Azhar of Cairo, the *Darul Uloom* at Deoband is the most important and respected theological academy of the Muslim World.'[16]

Traditional leaders like Maulana Mahmud Hasan, Ubaidullah Sindhi and Maulana Husain Ahmad Madani, among the *Deobandis* showed some awareness of the fact that Islam's public discourse needed a cosmopolitan and socially relevant component. They reached for knowledge that advanced the common objective, even if they did not always succeed in providing an effective one. Maulana Mahmud Hasan was among the founders of the Jamia Millia Islamia, a university established in 1920, with the express purpose of furnishing Muslims with skills and knowledge that would be relevant to their practical life in the outside world. For them, engagement in the political sphere alongside people of other faiths enabled them to broaden Islamic theological horizon in the public sphere.

In essence, *Darul Uloom* and its leaders signified, first, what was best for the Muslims of India both religiously and politically and secondly, through *Darul Uloom* they put into practice what they preached. In essence *Darul Uloom* was established to guide the Indian Muslims in a new emerging politico-socio-cultural setup in the country. Its aim was not just to act as an educational institution, but also to act as the fount of knowledge and character building and churn out alumni, who will be educated and morally upright. They were supposed to guide their co-religionists not just on religious issues but also on how to become effective and useful citizens of India. The leaders amongst the alumni participated shoulder to shoulder in India's freedom struggle along with other Indians, and after independence, became a guide to their co-religionists, on all matters religious and spiritual.

History of Darul Uloom

Darul Uloom is not just a *madrasah*, but also a movement, a spiritual movement, a *fikr* or *soch* (thinking), an ideology, which is closely linked with this country's history. In fact, the history of *Darul Uloom* and India's freedom movement are so intertwined that an impartial study of any one is not possible in isolation.

The Mughal rule in India spanned approximately 800 years of Muslims as rulers, yet no Islamic system was established in India. Moreover, a large part of the populace was unaffected by the religion of the rulers, and this has been the history of this country.

Historically, the Islamic system of education in India could be traced back to 159 *Hijri* (776 CE). At that time, the number of Muslims was very low but they did not face any opposition in spreading their religion or to establish their educational institutes or even follow their own personal law.

If we have to describe any person or figure responsible for the Islamic renaissance in India during the 1860s, then it was Shah Waliullah. After finishing his studies, he came to a conclusion that first, in the country a situation was evolving, under which different religions were trying to establish their hegemony, which might lead to a change in the ruling class and also establishment of a culture which would destroy the tolerant fabric of this country. To counter this, he had two solutions; first the Muslims should prepare a new team, whose educational and spiritual guidance would be able to safeguard the community's well-being.

For the Muslims, the two tools available to guard themselves and their co-religionists were the Holy *Qur`an* and the *Ahadeeth*. A basic thought in Islam, as enunciated in the Holy *Qur`an* is that the path to establish religious supremacy is through peaceful not violent means: Secondly, love and compassion are needed to rule or change hearts. Therefore, a need was felt to build a team of such intellectuals who by the force of their academic and religious qualifications and thought process could safeguard the interests of their religion.

Darul Uloom's, current *mohtamim* (vice chancellor) Maulana Abul Qasim Nomani spelling out the turn of events responsible for its establishment says:

The religious *madaris* were operational in India before 1886 also. Both, Maulana Qasim Nanautavi and Maulana Rasheed Ahmed Gangohi received religious education from Shah Abdul Ghani Muhaddis and modern education under Maulana Mamlook Ali. This shows that at that time there were religious education institutes run by the family of Shah Waliullah and Arabic section of Dilli College offered study of all modern subjects, in Delhi. However, once the complete rule of the Britishers was established after 1857, they wanted to break the Muslims psychologically as they had snatched power from them. On the other hand, to impose their culture they targeted religious education and culture of the earlier rulers, so they targeted and destroyed all Islamic religious educational institutions and established new centres where missionaries were appointed to impart education. They also made it well known that by their bearing and appearance the students will be Indians but their mental make-up will be Westernised by imparting such education.'

The Muslim leaders of the time analysed that since they had lost the political power it had become incumbent upon them to preserve their religious heritage and in turn, start a mechanism to transfer it intact to the future generations.

Shah Abdul Aziz Muhaddis Dehlavi had issued a *Fatwa* saying that now the country has been enslaved, and we have to get the nation freed, which influenced all our past and present leaders, as they are followers of those very leaders, who issued such a *Fatwa*. Even *Sheikh-ul Hind* Maulana Mahmud Hasan, who was the first student at *Darul Uloom* in an article, wondered whether Maulana Nanautavi had laid down the foundation of *Darul Uloom* just for facilitating education. The answer is in negative. Right from the beginning, even in the very act of founding *Darul Uloom*, both the issues i.e. to get the nation freed and secondly, consolidate our culture and religion, were the foremost ideals present. And no one individual was responsible for this. *Deobandi* leaders, who were guided by the thought and vision of Shah Waliullah, devised this plan.

This plan had two elements, one, defensive and second, reactive. Both these were positive; one was to attain freedom and second was to preserve culture and religion. The foremost was the freedom of the nation.

Darul Uloom was established ten years after the end of the first war of independence, or after the defeat for the leaders of the revolt. But as attaining freedom for the country was the foremost thought amongst the founders of *Darul Uloom*, they focussed on education but also realised the futility of waging an armed struggle against the colonial forces. *Sheikh-ul Hind* realised that Muslims of the country will have to wage a struggle along with other communities and religions. As any lead taken by them would not have been acceptable to a lot of other communities, they decided to join the wider freedom struggle and even chose a leader from amongst the other religionists. Thus, *Jamiat Ulema* gave full support to Gandhiji and introduced him to the whole country at its own expenses, and supported all his movements like Non-Cooperation and Civil Disobedience Movement.

Senior Hindi journalist and former Editor of *Dainik Jagran* and *Amar Ujala* newspapers, Ajay Upadhyay while deciphering the historical records which spell out the historical facts leading to the establishment of *Darul Uloom*, opines:

'As far as I understand, I feel that the first freedom struggle of 1857 laid the foundation stone of *Darul Uloom*, as people who were defeated at the hands of the colonial rulers felt that a proper planning is needed to oust the Britishers from India. The period from 1850 to 1880 is also known as a dark phase of the Indian history, as many records from 1857 to 1880 are unavailable to enlighten us of the happenings during that period. The only references are from the British side, and only from 1885 onwards when the Indian National Congress was formed. In this dark phase, the biggest source of light was the establishment of *Darul Uloom* in 1886, and the biggest attributes of this endeavour was to present a progressive Islam, its practices, its rituals.'

Islamic scholar Maulana Noorul Hasan Rashid Kandhalvi delving on the reasons responsible for the establishment of *Darul Uloom*, comments:

'After 1857 the social, religious and educational systems of Muslims particularly in and around Delhi and Western Uttar Pradesh was totally destroyed. Furthermore, the religious leadership in Delhi and in this area was also completely destroyed, as most of them were killed by Britishers and some of the surviving ones either left India or migrated to other princely states. So the surviving *Ulema* of those times tried to resurrect the religious system with whatever meager resources they had. Its beginning was in the shape of a *maktab* (primary school) and with the passage of time it not only became a strong tree but assumed the shape of a university, as it grew from strength to strength. The founders of *Darul Uloom* were really influential and if they had not taken this bold step then nobody else would have even dared or dreamt of taking such an initiative for many years to come.'

Maulana Arshad Madani, President of *Jamiat Ulema-i-Hind (A)* says:

'The people who established Deoband were the followers of a special ideology. They were not just teachers confined to imparting knowledge inside a *madrasah*, neither they were those who would prefer to sit in a *khanqah* (shrine) and pray with a *tasbih* (rosary). They fundamentally had a set purpose, which was to get the country independent. They utilised all their energies to formulate a plan, which called for raising oneself above religious affiliations, and to bind them together on human grounds, to make the foreign power ineffective in its nefarious designs to continue to rule the country. This was the salient feature of what could be described as the *Deobandi* thought.'

Former President of Maulana Azad University, Jodhpur and a leading Islamic scholar, Prof Akhtar-ul Wasey commenting on the reasons responsible for establishing the *Darul Uloom* is of the view that,

'The Indians suffered a defeat in 1857 at the hands of the British imperialist and expansionist forces, that defeat was not just militarily, but it was socio-political, economic, educational etc., in sum in all walks of life. After 1857, when the imperial power was established in all fields, the most disastrous steps, which they took, were against the educational system of the Muslims. Till that time the Muslim educational system in India was inclusive and used to produce *maulvis, imams, qaris* and *muftis* alongside the bureaucrats, jurists, accountants etc. The new educational system established by the British, made a divide between religious and worldly education. In such a scenario, with just one teacher and one student, the Indian Muslims started a new *madrasah*. Later, this initiative became a movement and institution in the shape of *Darul Uloom*, Deoband. And today this institution is fondly referred to as the Al Azhar of India.'

As the political power was taken away from the Muslims,

the effort was on to at least secure the religious identity of the Muslims in India. Due to this, they gave primary importance to religious studies. Secondly, the eight principles to manage *Darul Uloom* were conceived and implemented by Maulana Qasim Nanautavi. In effect they got people influenced by the ideals of *Darul Uloom* and when students started graduating from *Darul Uloom*, they were asked to go back to their villages or towns to establish a *maktab* there, which resulted in the spread of the *Darul Uloom's* philosophy in every nook and corner of the country. As a result, the students who finished *maktab* studies were sent to *Darul Uloom* for higher studies, thus swelling the ranks of people who believed in the *Darul Uloom's* philosophy. In fact, they established satellite *maktabs* and *madaris* and later on, they were joined to the main grid. In other words, in the social structure of Indian Muslims, these *maktabs* became the peripheral nerves and *Darul Uloom* became the main nerve centre.

The establishment of *Darul Uloom* was a revolutionary idea to propagate religious education, and simultaneously, it also became replicable. If you go deeper to gauge the real aim of establishing *Darul Uloom*, then first it was to strengthen the religious belief and convictions of the Indian Muslims and secondly, to challenge the imperialist or colonialist forces in the country with other like minded sections of the society. Furthermore, the alumni of *Darul Uloom* were not just confined to India but were spread across Central Asian and other South Asian countries, too besides a large number of African countries. When they returned to their countries after finishing their studies, they took with them not just the religious concepts but the concepts of nationalism and independence also.

Barbara D Metcalf (1980) writes that,

> 'The *madrasah's* founders, emulating the British bureaucratic style for educational institutions, in fact eschewed the informal pattern of education that the scene under the pomegranate tree conjures up. The school was conceived of as a distinct institution, not relegated to a wing of a mosque or home or dependent on the parent institution. When the school was founded, *Deobandi* scholars were aware of the religious diversity within India, and they made an effort to engage in dialogue with India's non-Muslim population. In 1875 and 1876, for example, *Deobandi* scholars participated in religious debates with Christian and Hindu scholars. They jointly fought with non-Muslims against the British during India's colonial resistance, and they also participated in non-violent struggles against colonial rule'.[1]

At that time, even in Deoband town Hindus formed 62.7 per cent of the total population of approximately 452,000 people.[2] Yet, the seminary was established in a Hindu-dominated city, as there was no religious animosity between the two communities then. Moreover, during the initial period of *Darul Uloom's* establishment, Hindus reportedly contributed to its operating expenses also.[3]

The President of *Jamiat Ulema-i-Hind* and former MP-Rajya Sabha, Maulana Mahmood Madani says:

> 'I would like to say that *Darul Uloom* is representative of *Manhaj-e Waliullahi* (Shah Waliullah's philosophy). Before the establishment of *Darul Uloom*, a formal or uniform system of education was not there for Muslims, except maybe, one or two small institutions. *Darul Uloom* emerged as a

centre for formal education in a unified manner continuing with *Manhaj-e Waliullahi*. Another unique feature of *Darul Uloom*, since the beginning, was that it followed a middle path or a path of *Istidlal*. Or you can say that when we talk about sects, *Darul Uloom* has always maintained a distance, it is not in opposition to *Barelawi* sect or *Ghair-muqallid* sects. Both of these are hardliners in their belief but *Darul Uloom* has always maintained a path of moderation.'

Prof Ebrahim Moosa, Professor of Islamic Studies at the University of Notre Dame in his book, *What is a Madrasa?* observes that,

'The contemporary south Asian *madrasah* retains some features of ancient scholastic tradition that values the role of a master-teacher, embraces didactic texts, fosters hermeneutical skills, and imparts a core knowledge of foundational teachings in every discipline. Teaching ancient texts seems to yield a diminishing harvest for students today given the gap between style and presentation of classical authors and the contemporary sensibilities of readers. A history of the authors, their texts, and social contexts as well as the features of the texts might instill a greater appreciation. The motivation of scholarly rivalry and varieties of scholarship only enhances and deepen an understanding of the various disciplines.'[4]

In essence *Darul Uloom* was set up as a centre for reawakening and guiding the Muslim populace of India, as per the norms laid down in the Holy *Qur`an* and the *Hadeeth*. Its purpose was not only to guide on religious matters but also on matters pertaining to the social and economic lives of the Muslims. It started functioning during a turbulent period of Indian history when Indians of all hues and shades were suffering under the clutches of colonial rule. *Darul Uloom* forged alliances with the nationalist forces and continued to fight the colonial rule shoulder to shoulder with the rest of the Indians. In the process, *Darul Uloom* became the guiding light for Muslims not just in India but in the entire Indian subcontinent and also amongst the countries under the British colonial rule or its enemies like the African and middle eastern countries and Turkey, which was the leading Islamic nation of that era, and was the thorn in the flesh of the British colonial empire and whose downfall was their prime target during the WW I, as later events proved. However, it continued to be a beacon of light for majority of *Sunni* schools throughout the world.

Shah Waliullah Dehlavi
The Patron Saint of Darul Uloom

The *Deobandi Ulema* in their actions and thought were guided largely by the philosophy of Shah Waliullah Dehlavi *(Rahmatullah Allaih-RA)* or *Fikr-e Waliullahi* (philosophy of Waliullah), as evident from the comments in the earlier chapter by different Islamic and *Deobandi* scholars. It is pertinent to note that Indian Muslims by and large are guided by the spiritual and worldly thoughts and philosophy of this Holy Saint now. He is also referred to as father of the Islamic Renaissance in India.[1]

Qutub Uddin Ahmed ibn 'Abd Al-Rahim popularly known as Shah Waliullah Dehlavi (1703-1762) was an influential Islamic reformer who sought to regenerate Muslim society in Asia. A prolific writer, he produced 51 important Islamic texts during his lifetime.

Through his writings and his teachings, as well as the life he led, Shah Waliullah Dehlavi inspired subsequent generations of Islamic followers who carried on his reformation mission after his death. Today, his writings represent his most important achievement, especially his translation of the Holy *Qur`an*, into Persian – a popular and court language of the time. This made the religious Islamic text accessible to a large number of people.

Shah Waliullah Dehlavi was born on 21 February 1703, in the town of Phulat in Muzaffarnagar, Uttar Pradesh, India, as the reign of Aurangzeb, the Mughal emperor of India, was nearing its end. (Aurangzeb died four years later, in 1707.) He was born as Qutub Uddin, but he would come to be better known as Shah Waliullah, an appellation that indicated his inherent goodness and spirituality.

His grandfather, Sheikh Wajih Uddin, was a high-ranking military officer in the army of Shah Jahan, who sided with Prince Aurangzeb in the war of succession. His father, Shah Abdur Rahim, was a Sufi and an illustrious scholar who helped compile the *Fataawa-i Alamgiri*, the huge written work of Islamic law. He taught at the *Madrasah-i Rahimiya*, a theological college, or seminary, that he helped establish. The institution would become an important part of the religious emancipation of Muslim India, as it provided a starting point for later religious reformers. Besides playing an important part in the religious emancipation of Indian Muslims, it also became a training ground for religious reformers like Shah Abdul Aziz, Syed Ahmad of Bareli, Maulavi Abdul Hai and Shah Ismail Shaheed. Writing about the teachings of Shah Abdur Rahim and his brother, Maulana Ubaidullah Sindhi observes,

> 'The essence of the teaching of the two brothers was the effort to discover a path which could be traversed together by the Muslim philosophers (the *Sufis* and the *Mutakallims*) and the Muslim Jurists (*Faqih*).'[2]

Shah Waliullah received his basic education from his

grandfather, but later his father provided him with his academic and spiritual education and guidance. Shah Waliullah was introduced to Islamic education when he was only five years old. Two years later, he had memorised the Holy *Qur`an*. Obviously, he was a precocious scholar. He was only ten years old when he was able to read from the *Interpretation* by *Ja'mi*, an acclaimed Arabic grammar book. Around this time, he also gained knowledge of *Tafseer, Hadeeth*, spiritualism, mysticism, metaphysics, logic, and *Ilm-ul Kalam*. Once introduced to Persian and Arabic languages, he was able to complete his lessons in one year. After that he concentrated on Arabic and Persian grammar and syntax. On top of all that, he studied medicine.

After his father's death, Shah Waliullah, who was then 17 years old, became a teacher at the *Madrasah-i Rahimiya*. He taught there for 12 years, providing guidance to fellow Muslims on spirituality and reformation. A deeply devout person, Shah Waliullah adhered strictly to the Islamic custom of offering prayers five times a day. The *Madrasah-i Rahimiya* would become the center of Islamic Renaissance in the Indian subcontinent, as it attracted scholars from all parts of the country. After their training, they carried the seminary's teaching throughout the Indian subcontinent.

Shah Waliullah's Travels to Arabia

In 1730, Shah Waliullah went on to pursue higher studies in Arabia. He studied at *madaris* at Makkah and Madinah, two renowned educational centres of the Islamic world, where he developed a reputation as a brilliant scholar. There he came into contact with the outstanding teachers of Hejaz. His favourite teacher was Sheikh Abu Tahir bin Ibrahim of Madinah. The Sheikh was an erudite scholar, possessing encyclopaedic knowledge; Shah Waliullah benefitted much from him too, and speaks highly of his piety, independence of judgement and scholarly talents. In all, he studied for 14 months in Madinah, where he received his *Sanad* in *Hadeeth*.

According to accounts, while he was in Arabia, Shah Waliullah received a vision of the Holy Prophet Mohammad (PBUH), who commanded that he should work to organise and then emancipate the Muslim community in India. Apparently in response to this vision, Shah Waliullah returned to Delhi on 9 July 1732, where he began what he considered, his life's mission.

Shah Waliullah as a Muslim Leader

He rose to be a great scholar of Islamic studies, endowed with saintly qualities. So great was his dedication to work that according to his talented son Shah Abdul Aziz: '...he was rarely ill and once he sat down to work after *Ishraq* (post-sunrise prayers) he would not change his posture till midday'.[3] He was a real genius, an intellectual giant who set himself the mission of educating the misguided Muslim masses with the true spirit of Islam. His task was the revival of Islam in the subcontinent, which had been clouded with mystic philosophy, and to bring it out in its pristine glory. He was a humble devotee to this cause, who resisted all temptations of personal glory.

In pursuing this mission, Shah Waliullah faced a formidable task. At the time, Indian Muslims were facing social, political, economical, and spiritual disorder. But Shah Waliullah identified the causes of the problems and indicated appropriate remedies. He was critical of the non-Islamic customs that had become integrated into Muslim society, mostly as a result of exposure to other religions. Specifically, he denounced extravagant marriage ceremonies and festivals.

Indeed, it is unfortunate that these customs still continue amongst the Muslims of India. Also, he determined the causes of the economic erosion in Muslim society and proposed appropriate changes, including greater distribution of wealth, a concept that predated the economic theories of Karl Marx, the 19th century philosopher and economist who critiqued capitalism and became known as the father of Communism.

But the larger, underlying problem, Shah Waliullah believed, was a lack of knowledge on the part of Muslims about Islam and the Holy *Qur`an*. This ignorance, he felt, was the source of all troubles that the Muslims endured.

Once settled in Delhi, Shah Waliullah began teaching students in the varied branches of Islamic learning, as well as preparing them to be scholars who would go out and reveal to the masses the true nature of Islam. Further, to help promote Islamic teachings and make it more comprehensible to lay people, he translated the Holy *Qur`an* into Persian, which was the common language at the time. He also tried to help settle the differences that separated Muslims into various sectarian groups. In this way, he rose to become a great leader as well as a scholar, and his followers recognised some saintly qualities in him. His ambitions were great yet selfless, and he saw his own mission as engineering the revival of Islam in India. A humble man, Shah Waliullah sought no personal reward but only greater glory for his fellow Muslims.

Besides being a deeply spiritual and noted scholar, Shah Waliullah was also politically astute. Not only did he have a keen grasp of regional and national politics; he also clearly understood the profound impact of economics. Based on what he saw, he promoted the concept of socio-economic equilibrium, and he deplored the accumulation of wealth, viewing it essentially as the proverbial root of all-evil in the world. Further, he advocated a social order that embraced Islamic principles of equality, fraternity, and brotherhood.

Shah Waliullah's Writings

As his letters to various political leaders suggest, Shah Waliullah exerted a great deal of influence through his use of the written word. A prolific writer, he assumed a lifetime task of producing standard works on Islamic learning. Within a period of 30 years, he wrote 51 books (23 in Arabic and 28 in Persian). Even today, some of his works are regarded as seminal in the entire sphere of Islamic literature.

His works can be classified into six categories. The first deals with the Holy *Qur`an*. It includes his translation of the Holy book into Persian, the literary language of the subcontinent then. According to him, the object of studying the Holy book is 'to reform human nature and correct the wrong beliefs and injurious actions'.

The second category deals with *Hadeeth*, in which he has left behind several works including Arabic and Persian commentaries on *Mu'atta*, the well-known collection of the traditions of the Holy Prophet (PBUH) compiled by Imam Malik. He attached great importance to this collection even greater than those of Imam Bukhari and Imam Muslim. He was an outstanding *Muhaddith* (legist) and links of all modern scholars of *Hadeeth* in the subcontinent can be traced to him.

Foremost among these modern traditionalists were his son and successor Shah Abdul Aziz and Syed Murtaza Bilgrami. Shah Waliullah wrote a number of books and pamphlets dealing with *Hadeeth*.

The third category deals with *Fiqh* or Islamic Jurisprudence, which includes *Insaaf-fi bayaan-i Sabab-il Ikhtilaaf,* which is a brief but very interesting and informative history of the Islamic Jurisprudence of the last six centuries.

The fourth category deals with his works based on mysticism. The fifth category pertains to his works on Muslim philosophy and *Ilm-i Kalam*. He also wrote a pamphlet on the principles of *Ijtihad* (independent interpretation) and *Taqlid* (conformity). In his *Principles of Ijtihad* he clarifies whether it is obligatory for a Muslim to adhere to one of the four recognised schools of Islamic Jurisprudence or whether he can exercise his own judgment. In the opinion of Shah Waliullah, a layman should rigidly follow his own *Imam* but a person well versed in Islamic law can exercise his own judgment, which should be in conformity with the practice of the Holy Prophet (PBUH).

But the most outstanding of all his works is *Hujjat Allah Al-Balighah (the profound evidence of Allah),* which deals with such aspects of Islam that are commonly sought after among all Muslim countries. In its introduction he observes:

'Some People think that there is no usefulness involved in the injunctions of Islamic law and that in actions and rewards as prescribed by God there is no beneficial purpose. They think that the commandments of Islamic law are similar to a master ordering his servant to lift a stone or touch a tree in order to test his obedience and that in this, there is no purpose except to impose a test so that if the servant obeys, he is rewarded, and if he disobeys, he is punished. This view is completely incorrect. The traditions of the Holy Prophet (PBUH) and consensus of opinion of those ages, contradict this view.' [4]

The sixth category deals with his works on the *Shia-*

Sunni problem, which had become somewhat acute in those days. His writings on this subject have done a great deal in simplifying this problem. His theories pertaining to economics and socialism are also revolutionary. His economic ideas can be found in *Hujjat Allah Al-Balighah, Al-Budur Al-Bazighah, Al-Tafhimat Al-Ilahiyah*, and *Izalat Al-Khafaand* and he may be considered the precursor of Karl Marx. One chapter in *Al-Budur Al-Bazighah* describes the evils of capitalism, which Shah Waliullah believed led to the fall of the Roman and Sassanid empires. Many of his theories relating to economics and socialism are now deemed revolutionary, and may be considered to be a forerunner to Marx. In *Izalat al-Khafa'an*, another of his best-known works, Shah Waliullah fully described the idea of the political revolution that he envisioned.

Writing about his works in the *History of the Freedom Movement*, Sheikh Mohammad Ikram states:

'Shah Waliullah wrote learned works and initiated powerful and beneficial movements, but perhaps no less important are the invisible qualities of approach and outlook, which he bequeathed to Muslim religious thought in the Indo-Pakistan subcontinent. His work is characterised by knowledge, insight, moderation and tolerance, but the quality on which he laid the greatest emphasis, in theory and in practice, was *Adl* or *Adalat* (justice/fairness). His works and views bear ample testimony to the ways he observed this principle in practice and he lost few opportunities of emphasising in theory its role in maintaining the social fabric.'[5]

Shah Waliullah introduced several reforms in religious and economic spheres. He was the first person to translate the

Holy *Qur`an* in Persian, which was the court language at that time, and a practice that was later usefully followed by others. His own son, Shah Abdul Aziz, later translated the Holy book into Urdu, the language of Muslim masses in India at that time. Also during the Mughal era, there had been conflict between orthodox Islam revived under Mujaddid Alf-e Sani, championed by Aurangzeb and heterodoxy introduced by Akbar and championed by Dara Shikoh. The reign of orthodox Aurangzeb created aversion to Sufism and led to the advent of extreme puritanism. Shah Waliullah struck a balance between the two extremes and retained the virtues of both.

He was born in an atmosphere that was deeply imbued with the spirit of *Sufism*. His father was a well-known *Sufi*. In his early age, he came under the influence of Ibn Tamiyya, a great religious reformer. During his stay in Hejaz, he came into contact with scholars who were influenced by *Wahhabism*. This provided a check to his blind following of *Sufism*. But unlike *Wahhabis*, he did not totally discard *Sufism*. He was aware of the services rendered by *Sufis* in popularising Islam in the subcontinent and the spiritual self, developed by the truly Islamic form of *Sufism*. Yet, he was also highly critical of the decadent and traditional form of *Sufism*, which borders on the verge of asceticism and is, therefore, averse to true Islam. In his *Wasiyat Nama* (Will) he observes:

'And the next advice (*Wasiyat*) is that one should not entrust one's affairs to and become a disciple of the Saints of this period who are given to a number of irregularities.' Shah Waliullah urged for the reform and discipline of *Sufism* and not its rejection. He wrote several pamphlets on this subject in which he analysed the evils and virtues of *Sufism*.

'With these books,' writes Maulana Manazir Ahsan Gilani,

'the disputes between the *Sufis* and the *Ulema*, came to an end. By giving an Islamic interpretation to the *Sufi* doctrines, Shah Waliullah removed the distaste, which the *Ulema* had felt for *Sufism* and the *Sufis*.'[6]

Shah Waliullah has, therefore, not only bridged the gulf between the *Sufis* and the *Ulema* but also harmonised the differences prevalent among different sects of *Sufis*. His principles on the subject were put into practice in the great theological college of Deoband, which had among its patrons such well-known *Sufis* like Maulana Rasheed Ahmad Gangohi and Maulana Ashraf Ali Thanvi.

Shah Waliullah's ideas and values came in response to the time in which he was born, and which has been described as an era of decadence. His ideal vision for the Muslim society was one where all individuals enjoyed complete freedom and rulers based their decisions on the Holy *Qur`an*. He was critical of the idle rich, such as the Mughal rulers and India's nobility. He is further quoted as writing about this element of society: 'Oh Amirs! Do you not fear God? (How is it that) you have so completely thrown yourself into the pursuit of momentary pleasures and have neglected those people who have been committed to your care! The result is that the strong are devouring the (weak) people.'[7]

Shah Waliullah's Continued Influence After His Death

After a lifetime devoted to teaching and writing about Islam, Shah Waliullah died on 20 August 1762. The Muslim leader and reformer was 59 years old. He was buried next to his father in *Mehndiyaan*, a prominent graveyard in New Delhi, India.

After his death, his son, Shah Abdul Aziz, along with his

followers and generations of successors, continued his mission to regenerate the Muslim faith.

Shah Waliullah was of the opinion that intellectual revolution should precede political change. He did not contemplate a change in the political or social set-up through a bloody revolution. He wanted to bring a revolutionary change in the society through peaceful means. In his well-known book, *Izalat Al-Khafa'an*, he discusses the ideology of the political revolution, which he envisaged.

No scholar of medieval India had understood the various aspects of civics as had been done by Shah Waliullah. He considered 'self-consciousness' as a prerequisite to 'political consciousness'. He has dealt in detail with the factors, which contribute towards the growth of civil consciousness in his immortal work *Hujjat Allah Al-Balighah*.

Shah Waliullah was, perhaps, the only Muslim scholar of medieval India who realised the importance of economics in a social and political set-up. He advocated the maintenance of economic equilibrium in the society and strongly criticised the accumulation of wealth, which leads to all sorts of evils in the world. He had visualised a social order based on economic equality, fraternity and brotherhood which were the principles governing Islamic socialist practices during the time of the pious Caliphs.

Born in an age of decadence and chaos, Shah Waliullah strove for a world of peace and prosperity. He made a singular contribution to the socio-economic thought of mediaeval India and visualised a Muslim society in which the individual enjoyed the fullest freedom, consistent with the maximum good of all. In such an ideal Islamic state, the ruler was to be governed by the Holy *Qur`an* and the *Sunnah*. No economic exploitation was to be tolerated in such a state and the individual was free to earn his living by fair means.

His seminary, *Madrasah-i-Rahimiya* became the centre of Islamic Renaissance in the subcontinent. Here, scholars flocked from four corners of the country and after being trained, became the torch bearers of the freedom movement in the subcontinent. The *madrasah* had in fact, become the nucleus of the revolutionary movement for the reconstruction of religious thought in Islam. It produced many dedicated workers who carried on their preacher's mission with a missionary zeal. Among these were Maulana Mohammad Ashiq of Phulat, Maulana Noorullah of Budhana, Maulana Amin Kashmiri, Shah Abu Saeed of Rai Bareli and his own son, Shah Abdul Aziz who was initiated into the religious and political philosophy of his father.

Shah Waliullah is still highly respected by Muslims throughout Asia. His teachings and tradition live on with the *Deoband* and *Barelawi* movements. Meanwhile, Shah Waliullah's influence continues to be felt in many religious, social, and political matters.

Commenting on the role played by Shah Waliullah's philosophy and thought on the founding *Ulema* of *Darul Uloom*, Maulana Rasheed Kandhalvi says,

'Darul Uloom's basic thought flowed from the spirit of Sheikh Waliullah, as all the founders had seen and practiced the social, economic, political and religious thought of Sheikh Waliullah and his descendants. Further, all of them had studied at Dilli College, which was started by Maulana Mamlook Ali, and that *madrasah* could be compared to any university of today's age. It taught various modern subjects; students and teachers were not just Muslims, but also Hindus, Sikhs, Christians,

Buddhists etc. So we can say that to a certain extent, teachers and students of the Dilli College also influenced the syllabus of *Darul Uloom*. In the initial years all subjects including elementary subjects were taught here.'

Commenting on the role played by Shah Waliullah's philosophy and thought on founding *Ulema* of *Darul Uloom*, Maulana Asrarul Haq Qasmi said,

'If we have to describe any person or figure responsible for the Islamic Renaissance in India of those times then it was Shah Waliullah. After finishing his studies he came to the conclusion that first, in the country a situation was evolving, under which different religions were trying to establish their hegemony. This might ultimately lead to a change in the ruling class and also establishment of a *tehzeeb* (culture) which will destroy the tolerant fabric of this country. To counter this, he had two solutions, first, the Muslims should prepare a new team which by educational and spiritual guidance be able to safeguard the community's well-being. For the Muslims the two tools, which are available to guard themselves and their co-religionists, are the Holy *Qur`an* and the *Hadeeth*. A basic thought which has been given by Islam and has been enunciated in the Holy *Qur`an* is that if you want to establish your religious supremacy then the manner to achieve this is through peaceful not violent means. Secondly, if you want to rule or change the hearts then love and compassion are needed. This meant that a need was felt to build a team of such intellectuals who by the force of their academic and religious qualifications and thought process could safeguard the interests of their religion.'

Shah Waliullah decided to make the teachings of the Holy *Qur`an* available to all so that they were able to understand the meaning and essence of the Holy book. For this purpose, he first translated the Holy *Qur`an* in Persian, as translation of the Holy *Qur`an* from Arabic to any other language was not permitted then. He took this revolutionary step, for which he had to face a lot of criticism, but he did not pay any heed to his critics. He was confident that till the time you do not translate the Holy *Qur`an* in the language of the court or the one which is widely used by the populace, you will not be able to transmit the message and the message will be lost amongst those who speak or understand an alien language.

Secondly, he tried to introduce this to the wider populace through a team of religious scholars who could combine the *brahin* (reasoning) to maintain their religious identity, with reference to the Prophet's (PBUH) last sermon which summarised that the last Prophet (PBUH) was sent so he could establish a true religion not through use of force but through conviction and principles. 'O People, no prophet or apostle will come after me, and no new faith will be born. Reason well, therefore, O people, and understand words, which I convey to you. I leave behind me two things, the *Qur`an* and my example, the *Sunnah*, and if you follow these you will never go astray', said Prophet Mohammad (PBUH) in his last sermon.

Thirdly, he (Shah Waliullah) introduced Islam to the wider populace. Even today, there is a common complaint that Islam is merely a name of some rituals and religious practices, and it has no role to play in other walks of life. So, Islam is a private religion thus, why do you bring it to all walks of life? We ourselves are to be blamed for this! We, as Muslims have not been able to introduce to people of other faiths the all-pervasive nature of Islam, and even we have not been able to follow its tenets completely.

Islam describes a living human being as one who possesses both the knowledge and the etiquette. If he is equipped with these then he will never indulge in tyranny or usurp the rights of others.

Shah Waliullah introduced Indians to this Islamic philosophy and thought on politics, sociology, and economics and on every walk of life through his various books.

Shah Waliullah was the first person in India, who was able to say that kingship is bound to end in India and a quasi-democratic system would prosper in the world.

Expressing more or less the sentiments expressed by Maulana Asrar, Maulana Mahmood Madani says:

'I'll say that *Darul Uloom* is a representative of *Manhaj-e Waliullahi*. Albeit before the establishment of *Darul Uloom* a formal or uniform system of education was not there for Muslims except maybe one or two small institutions. *Darul Uloom* emerged as a centre for formal education in a unified manner continuing with *Manhaj-e Waliullahi*, another unique feature of *Darul Uloom* since the beginning was that it followed a middle path or a path of *etedaal* - moderation. Or you can say that when we talk about sects, *Darul Uloom* has always maintained a distance, it is not in opposition to *Barelawi* sect or *ghair-muqallid* sects. Both of these are hardliners in their belief but *Darul Uloom* has always maintained a path of moderation.'

Maulana Wahiduddin Khan also concurs with others by saying:

'In fact *Darul Uloom* was the revival of Shah Waliullah's

movement, who wanted to spread the knowledge of the Holy *Qur`an* and *Hadeeth*. This is evident in *Darul Uloom* also, where due prominence is given to the learning of *Hadeeth* and the *Alim* teaching *Hadeeth* is referred to as *Sheikh-ul Hadeeth* - the top most post in the academic hierarchy of *Darul Uloom*. The spiritual founder of *Darul Uloom* was Shah Waliullah and the practical founder was Maulana Qasim Nanautavi.'

'Shah Sahib, as an intellectual could foresee into the future clearly and precisely, so he devised an action plan for the Muslims. Before he passed away at the age of 59 years, Shah Sahib very astutely laid down the fundamentals on which Muslims should traverse. He was a revolutionary in the sense that much before the concepts of coexistence and tolerance came into vogue, he could lay down the foundation on which Muslims should base their educational edifice and blended it very judiciously with the surroundings in which it had to flourish. As evidenced by views of our leading scholars, almost all the founding fathers of *Darul Uloom* were guided by Shah Waliullah's philosophy and thought, which was in evidence further down the road, when these leaders took a conscientious decision, during the country's freedom struggle, of remaining in India and participating in the freedom struggle with people of all creeds, castes and religions to attain a common goal. And to me personally Shah Sahib's philosophy and ideals have become more pertinent for the Muslims to act upon given the situation in the country, as until and unless you yourself are not guided by lofty principles and worthy leaders, you can't give a fight to elements detrimental to you and your faith.'

Shah Waliullah's contribution to *Darul Uloom* could be gauged from the fact that even 153 years after the establishment of *Darul Uloom*, Shah Waliullah's teachings and thoughts continue to guide and inspire the students, faculty and administration of *Darul Uloom*. His teachings of adopting a middle path in every matter continues to influence the leaders of *Darul Uloom* even today. And perhaps this is one of the key reasons that over time the influence of *Darul Uloom* has continued to spread, influencing not just Muslims of India but millions across the world.

Shah Waliullah hoped for the restoration of a stable Muslim rule, in which the *Ulema* would play an important role. Unlike them, he explicitly analysed the basis of the arrangement between the ruler and *Ulema* and argued the necessity of their complementary functions and the need for proper balance between the two. The importance of appropriate political leadership was as self-evident to him as was the importance of religious leadership. He understood history to follow an evolutionary pattern, in which the society progressed through increasingly complex and encompassing stages from primitive to urban to monarchial and finally to universal orders.[8]

Shah Waliullah's success in mastering the intellectual Islamic traditions gave him his influence. His success, however, rested neither in curricular and institutional innovation nor in the compilation of mere commentaries, but in a major individual effort at intellectual synthesis and systemisation, an unprecedented *tatbiq* (implementation) of the whole range of Islamic knowledge. Troubled by the disorder he saw around him, perhaps even sensing that he was at the end of an age, he sought to stem the tide of decline by consolidating and clarifying the entire body of the Islamic tradition. Shah Sahab understood that the knowledge of truth would bring Muslims to religious obedience that would end the divisions and deviations he so greatly deplored. He felt himself uniquely endowed by divine gifts for the task, as he understood it, never before attempted. His *Hujjat Allah Al-Balighah* is a testament to his efforts to elucidate and enshrine the glorious intellect of the faith and to coax Indian Muslims to a path of salvation besides contributing positively to society as well.

Madrasahs in India Prior to 1896

Madrasahs have played an important role in the history of Islamic civilisation. They have been powerful nodes in the learning system and have been harbingers of several revolutionary achievements in fields as diverse as jurisprudence, philosophy, astronomy, science, religion, literature and medicine. It was only when the Golden Age of Islam began to decline that the *madrasahs* lost their academic and intellectual purity, and ceded prime space to Western-oriented education.

The spread of *madrasahs* played a key role in the consolidation of doctrinal positions and legal thinking which now form the dominant position among *Sunnis*. In time, the *Shias* developed their own religious seminaries, called *Hawzas*, which play a similar role. Some of the most famous *madrasahs* are the Deoband in India, Al Azhar in Egypt, *Hawzas* of Qum in Iran and the *Al Zaytunah* in Tunisia.[1]

Moin Qazi (2017) in his article 'Darul Uloom Deoband: *Islamic teaching Madrasahs*' in *Daily O* opines that the *madrasah* system is 1,000 years old. The first major academic institution in the Muslim world, however, was founded by Nizam-ul-Mulk Abu Ali al-Hasan al-Tusi (1018-1092), the celebrated Persian scholar and vizier of the Seljuk Empire.[2]

Later, Nizam-ul-Mulk established numerous *madrasahs* all over the empire that in addition to providing Islamic knowledge, imparted secular education in the fields of science, philosophy, public administration and governance. The earliest recorded South Asian *madrasah* was established in Ajmer in India in 1191.

Prof Zafarul Islam Khan (2010) in his article *The Origins of Madrasahs*, in *The Milli Gazette* opines that *madrasah* education is neither a by-product of any particular historical event or emergent situation, nor does its foundation and functioning solely depend on the state support or patronage of political authorities. This is actually an in-built system of Muslim society, which worked without any break for for the spread of education among Muslim masses through the ages.[3]

In the case of India, it may be surprising but it's a fact that the establishment of *madrasahs* goes back to pre-Muslim period, as the foundation of the *madrasah* education was laid by Arab traders initially in the form of *maktabs* in South India (especially in Malabar) in the last part of the seventh century. This was the time when they had started residing along with their families in their newly established colonies in South of India, after establishing trade links with India as spice traders. During the Arab rule in Sind (8-10th centuries), the *madrasah* education got formal shape, as they were set up in several towns in this region, which had sprung up as centres of Islamic culture and civilisation.

Kashif-ul Huda (2010) in his article *System of Islamic Education in Kerala* opines that the system of Islamic education must have started at the same time as the first few mosques were established in Kerala. This system evolved over a thousand-year period.[4]

In Kerala, *Maktabs* or *Othupallis* initiated the spread of education. They were not quite different from their counterparts in North India or other Muslim countries. *Othupallis* are single teacher schools set up in neighbourhood mosques. The Imam of the mosque was also the teacher at the *Othupalli* and imparted basic Islamic education to the children of the area. Students were taught *Surahs* and *duas* from the Holy *Qur'an* and learned to read Arabic. They also learnt how to pray and other basic Islamic teachings were also imparted to them. Like other states, in Kerala too, the teaching of Islamic knowledge started at *maktabs* leading to the *madrasahs*, which was also a part of the local milieu as elsewhere. Their running costs were either given as grants by the local king or landlords or the rich trading community.

When Sind acquired prominence, a large number of men of learning and erudition migrated from Arabia to this land and made it their permanent home. Within a short period of time, Debal, Mansura and Multan became important centres of Islamic culture in Sind. In the early days, Debal, a part of India, became a centre of trade and commerce and gradually became thickly populated by the Arabs. A good number of educational centres or *maktabs* were housed within the mosques. There were also some *maktabs* (of secondary stage) in Debal. The syllabus included the study of *Hadeeth* and *Tafseer*. *Madrasah* education also flourished in Mansura, the capital of Sind. Qazi Abdul Abbas Ahmad al-Mansuri and Ahmad bin Muhammad Mansur, were among the eminent teachers at Mansura in the last part of the tenth century.[5]

Multan was the most important centre of Islamic learning after Mansura. Even though the first proper *madrasah* in Multan was established much later by Nasir Uddin Qubacha, Abul Hasan Ali bin Amir bin Hakam is reported to have founded a large centre of learning at the great mosque of the city.

Education Under the Early Turks in India

Sultan Mahmud Ghaznavi was the most illustrious patron of sciences. He raided India seventeen times but had no desire to conquer and rule the country. That is why, perhaps, he did nothing for the promotion of education in India. But he is reported to have bestowed the princely sum of 400,000 *Dinars* annually on learned men and poets. Since his zeal for education was not confined to mere support of learned men, he also founded permanent institutions for the promotion of learning in Ghazni. Many great scholars flocked to his court such as Al-Biruni, Ibn Sina and Firdausi. According to a chronicler, he founded a *madrasah* at Ghazni and supplied it with a vast collection of books in various languages. For the maintenance of this establishment, he apportioned a large sum of money besides allotting sufficient funds for students and learned men to instruct youth in the arts and sciences. Thus Mahmud, known for his militarism, was also a great patron of learning and indeed, in the words of a medieval chronicler, Mohammed Kasim Ferishta, 'no king had ever more learned men at his court than Sultan Mahmud Ghaznavi'.

Sultan Mahmud, his son and successor followed the traditions set by his father by erecting magnificent public buildings including *maktabs* and *madrasahs*; making provision for their maintenance by rich and adequate endowments, thus maintaining the attractiveness of Ghazni for learned men. He paid particular attention to diffusion of learning, and placing these benefits within easy reach of the public by establishing educational institutions in several cities of his dominions including Punjab. During his reign, Arabic and Persian literature acquired a rich storage of knowledge through interaction with both Sanskrit and Greek literature. Mathematics, astronomy, astrology, philosophy, medicine and pharmacology, which had reached high levels of excellence in India, were the favourite subjects of study with Muslim scholars. Translation of Indian works, including a large portion of narrative literature, into Arabic and Persian provided an added incentive to their eagerness to imbibe more knowledge through these sources.[6]

The real foundation of Turkish rule in India was laid by Muhammad Ghori (Sultan Shahab Uddin of Ghor) in the year 1191-92. The later Ghaznavids transferred their capital from Ghazni to Lahore, which became a centre of Muslim learning in the twelfth century. After the Ghori conquest, the seat of political authority shifted from Lahore to Delhi and gradually, by the middle of the thirteenth century, Delhi became a great centre of Muslim learning in the East.

The Ghori rulers adopted a pattern of education, which reached its zenith during the Ghaznavid rule, and spread all over the country from Delhi. Muhammad Ghori established several *madrasahs* at Ajmer, the first of their kind in India. Muhammad Ghori's reign was a very stormy one. He could not develop any systematic and planned policy for the spread of Muslim education in India. Yet according to one opinion, the study of *Fiqh* was developed in India during this period.

The Ilbarites' Initiatives in Education

Qutub Uddin Aibak, who was the first of the Ilbarite (Slave) Sultans of Delhi, built a number of mosques in various parts of his dominion. These became centres of both religious and secular learning. His successor, Iltutmish was the first to establish a *madrasah* in Delhi, which he named *Madrasah-i-Muizzi* after Shihab Uddin Muhammad Ghori. A *madrasah* of the same name was also founded at Badaun, which became yet another centre of Islamic culture in northern India.[7]

Iltutmish also gave good education to his daughter Raziya. She herself later encouraged and patronised educational institutions. The existence of the *Muizzi Madrasah* in a flourishing state during her reign is evidence of her interest in spreading education. However, she could not achieve much in the field due to the short period of her rule.

The Madrasah Growth in Deccan and South India

Hasan Gangu Bahmani was the first Bahman who accepted service under a Muslim prince in the Deccan. This marks the period during which all the Deccan kings invariably entrusted the management of revenue to the locals.

Mujahid Shah Bahmani, who ruled for about twenty years after Hasan Gangu was noted for his fluency in Turkish language. His successor Mahmud Shah was a patron of learning and many poets from Arabia and Persia came to his court. The Sultan founded a *madrasah* in the Deccan in 1378 to provide education to orphans. The government provided them boarding and lodging. Learned teachers were engaged for their tuition. He established *maktabs* and *madrasahs* in several other cities of his dominion such as Gulbarga, Bidar,

Qandhar, Ellichpur, Daulatabad, besides other places and provided substantial endowments for their maintenance.[8]

The next king, Firoz Shah, was a great lover of astronomy. He was well versed in many sciences and was fond of philosophy. His brother and successor, Ahmad Shah Bahmani, followed in his footsteps and gave several villages and extensive lands near Gulbarga to Sayyed Muhammad *Gesu Daraz* and built for him a magnificent *madrasah* near Gulbarga.

A noteworthy feature of his reign was the munificence of Mahmud Gawan, his minister for literary pursuits, who established *madrasahs* throughout the kingdom.[9] Thus, it is said, *madrasah* education was so widespread that there was scarcely a town or a city from where learned men had not derived advantage. The famous *madrasah* at Bidar, known after his own name as *Madrasah-i Mahmud Gawan*, was also built by him two years before his death. It had a mosque attached to it to impart religious education along with secular learning. It was even equipped with a library that contained 3,000 books. Moreover, 3,500 books were obtained from Mahmud Gawan's house. The reign of Mahmud Shah Bahman II is a good example of the extent to which the deep interest of a king can spread education.

Adil Shah, the founder of the kingdom of Bijapur was an educated person who took great interest in literature. His reign was noted for its patronage to Islamic learning and for a rich library containing a rare collection of manuscripts on Islamic studies.

Teachings on Islamic sciences were organised at Asar Sharif, a famous mosque at Bijapur.[10] The institution was developed by Adil Shah into twin *madrasahs*. He founded another *madrasah* at Bijapur under Amir Fatah Ullah Shiraz.

Ismail Adil Shah, the successor of Adil Shah kept up the reputation of his house with his literary pursuits.

During the reign of Ibrahim Adil Shah I, public accounts were kept in *Hindavi*, instead of Persian, and many Brahmins were appointed for this purpose. Soon these Brahmins acquired great influence in the government. During the reign of Yusuf Adil Shah, the Hindus were able to exercise considerable power in the king's revenue department. This gives an evidence of increasing interaction between the two communities and their languages. While Yusuf Adil Shah invited artists and scholars from Persia and Turkey, Ibrahim Adil Shah II, himself was an eminent poet. In his reign Pandit Narhari, a court poet, composed the poetic excellence on his master, called, *Nauras Manzarf*. Shri Laxmipathi, a disciple of Pandit Rukmangada composed a number of Marathi and Hindi devotional songs set in musical *Ragas*. Swamy Yadvendra was also a prominent courtier, who contributed to Marathi literature. Muhammad Quli Qutub Shah is highly reputed for his patronage and encouragement of education in Golconda. He built the *Chahar Minar* and opened a *madrasah* there. He also built several other *madrasahs* and public seminaries, all of which were properly equipped. Learned men were appointed and received liberal remuneration for their services. Qutub Shah also set up a *madrasah* outside the fort of Golconda. One of the *madrasahs* was close to Hyderabad. Apart from the bigger *madrasahs* in southern India, there were *maktabs* attached to the houses of the teachers.

The rulers of Ahmadnagar made arrangements for free education and lodging for the poor and the orphans. In about 1563, Burhan Nizam Shah established *Madrasah Isna Ashriya*, facing the fort of Ahmadnagar. He also founded *Madrasah-tut*

Tahiriyya, inside the fort.[11]

Hinawar, an important town situated in the South-western part of the Indian peninsula, was the capital of Sultan Jalal Uddin Ahsan Shah, the founder of the independent kingdom of Madura. One of the most powerful rulers of Hinawar, he was keenly interested in advancing education in his kingdom. Ibn Battuta, the famous traveller, who visited his kingdom, writes that 'there were as many as twenty-three *madrasahs* for boys, and thirteen for girls in his capital'.

Earlier Madrasahs in Central and Western India

In Malwa (currently Madhya Pradesh), Sultan Mahmud Khalji was a great promoter of learning and literature. During his long rule of over thirty years, he encouraged learned men to such an extent that Malwa became an important centre of learning. He had founded a *madrasah* at Sarangpur, where special arrangements were made for teaching arts and crafts to women as well.[12]

Many distinguished philosophers and *maulanas* from other countries not only came to this place, but were also attracted to the madrasahs that Mahmud had founded in different parts of his dominion. One of these was situated in the capital, in close proximity to the mosque of Sultan Hoshang Shah.

Hoshang Shah founded a *madrasah* at Shadiabad Mandu in about 1475. His successor, Mahmud Shah, established many *madrasahs* in Mandu and sanctioned a grant for teachers and the students. His successor, Ghiyas Uddin Mahmud Shah I, founded two *madrasahs* at Ghiyasiya and Zafarabad. He laid stress on women's education and his *mahalsara* (women's wing of the palace) made arrangements for teaching Holy *Qur`an* and *Hadeeth* to women to equip them to learn the Holy *Qur`an* and Islamic law.

In Burhanpur, the capital of Khandesh, there was at least one *madrasah*. In Gwalior, there was a *madrasah* founded by Rahim Das of Gwalior, mentions Kuldeep Kaur, in her book *Madrasa Education in India*. Men of letters from Persia, Arabia and Turkey found it worthwhile to settle in Gujarat. Sultan Ahmad Shah (1411-1441) built the city of Ahmedabad and adorned it with magnificent *maktabs* and *madrasahs*, the remains of which remind us of their past glory even today. Maulavi Shirazi, a poet in the court of Ahmed Shah I, composed the *History of Gujarat* in Persian verse. In the reign of Ahmad Shah I, there were a number of *madrasahs* in Ahmadabad. Similarly, Sultan Mahmud II also upheld the traditions of his forefathers by expressing his solicitousness for learned men and by building *madrasahs*. However, the earliest *madrasah* recorded to have existed in Gujarat was established in 1038 at Baroch (Bharuch). The founder was Baba Raihan, a scholar from Khorasan. Qazi Zainul Abidin the grandfather of Qazi Nur Uddin of Baroch, refers to it in his memoirs by the name *Madrasah Maulana Ishaq bin Abdul Wahhab*.[13]

This *madrasah* exists even today, though shorn of its former glory. An Ishaq boarding house is still in existence in the locality. It was Ahmadabad, the capital of Gujarat, where the great and largest number of *madrasahs* existed. A great saint *Sheikh* Ahmad Khattu, came to Gujarat in 1399 and settled in Sarkhej. He was one of the four Ahmads who participated in the founding of the city of Ahmadabad. After his death, he was buried at Sarkhej and Sultan Muhammad Shah II erected a splendid mausoleum at the place where the saint had lived. A big *madrasah* sprang up at Sarkhej in 1466 during the reign of Sultan Qutub Uddin, the son of Muhammad Shah II.

One of the greatest *Sufis* of Gujarat, Saiyid Usman Shamai-Bushani, founded a *madrasah* on the banks of river Sabarmati. It gradually developed into one of the biggest and most famous *madrasahs* of Gujarat. The place soon began to be called Usmanpura after this great teacher. Sultan Muhammad Shah was a great devotee of this teacher saint and showed his reverence for him by building a *madrasah* at Usmanpura. Sultan Muzaffar II built a seminary for Shah Wajih Uddin. It was later rebuilt as a *madrasah* by Sadiq Khan. Shah Wajih Uddin spent sixty-five years of his life teaching here.

Another notable madrasa at Ahmadabad was the *Madrasah-i Saif Khan* built in 1622. John Briggs (1849) in his *Cities of Gujarashtra* mentions a *madrasah* built by Alam Khan Ghazi in 1636 during the reign of Shahjahan. It was situated on the Southeast corner of the river Bhadra with its entrance in the East. In 1820, it was converted into a district jail. Yet another famous *madrasah* was built in Ahmadabad by Nawab Akram Uddin Khan, the Sadr of Ahmadabad, for the celebrated teacher Maulana Nur Uddin, at a cost of over Rupees one lakh. The foundation was laid in 1690 and it was completed in 1697. Shujaat Khan's *madrasah* was built and maintained in Ahmadabad in keeping with the traditions set by some noblemen.

An important *madrasah* in Pattan, was attached to the tomb of Sheikh Hisam Uddin Multani, where Maulana Taj Uddin and his son Muhammad bin Taj lectured on *Hadeeth*. In the middle of the sixteenth century, there was another *madrasah* in Pattan run by Sheikh Abdul Latif-al Fatani, who was especially interested in *Tajwid* and *Qirat*. Haji Zahid Baig, a rich merchant of Surat, built a *madrasah* adjoining

Saiyid Muhammad's tomb. Zafaryab Khan and his grandson Haji Miyan founded a Baradari, a *madrasah* and a mosque in the name of their teacher, Shah Qutub Uddin.[14]

Earlier Madrasahs of Northern India

In Kashmir, Sultan Qutub Uddin Kashmiri founded a big *madrasah* at Qutbuddin Pura in about 1420 and appointed Sajjad Jamal Uddin as the lecturer in *Hadeeth*.[15]

Sultan Zainul Abideen established a residential *madrasah* near Srinagar. His successor, Sultan Husain Khan Chack, also founded a great *madrasah* and appointed a host of reputed teachers, who made significant contributions in the spread of *madrasah* education in Srinagar and Kashmir. During the reign of Akbar, Husain Khan built many *madrasahs* in his kingdom and presented the Pargana (district) of Asapur as an endowment.

Husain Shah Langa of Multan will always be remembered for the impetus he gave to education by setting up several *maktabs*, seminaries and *madrasahs* staffed by talented teachers. Husain Mirza, the last of the Langa dynasty, also contributed to the progress of education in his kingdom. He encouraged and patronised well-known scholars, among them Saad Ullah Lahori and Maulana Abdur Rehman Jami.

In Sind some of the *madrasahs* and *maktabs* established by the Saeyeds of Rohri, have survived the passage of time and their minarets and domed-roofs dominate the picturesque landscape of that part of the province. Nasir Uddin Qubacha, who ruled Sindh, about the beginning of the thirteenth century and later Shah Beg Arghun, in the third decade of the sixteenth century, were both exceedingly well read. Many learned men, driven out of Ghazni and Ghor by the ruthless ravages of Chengiz Khan, took asylum at the court of Nasir

Uddin Qubacha. Alexander Hamilton, who visited India during the reign of Aurangzeb, writes that only in Thatta, there were four hundred schools for different subjects and art and craft. During Ibrahim Lodhi's reign (1402-1440) the court of Jaunpur far outshone that of Delhi and was the resort for all the learned men of the East.[16]

Sultan Ibrahim patronised *madrasah* education to such a high degree that his capital city Jaunpur, became famous as an important centre of education, to which hundreds flocked from far and near for higher education. It produced men like *Sheikh* Allahdad Jaunpuri, Zahir Dilawari, Qazi Shahab Uddin Daulatabadi, Maulana Ali Ahmad, Maulana Hasan Bakhshi and Nurul Haq.

About the middle of the fifteenth century, Bibi Raji, the wife of Mahmud Shah, (son of Sultan Ibrahim) built Jami Mosque, a *madrasah* and a monastery under the name of *Namazgah*. She also awarded stipends to students and teachers. The famous Itala Mosque of Jaunpur was the *madrasah* of Shahab Uddin Daulatabadi. Founded by Sheikh Muhammad Afdalul Usmani, it enjoyed great reputation.

There was also a *madrasah* of Sheikh Muhammad Rashid Mustafaul Usmani Jaunpuri at Mirmast. This grand *madrasah* was situated on the bank of river Ganga in a lofty building along with a mosque and a hostel for teachers and students. One of its outstanding students was Sheikh Nizam Uddin Lakhnavi.

During Humayun's reign, Jaunpur continued to enjoy its high reputation as a centre of learning and remained so through Jahangir's reign up to the time of Shah Jahan, who gave it the name of *Shiraz-i Hind*.

In the late medieval times, Lucknow became famous for

its renowned *madrasah* of Sheikh Nizam Uddin Sihalvi at Firangi Mahal.

The *madrasah* of Qazi Abdul Qadirul Umri was also a famous institution. Other *madrasahs* were Abdul Qadar bin Ahmad's *madrasah* at Amethi and Sheikh Pir Muhammad's *madrasah* at Lucknow, which was situated on the bank of the river Gomti. For a long time, this *madrasah* was a meeting place for the learned men of the state. Early in the nineteenth century, the king of Awadh, Amjad Ali Shah also founded a great *madrasah* at Lucknow.[17]

Famous Madrasahs of Eastern India

Ikhtiyar al-Din Muhammad Bakhtyar Khalji's kingdom extended up to the town of Nadia in Bengal in 1197. After consolidating his conquest, he set up a new city called Rangpura; which was studded with various *maktabs* and *madrasahs*. Similarly, Hisam Uddin Husain Khalji, who had conquered the small territory of Sultan Ghiyas Uddin I, (1212-1227) made Lakhnauti (also known as Gour) in Malda district his capital. Scholars, artists and saints thronged here to enjoy royal patronage. As a result, a number of *madrasahs* sprang up in the city. Ghiyas Uddin II, his successor established the historic *Madrasah* of *Dars Bari* situated near Umiarpur village. Husain Shah and Nusrat Shah were patrons of both Hindu and Muslim literature. They founded *maktabs* and *madrasahs* in their kingdom and offered plenty of endowments for their maintenance.[18]

Husain Shah had also founded a *madrasah* as a memorial to the famous saint Qutbul Alam. In *Khurshid-i-Jahan-Numa*, Ilahi Bakhsh Husaini mentions about a *madrasah* in Ghurashahid (a residential quarter in Gour) in the neighbourhood of the residence of Ghulam Husain, the well-known author of the *Riyaz-ul Salatin*.

Shaista Khan, the uncle of Aurangzeb built a mosque and a *madrasah* on the bank of a river in Dacca during his tenure as a governor there (1664-1680).

Another mosque with a *madrasah* was built by Muhammad Azim in Azimpur (Dacca). This mosque was a double storeyed structure, with its upper portion housing the *madrasah*. Later, in the eighteenth century, Maulana Abdul Ali established a *madrasah* at Buhar, Burdwan. But with time, it was closed and its rich collection of books was sent to the Imperial Library (now National Library, Calcutta) where its memory survives in the 'Buhar Section'.[19]

Similarly, there is a village called Mangalkot, which once used to be the meeting place of great *Ulema* and saints of the age. Maulana Hameed Uddin Bengali, a disciple of Sheikh Ahmad Sirhindi, had a monastery there which continues to be maintained by his followers. This *madrasah* known as Mangalkot *Madrasah* has gradually deteriorated.

The entire stock of the literary material (comprising 704 volumes-460 published and 244 manuscripts) was sent to the *Madrasah-e Aliya* library in Calcutta, in 1928, later to be shifted to the *Madrasah-e Aliya* in Dacca, where they are housed under 'Mangalkot Section'. The *Katra Madrasah* of Murshidabad speaks of the glorious history of *madrasahs* built by Murshid Quli Khan, who also built many *maktabs* and *madrasahs* in the town.[20]

Towards the end of the eighteenth century, there were also some small educational institutions at Silapur in Bengal. Here, both Hindus and Muslims were taught Persian and Arabic. Generally, these *madrasahs* were built at the side of mosques or vice versa. In far off places where only mosques were built, they served the purpose of both a mosque and a *maktab*.[21]

An interesting point to mention here is that Warren Hastings, the British Governor General of East India Company established the *Aliah Madrasah*, one of the oldest modern-style educational institutes in Asia, and first in India in October 1780 near Sealdah in Calcutta. A number of titles were used for it, such as Islamic College of Calcutta, Calcutta *Madrasah*, Calcutta Mohammedan College and *Madrasah-e-Aliah*. This *madrasah* was awarded the status of a university by the state government of West Bengal in 2008.[22]

After the establishment of Delhi Sultanate in the beginning of the thirteenth century, *madrasah* education developed and with the expansion of the Muslim state, a series of *madrasahs* were established in different parts of the country. This tradition got firmly established and further developed during the Mughal rule (1526-1857).

In fact, it had been a popular practice on the part of Muslim rulers to make arrangements for the construction of mosques and setting up centres of religious education (i.e. *maktabs* and *madrasahs*) in the territories that came under their control. Moreover, many *Ulema* of the period themselves took up the task of teaching especially the main subjects of Islamic learning in local mosques or at their own houses which had flourished in the form of individual centres of teaching and functioned just like *madrasahs*.

Maulana Manazir Ahsan (1955) comments that it has become a general practice on the part of modern writers on the *madrasah* movement or *madrasah* education in India to trace its origin to the post-1857 deplorable condition of the Indian Muslims or to link it to the degeneration of their religious and social life in that period. But in view of the historical facts it would be erroneous to conclude that in India, *madaris* came to be founded after 1857 mainly to cope with the problems of Muslim society, particularly to provide safeguards against the onslaught of western culture and civilisation and to uplift their socio-cultural status.[23]

Of course, it cannot be denied that in the post-1857 period, the *madrasah* movement was revived and further strengthened. A section of the Indian *Ulema* devoted themselves fully to this cause and made significant contributions to establish new *madrasahs* and expand the old ones under the Waliullahi movement.

It should not be overlooked that educational facility in medieval India was available through three means: formal institutions (in the form of *maktabs* and *madaris*), informal institutions (in the shape of individual centres of teachings) and private teachers and tutors (known as *muallim* or *ataleeq*).

As a matter of fact, in those days, the second type of institutions were found in a very large number, under which *Ulema* or learned persons imparted knowledge or gave lectures on different subjects, sitting in a mosque or at their own houses. This system was in vogue at the primary as well as higher level. Further, during the Muslim rule in India, in big cities and towns, the grand and spacious mosques used to have a series of *hujrahs* (side rooms) at least on two sides of the courtyard, which were meant mainly for the students and teachers.

In fact, these mosques also served as a *madrasah* or educational institution, as has been rightly observed by Maulana Abul Hasan Nadwi. Many *Ulema* or theologians, as stated above, performed this work voluntarily considering it as a *kaar-e-khair* (noble deed) or source of *baith-e-swab* (divine reward).

Significantly, there are enough examples that some of the state officials and *Sufis* also showed keen interest in teaching work and spared some time daily for this purpose at their place of work or *khanqah* (monastery) respectively. Maulana Manazir Ahsan Gilani has rightly observed in his book *Hindustan mein Musalmanon ka Nizam-i-Talim wa Tarbiyat* that during Muslim rule in India the conduct of the teaching work depended on the establishment of *madrasahs* or formal institutions.[24] Wherever any *Alim* or scholar (interested in teaching) sat and started teaching, it became a *madrasah* and students or seekers of knowledge flocked to him availing of his *dars* or lectures. It may be a mosque, a house, a *khanqah*, a court, a palace or the *deorhi* (outer entrance room of a building) of a *zamindar*.

This situation was more vividly depicted by the eminent writer and noted educational thinker Allama Shibli Nomani (1933) thus,

'In the old dictum a college used to be the name of a person. Wherever he sat down that became a college surrounded by a huge gathering of students or seekers of knowledge. Whatever was uttered by him in day and night that served as a lecture and in this way his talking, movement, manners and behaviour all formed part of his silent lectures. Gradually, the circle of teachers as well as that of students used to expand, till after some time this living college got developed in the form of a university or *Jami-i Azam*. In present days, (learned) persons are ascribed to a college or an institution and at that time they were ascribed to a person (teacher).'[25]

Under the Mughals this tradition was further strengthened with the development of the state resources, expansion of the Muslim territories and rising number of *Ulema* and scholars.

What is more important to point out in this regard is that these informal institutions very well served the purpose of *madaris* as the details of their working show. Additionally, the contemporary historians inform us that some of the Sultans had made special arrangements for the education of male and female slaves. In the reign of Firoz Shah Tughlaq (1351-1388), thousands of slaves got education and training at the state's expenses not only in *Ulum-i Naqliyyah* (traditional sciences), but also in crafts and mechanical works.[26] In the same way Sultan Ghiyasuddin Mahmud Khalji (1469-1500), an independent ruler of Malwa, took special care in providing religious education to female slaves and for this purpose he appointed a number of teachers in the royal *harem*.[27] Such examples suggest that the Muslim rulers of medieval India had interest in the education of different sections of society and further dispels the misgiving that they were only concerned with the education of the elite.

This history of *madrasahs* in India leads one to conclude that the *madrasah* education is very deeply rooted in the Muslim civilisation and in India this noble tradition existed much before the Islamic rule began and was firmly established during the Mughal rule. As a matter of fact, the series of *madrasahs*, which flourish in modern India, are a continuation of the same well-established practice, for which the significant contribution of *Ulema*, scholars and rulers of medieval India cannot be denied.

Educational System in Darul Uloom

During the last twenty-five years or so, *madrasah* education in India has been a subject of focus and interest besides intense debate and prominence both in the educational and research circles, in addition to media and of course in the civil and political discourse of the country.

Every educational institute is based and structured around the philosophies and interests of its founders. This foundational ideology not only helps in establishing the institute and also differentiating it from others but makes it unique through the subjects taught, courses offered and quality of its faculty and alumni. *Darul Uloom* is also not different in this regard. The foundational ideology of its founding fathers has been discussed earlier and in this chapter we will delve into the study pattern followed at *Darul Uloom* from lower to higher classes, input of its academics and the results thereof. But first a word on what a *madrasah* is.

In the subcontinent under Islamic system of education, the first step by a child towards education is taken at a

Maktab, This is essentially an elementary school where children are introduced to the alphabets and writing, and reading elementary books relating to Arabic and Urdu and the Urdu. They are also introduced to the Holy *Qur`an* by memorising the last *Para* (chapter) as this consists of shorter *Surahs* (verses) which are easier to learn and memorise, and which most people recite during the *Namaaz*. The next step after finishing *maktab* is a *madrasah*, which is a centre for imparting elementary or secondary education. You can earn the *sanad* (degree) of a *Fazil* after completing a set eight-year course. Usually *madaris* are set alongside a mosque, but to become an *Alim* you have to attend a centre of excellence or a seminary where the students specialise in *Fiqh* (jurisprudence), *Tajweed* (the rules for pronouncing the Arabic language when reciting the Holy Qur`an) or *Qirat* (cantillation). A *Fazil* is equivalent to a Diploma holder whereas an *Alim* is a graduate of a university. *Darul Uloom* was the first such seminary which was established in India and many other lesser-known *madrasahs* are either affiliated to it or follow the curriculum prescribed by it.

While a *madrasah* now refers to any type of school imparting religious knowledge, the term *madrasah* was originally used to refer more specifically to a medieval Islamic centre of learning, mainly teaching Islamic law and theology, usually affiliated with a mosque, and funded by a charitable trust known as *Waqf*.[1] Financially, the school used to be wholly dependent on public contributions, mostly in the form of annual pledges, not on fixed holdings of *Waqf* or pious endowments contributed by noble patrons.

Madaris were largely centred on the study of *fiqh* (Islamic jurisprudence) and issuing the *Ijazah al-tadris wa-al-ifta'* (license to teach and issue legal opinions). The Islamic legal education system had its origins in the ninth century after the formation of the *madhahib* (schools of jurisprudence). George Makdisi considers the *Ijazah* to be the origin of the European doctorate's degree.[2] However, in an earlier article, he considered the *Ijazah* to be 'fundamentally equivalent' to the medieval doctorate, since the latter was awarded by an individual teacher-scholar not obliged to follow any formal criteria, whereas the former was conferred on the student by the collective authority of the faculty.[3]

To obtain an *Ijazah*, a student 'had to study in a guild school of law, usually four years for the basic undergraduate course' and ten or more years for a post-graduate course. The 'doctorate was obtained after an oral examination to determine the originality of the candidate's thesis', and to test the student's 'ability to defend them against all objections, in disputations set up for the purpose'. These were scholarly exercises practiced throughout the student's 'career as a graduate student of law'. After students completed their post-graduate education, they were awarded *Ijazahs* which gave them the status of a *Faqih* – a scholar of Islamic jurisprudence; *Mufti* – a scholar competent in issuing *Fatwas*', and *Mudarris* – a teacher.[4]

The Arabic term *Ijazah al-tadris* was awarded to Islamic scholars who were qualified to teach. According to Makdisi, the Latin title *licentia docendi* 'licence to teach' in the European university may have been a translation of the Arabic, but the underlying concept was very different.[5] A significant difference between the *Ijazah al-tadris* and the *licentia docendi* was that the former was awarded by the individual scholar-teacher, while the latter was awarded by the chief official of the university, who represented the collective faculty, rather than the individual scholar-teacher relationship.[6]

Much of the study in the *madrasah*-college centered on examining whether certain opinions of law were orthodox.

This scholarly process of 'determining orthodoxy' began with a question which the Muslim layman, called *mustaftī*, presented to a jurist-consultant, called *Mufti*, soliciting from him a response, called *Fatwa*, a legal opinion (the religious law of Islam covers civil as well as religious matters). The *Mufti* (professor of legal opinions) took this question, studied it, and researched it intensively in the sacred scriptures, in order to find a solution. This process of scholarly research was called *Ijtihad*, literally, 'the exertion of one's efforts to the utmost limit'.[7]

Before describing the curriculum of the *Darul Uloom* it will be pertinent to relate a short history of the syllabi of Arabic sciences, as given on *Darul Uloom's* website so that the academic tendencies, right from the first decade of Islam to the present day, can be understood better.[8]

In the prophetic era, education began with the Holy *Qur`an*. During the caliphate of the second Caliph, Hazrat umar, special arrangements were made, along with the teaching of the Holy *Qur`an* for the teaching and learning, and dissemination and publication of the *Hadeeth* also. As time rolled on and educational needs multiplied, disciplines also continued to be added. Till the middle of the second *Hijri* (Islamic century), arts and sciences were restricted to the Holy *Qur`an*, *Hadeeth*, *Fiqh* and the Arabic philosophy and poetry. Thereafter, till the end of the fourth *Hijri*, which is called the age of invention and redaction, the invention of different arts and sciences and their translations came into being along with civilisational growth and progress, and as per necessity some arts also began to be taught. As such, *Hadeeth, Tafseer, Fiqh,*

Principles of *Fiqh*, Grammar, Lexicon and Syntax, Arabic philosophy, poetry and History were considered the subjects for scholastic education of that period. Medicine, Astrology, Astronomy and some other Greek sciences were also being added to this syllabus.

Between the fifth and the seventh *Hijri* the science of Dialectics or Scholastic Theology was established through Imam Ghazali. For its support, besides the afore-said sciences, noetic sciences like Logic, Philosophy, etc. also became a necessary ingredient in the curriculum of the Islamic schools and universities.

Though these sciences were more or less current, nevertheless in all the Islamic countries, the impact of national, local and ethnic influences was inevitable. Since Arab families had settled in great numbers in countries like Egypt, Syria, etc. in great numbers, giving predominance to Arab leanings sciences like *Tafseer, Hadeeth* and *Asma al-Rijal* were comparatively paid more heed to. In Andalusia (Spain), literature, poetry and history had acquired great importance. In Iran, logic and philosophy were predominant, and in Khurasan (Persia) and Transoxiana (Central Asia), *Fiqh,* Principles of *Fiqh* and *Tasawwuf* (Sufism) were more in vogue. At the same time, however, due to the influences of the milieu and demands of the environment, the process of change and alteration in the syllabi has often taken place in different periods in one and the same country.

Although the Muslims had reached India in the first *Hijri* (622 CE) and a pretty good increase in the numbers took place by the beginning of the fifth *Hijri* (1009 CE), that is, during Sultan Mahmud Ghaznavi's period. Besides Sind, the area of Punjab too had been included in the Islamic dominions, and Muslims real influence started from the beginning of seventh *Hijri*, i.e. from the regime of Sultan Shahab Uddin Ghouri (597/1191 - 602/1205). It was that period when in Khurasan, Transoxiana, along with *Tafseer* and *Hadeeth*, Grammar and Syntax, Rhetoric and Literature, Jurisprudence, Logic, Scholastic Theology and *Tasawwuf* were considered the standard learning wherein Jurisprudence and the Principles of Jurisprudence held higher importance. The Muslims who had come to India had mostly come from these countries, naturally therefore, they attached more importance to their Islamic leanings, which was inevitable. As such, all these sciences were included and were made a part and parcel of the syllabi of *madrasahs* of that era in India.

On the issue of *Darul Uloom's* syllabus or study pattern, Late Maulana Wahiduddin Khan said:

'*Darul Uloom's* syllabus was and is largely based on the *Fiqh* and *Hadeeth* of Imam Abu Hanifa. As far as *Mantiq* (logic) and *Falsafa* (philosophy) are concerned, books written by Maulana Nizam Uddin are still prescribed in the *Darul Uloom's* syllabus. Though Arabic teaching was also a part of the curriculum, yet the students and teachers refrained from interacting with each other in Arabic except during classes, though they were masters of the language. However, after 1947 Maulana Wahid-uz Zaman Kairanavi started a movement to practice speaking Arabic.'

Prof Akhtar-ul Wasey, commenting on the original syllabus at *Darul Uloom* says that:

'The syllabus prepared by Hujjat-ul Islam Maulana Qasim Nanautavi, gave a fair preference to vocational studies also, now known as Skills Management. He also included medicine, bookbinding, leather craft, calligraphy and other trades because he wanted the graduates of *Darul Uloom* not to be dependent on any one else for their livelihood. His main idea was that after graduating from *Darul Uloom*, they'd start their own businesses and in spare time propagate Islam. And in reality turned them into self-reliant individuals.'

Maulana Arshad Madani commenting on the study pattern followed at *Darul Uloom* says:

'In the initial years, Deoband followed a system which had an educational plan spanned over eight years, and covered all the subjects which were taught till 11th standard in modern schools e.g. Geography, Mathematics, Economics, Civics, along with religious topics where they underwent the basic and advanced training of the Holy *Qur`an* and *Hadeeth*. Since the Muslim rule had come to an end in the country, so the founders of *Darul Uloom* were firm believers in turning out such a system where one should be imparted both the religious and contemporary subjects. Religious issues comprised of religious teachings, way of observing rituals but the third and most important is tolerance and coexistence, so that whosoever completed his education at *Darul Uloom* should turn out to be an all encompassing human being, not just a religious scholar. So that he should not be isolated in the society but should stand shoulder to shoulder with other communities also.'

The Principal of *Nadwa-tul Ulema*, Lucknow, Maulana Saeed-ur Rehman Azmi is of the view that:

'Their aim was to turn out a product who will be well-equipped to carry on the task of propagation and introduction of religion, apart from being an important part of the community and establish an atmosphere of tolerance. In the initial phase, they also included *mantiq* (reasoning) and *falsafa* (philosophy) and even *riyazi* (mathematics).'

Maulana Mahmood Madani commenting on the ideals enshrined in the syllabus at Darul Uloom says:

'The first and foremost ideal of this movement was to reawaken the religious soul of the Muslim *ummah*. *Alhamdulillah, Darul Uloom* has been a success in this endeavour, it became the mother of all *madaris* in India.'

On the issue of the syllabus and educational system followed at *Darul Uloom*, Maulana Mahmood is of the view that 'Yes, financial independence is necessary', but he asserts that not just *Darul Uloom* but Indian *madaris* of any sect in India are not producing a product which is not gainfully employed. At the same time, taking a swipe at the modern educational system, he says that there are six crore post-graduates without any gainful employment whereas you'll not be able to find any *madrasah* graduate who is not gainfully employed. He further tries to elaborate that nowadays the main constituent of students at *madaris* comes from lower-middle class or even the most backward class, so at the best you can turn them into a product which is gainfully employed after finishing his studies. He adds, 'Yes, there is always a need for improvement and I'm of the view that we should improve our syllabus, which could churn out people with a thinking caliber, because no society can survive or develop if it has no thinkers to analyse and guide the rest of the society.'

Maulana. Khalid Saifullah Rahmani commenting on *Darul Uloom's* syllabus says:

'The syllabi always functions in consonance with the current demands of that particular era, it is not a mechanism which would be identical in all the ages. So the basic subjects such as the *Holy Qur`an, Hadeeth, Fiqh* etc. can't be changed but other related subjects and books could be changed and have been changed at *Darul Uloom*, keeping in view the current demands and aspirations.'

According to Maulana Rahmani, many new books on Arabic grammar and literature have been included along with English being introduced up to a certain standard and then after graduation an intensive English language programme has been launched along with Computer and Internet learning departments, to keep the students abreast of new technologies.

Maulana Abul Qasim Nomani commenting on the current syllabus of *Darul Uloom* and the need to change it with times says that:

'In our syllabus we have two divisions, one is imparting *Uloom-e Maqsood* (theology); which comprises of the study and teaching of *Hadeeth, Usool-e Hadeeth, Fiqh, Usool-e Fiqh, Tafseer, Usool-e Tafseer* and some subjects related purely to *deeniyat*. The other is *Uloom-e Aaliya*, which are the means to attain *Uloom-e Maqsood*, comprising of *Adab* (literature), *Balaghat* (eloquence in rhetoric), *Mantiq* (logic), *Falsafa* (philosophy), and *Riyazi* (mathematics). In the initial years of foundation of *Darul Uloom, Uloom-e Maqsood* were taught religiously but others such as *Mantiq, Falsafa* or *Maqoolat* were also laid stress upon, as during that time it was considered paramount to be an expert in these fields also, but over the years these subjects lost importance and books were changed or completely given-up.'

According to Maulana Nomani, it could be said that the core books related to religious subjects have not been changed, but subsidiary subjects have witnessed change due to their relevance in that period. Similarly, it could be said about the vocational subjects too, earlier, special stress was given to calligraphy as every book was stencilled by a calligrapher. With the advent of computer, typing in Urdu and Arabic has become easier than having it calligraphed, but then calligraphy has now been given the status of an art form, though earlier it was taught as a means of sustenance, the same could be said about foundry work, leather work etc. Thus, keeping pace with the times has always been a feature of *Darul Uloom*, so that its graduates are in tune with the current age. Now, *Darul Uloom* has departments for English and computer education, as the need and demand for these subjects is increasing day by day and our students want to keep pace with modern society.

Here it would be pertinent to describe what a *Maslak* is. Prof Moosa in his book *What is a Madrasa?* offers the view that every *madrasah* narrates its own version of institutional memory and showcases its theological goods of authenticity. Representatives of the *Deoband* school, explain their *Maslak* as: not merely devotion to principles or the worship of personalities; neither do they (adherents of the *Deobandi Maslak*) view literature on religion and religious instructions as sufficient on their own, nor do they place reliance and trust in the views and acts of role-models alone. Rather, it is an amalgam of principles, rules, individual stories and personal biographies. In short, literature on religion is only acceptable on condition that it involves the lived companionship of the righteous and allows for the formation of a virtuous temperament (*Maslak*). To ignore any aspect of this is impermissible.[9]

Commenting on the study pattern at *Darul Uloom*, Prof Wasey says:

> 'See, one interesting aspect of *Darul Uloom* is that it is the centre of *Sunni Hanafi* Islam and the students who came from Afghanistan, Central Asian and South Asian countries and some even from certain parts of Iran, for them *Darul Uloom* was a natural choice as they themselves belonged to the Sunni Hanafi sect.'

The goal of *Darul Uloom* was to train well-educated *Ulema* who would be dedicated to a reformed Islam. Such *Ulema* would become prayer leaders, writers, preachers and teachers, and thus, in turn, disseminate their learning. To this end, the school set formal requirements for admissions and matriculation.[10]

Maulana Hakim Sayyid Abdul Hai Lakhnavi has fixed the following four phases of the old Indian curriculum at Indian *madaris*.[11]

First Phase

This phase lasted from seventh *Hijri* (1203-1299 CE) to the tenth *Hijri* (1495-1591 CE). For more or less two hundred years the acquirement of the following disciplines was considered the standard of learning: Grammar, Syntax, Literature, Rhetoric, *Fiqh*, Principles of *Fiqh*, Logic, Scholastic Theology, *Tasawwuf, Tafseer and Hadeeth.*

During this period, for the *Ulema Fiqh* and *Usool-e Fiqh* were considered the highest criterion of learning and merit. In *Hadeeth* the study of *Mashariq al-Anwar* alone was considered sufficient, and for more understanding and expertise in *Hadeeth,* the *Masabih* was the ultimate text.

The peculiarities that are seen in the curriculum of this period were the result of the inclination of the conquerors of India. The people who laid the foundation of Islamic state in India had come from Ghazni and Ghor (both in Afghanistan). In these places, proficiency in *Fiqh* and *Usool-e Fiqh* was considered a diploma of distinction; the rank of jurisprudential traditions in these countries was very high, so the new dispensation in India followed its old traditions as regards to the Islamic education.[12]

Second Phase

In the late ninth *Hijri*, Sheikh Abd Ullah and Sheikh Aziz Ullah, in order to somewhat elevate the previous standard introduced Qazi Adad's books, *Matal'e* and *Mawaqif,* and Sukaki's *Miftah al-Ulum* in the syllabi. Badauni has said about the two:

> 'Both these respectable men came to India (Hindustan) at the time of the devastation of Multan. They brought rational sciences into vogue in that land; earlier than this, in logic and scholastic theology nothing but *Sharah-e Shamsiah* and *Sharah-e Saha'if* were current'.[12]

At the end of this period Sheikh Abdul Haq Muhaddis Dehlavi, having studied the science of *Hadeeth* under *Ulema* of the two holy cities (Makkah and Madinah), tried to encourage and bring into vogue the study of the science of *Hadeeth*. After him his son, Sheikh Nurul Haq, also tried to spread the study of *Hadeeth* but did not meet with much success.

Third Phase

The people's aspirations had increased due to the change that took place in the syllabus of the second period and now they wanted to raise the standard of proficiency still further. Mir Fateh Ullah came to India from Shiraz. Mughal Emperor Akbar welcomed him by awarding him the title of *Adad-al Mulk*. He made some new additions to the previous syllabi, which the *Ulema* readily accepted. In his *Maasir Al-Ikram*, Mir Ghulam Ali Azad Bilgrami (1910) writes:

> 'He (Mir Fatheh Ullah Shirazi) brought the works of the later *Ulema* of the *Vilayat* (Persia) like Muhaqqiq Dawwani, Mir Sadr Uddin, Mir Ghiyas Uddin Mansoor, and Mirza Jan Mir, to India and introduced them into the circle of study, and a large crowd of attendants derived benefit from the Mir's assembly; and from that time the rational sciences gained a new currency.'[13]

In those days the centre of gravity of knowledge had shifted from Delhi to Lucknow. Moreover, the new relations that had developed with Iran during the period of Humayun and Akbar gradually produced a new change in the academic culture in India. Through the influence of the Iranian nobles and *Ulema* of the Mughal Court, Logic and Philosophy, which were *ab initio* considered the highest criterion of learning in Iran, were gaining superiority there over other sciences; but this restructuring of the course could not gain general popularity in India, in spite of the official patronage. [14]

Fourth Phase

The fourth period began from the twelfth *Hijri* (1688 to 1785 CE). Its founder was Mulla Nizam Uddin Sihalvi, who was the contemporary of Hazrat Shah Waliullah. The curriculum known as *Dars-e Nizami*, which is currently taught in all the Arabic schools, is a relic of him. Adding something more to the syllabi of the third period, Mulla Nizam Uddin prepared a new syllabus. [15]

However, there is a little controversy here, as Maulana Rashid Kandhalvi is of the view that Mulla Nizam Uddin didn't contribute to or formulate any syllabus, which could be called as *Dars-e Nizami*. In his article *Syllabus at Darul Uloom, Deoband* and *Mazahir Uloom, Saharanpur*, published in *Al Furqan* of June 2007, he wrote,

'There is no conclusive proof that the syllabus which is prescribed at these two leading institutes in any way was prescribed by Mulla Nizam Uddin'. He writes that 'references to Mulla Nizam and his works can be found in *Ma'asir Al Ikram* by Ghulam Ali Azad Bilgrami published in 1910, wherein no reference to any syllabus written or prescribed by him could be found. Further, in *Tazkar-e Ulema-e Hind* published in 1914 Maulvi Rehman Ali Anami has also not referred to any such syllabus. Even Mohammed Raza Ansari, who has penned a very literary and well-researched book, *Dars-e Nizami* on Mulla Nizam and his family, has devoted one full chapter to the topic but even that chapter fails to provide any clue that Mulla Nizam formulated any new syllabus.' Maulana Rashid further wrote that, 'some of the books prescribed as essential readings in *Dars-e Nizami* have been prescribed for ages and some books included in the essential readings were written after the death of Mulla Nizam, so it can't be concluded irrefutably that any such syllabus, which is known as *Dars-e Nizami* was ever prescribed by Mulla Nizam Uddin.'

Here it would be pertinent to point out that the first version of the so-called *Dars-e Nizami* was originally conceived by Mulla Qutub Uddin of Sihali (Barabanki) during the reign of Aurungzeb by way of reform to the *madrasahs'* education. The need to review the *Dars-e Nizami* was felt by Mulla Nizam Uddin, son of Mulla Qutub Uddin, because the early medieval *madrasah* education in India lacked a uniform syllabus. Each *maktab* and *madrasah* had different books for the students on languages *Tafseer, Hadeeth,* logic etc., instead of following a unified pattern.

Prof Moosa in *What is a Madrasa?* comments that posterity remembers Mulla Nizam Uddin for his ability to select classical texts for an educational syllabus that produced highly skilled and literate scholars, bureaucrats, writers, and intellectuals in his day. At the time, the beauty of Nizami curriculum, *Dars-e Nizami,* named after its author Nizam Uddin, was that each text was carefully selected for its pedagogical merits commensurate with the level of development of a student. Despite many mutations over the centuries, the curriculum still caries his imprint and is to this day, taught in thousands of *madrasahs* in South Asia and beyond. From the outset Nizam Uddin's goal was to produce a graduate who would think logically, acquire excellent writing and linguistic skills, and above all know enough about Islam as a religious tradition to address issues beyond basic questions of religious practice.[15]

In the middle of the thirteenth *Hijri or* eighteenth century there were three centres of Islamic education in India: Delhi, Lucknow and Khairabad. (In the last chapter we have seen that these centres changed with change of power and rise and fall of various kingdoms). Though the syllabi of the three were somewhat common, the points of view of all the three were different. More attention was being paid to *Hadeeth* and *Tafseer* in Delhi. Hazrat Shah Waliullah's family was assiduously busy in the dissemination and teaching of the Holy *Qur'an* and the *Sunnah*, and the anorectics were of a secondary position. In Lucknow, the old seventh *Hijri* tenor was dominant over the *Ulema* of Farangi Mahal, and *Fiqh* and *Principles of Fiqh* had more importance in their centre. In *Tafseer*, *Jalalayn* and *Baizavi*, and in *Hadeeth*, *Mishkat al-Masabih* alone, were considered sufficient. The academic subject at the Khairabad centre was virtually restricted to logic and philosophy; these subjects were taught with such care and assiduity that the teaching of all other sciences had almost become eclipsed before them.[16]

Prof Moosa is of the view that from the beginning of Islamic education in the Indian subcontinent to the present day, the *madrasah* curriculum underwent alteration during five phases. Each phase is distinguished by the addition or subtraction of texts and changes in the focus of curricular design.

By this historical reckoning, Mulla Nizam's curriculum in the eighteenth century fits into the fourth stage of a venerable trajectory of Islamic education. It serves as a capstone to a six-centuries long tradition of an identifiably Muslim intellectual and scholarly tradition in India. It is representative of a hybrid Arabic-Islamic and Indo-Persian tradition of learning. As such, the Nizami curriculum is the most successful and durable version of that long-established knowledge tradition. Some texts used in this curriculum had already been introduced to the community of scholars in India as far back as the fourteenth century.

Prof Moosa further comments that Nizam Uddin's pedagogical method was to stress upon the rational core of the Muslim intellectual tradition; he selected specific texts for each subject area. He and other Muslim thinkers, like Shah Waliullah, were of the same mind on the question of rationality. Shah Waliullah explicitly mentioned that divine inspiration had guided him to present Islam's teachings in 'loose fitting garments with an abundance of demonstrative proof (*burhan*)'. Nizam Uddin's intent was also clear: to resuscitate the Muslim rational tradition was the best defence against perceived cultural and political threats from India's new political masters. As a mainstay, the Nizami curriculum thus enjoyed a status akin to that of a canon in the *madrasah* tradition.[17]

Darul Uloom's Curriculum

By the second half of the thirteenth *Hijri* (1785 to 1883 CE) the educational centrality of Delhi and Khairabad had come to an end; however, some light of knowledge still lingered in on in Lucknow. Although the centrality of these places had ended, the distinctive peculiarities of all these three centres were more or less present in all the Arabic schools of India.[18]

The *Darul Uloom*, Deoband, has not only preserved the prominence of these sciences but has also played an important role in developing them. The peculiarities of all these three places (Delhi, Khairabad, Lucknow) have been gathered in the syllabus of the *Darul Uloom*, and the syllabus thus prepared with their amalgamation has been in force for more or less a century-and-a-half in all the Arabic schools in the country. At some places other modern syllabi are also current. Amongst such seminaries the position of *Nadwa-tul Ulema*, Lucknow, is most conspicuous, but this change is not very common, and more or less 90 per cent of the *madaris* follow *Dars-e Nizami* or in other words the one followed at *Darul Uloom*.

The present syllabus consists of four stages: Primary, Middle, High (Graduate stage) and Masters (Postgraduate stage). After the successful completion of this eight-year course of the Arabic classes the student becomes eligible for receiving the Graduate Degree (*Sanad-e Faraghat*) of the *Darul Uloom*. The postgraduate class is not compulsory; if a student wants to acquire specialisation in any subject or topic, he can take admission in the postgraduate class and continue his education. The curriculum of the *Darul Uloom*, Deoband, as detailed in Annex A, lists the subjects taught and books prescribed for an eight-year course, currently.[19]

Prof Moosa is of the view that representatives of the *madrasah*-sphere often point to one dimension that sets them apart from other institutions of learning like colleges and universities: theirs is a life that is matched by a life of practice. Learning the theory of Islamic comportment is one thing, to internalise a spiritual discipline in one's life is another. Teaching young people both the knowledge and the practice of a moral life is the fundamental purpose of the *madrasahs* of South Asia and their equivalent institutions around the globe. *Madrasah* life is centered on one's self-formation. Prayers are an inseparable part of practice and discipline.[21]

Primary Classes

According to the rules of the *Darul Uloom*, the completion of the following primary course is necessary for reaching the said 'Arabic Classes'.

The Holy *Qur`an* Class:

(1) First of all, it is necessary to at least be able to read the Holy *Qur`an*. Before the reading of the Holy *Qur`an*, generally the primer, which is known as *Qaida-e Baghdadi* is taught. The

ability to read the Holy *Qur`an* takes more or less two years. This period is for those small children who may have started to read at the age of five years and may have average intelligence; intelligent children can complete the reading of the Holy *Qur`an* in a much shorter time.

The period of committing the Holy *Qur`an* to memory is more or less three years.

(2) After completing the Holy *Qur`an*, the learning of Urdu and Persian is also necessary, but the Department of Cantillation is also there for those children who wish to be trained in cantillation after having memorised the Holy *Qur`an*.

The Cantillation Class: In this class, along with the practice of cantillation, the following books are also taught:

Jamal-al Qur`an, Ma'rifat-al Waqoof, Fawa'id-e Makkia, Sharah Al-Shatibia, Al-Rayyan Sharh, and Sharah Tayyaba.

This is a two-year course. It has been made compulsory for every student of the Arabic class that, along with other lessons, he should take admission for one period in this department and should practice to read at least the *Para-e Amm* with cantillation.

(3) Urdu Deeniyaat (Theology in Urdu): At the Department of Urdu Deeniyaat, besides the teaching of Theology in Urdu, arithmetic and other subjects are also taught. The course of this department is spread over four years.

(4) The Persian Class: At the Department of Persian, primary books of Persian prose and poetry, arithmetic, geography, Hindi and Arabic grammar are included in the course.

Over and above the primary classes additional classes for practice and teaching are as follows:

(1) Modern Sciences: This department teaches English language and contemporary sciences through a one-year course.

(2) Practice of Fatwa-writing (Ifta): There is a department to acquire articulacy in fatwa-writing and also for those who may graduate in the *Daura-e Hadeeth*. The period of training of this too, is one year.

(3) Jamia-e Tibbia: An educational department of the *Darul Uloom* is *Jamia-e Tibbia* also. Its course extends over four years and its syllabus consists of books of the Unani system of medicine as well as books of allopathic system of medicine.

(4) Department of Calligraphy: Graduates of the *Daura-e Hadeeth* can take admission in this department also. The period of practice here is one year. This department also renders the service of correcting and improving the handwriting of the students of the Arabic classes.[22]

On observing this syllabus of the *Darul Uloom* the question arises: 'Why were not the modern sciences, which had already reached India at the time this syllabus was compiled included in it?' The reason for this non-inclusion, according to Hazrat Nanautavi, was that these subjects were being taught in the government schools that had been established in the country at various places and everyone could take advantage of these. On the contrary, the old sciences were in a state of abandonment and there was not even a second-rate arrangement for teaching them. Moreover, in this syllabus itself, attention had been paid to the creation of such ability in the student that he might acquire knowledge of other sciences through self-study. This question had also cropped up at the inception of the *Darul Uloom* itself. On the occasion of the convocation of 1873 *(Hijri 1290)* Hazrat Nanautavi challenged and answered this question elaborately. He said:

'For the education of all, and to study the rational and traditional sciences and to acquire competency therein, this *madrasah* and the *madrasah* at Saharanpur are, no doubt, an excellent provision; and if it pleases Allah, the alumni here, provided they complete the curriculum, can easily and quickly acquire the remaining ancient and modern sciences by dint of the power of their ability.... Notwithstanding all this, even if some loss is conceivable supposedly due to lack of practice in some of the modern subjects, then due to want of ability and absence of the knowledge of religious sciences the students of those schools ought to be considered inferior to the students of this *madrasah*.... Hence, it was considered necessary to spend money for the traditional sciences, as also for those disciplines which certainly develop ability for the conventional (religious) as well as the modern sciences.

Secondly, the acquisition of numerous sciences at one and the same time proves detrimental to ability in respect of all the sciences. Of course, after acquiring the knowledge of intelligence developing subjects, which have been especially prescribed for the acquisition of ability, if the old and new arts (subjects) too are acquired, the span of time required for their acquirement will, of course, remain equal. The objective will be achieved well enough through its antecedence and subsequence, as also the ability of each science and hence the reason-developing sciences were also introduced, along with the traditional sciences, in the curriculum. Hereafter, if the students of this *madrasah*, joining government schools, acquire knowledge of the modern subjects, this thing would shore up their accomplishments much more.'[23]

On another occasion, replying to the objection that modern sciences have not been included in the curriculum of the *Darul Uloom*, he said:

'There is no arrangement here at all for the teaching of the worldly sciences. The answer (to this objection) firstly is that there ought to be a treatment of the disease. To take medicine for a disease, which is not there, is useless.'[24]

Teaching Pattern at Darul Uloom

The pattern of teaching at *Darul Uloom* can be divided into three grades: Primary, Intermediate, and High.

The aim before the teachers in the primary grades is to create the ability in the students to comprehend the contents of a holy book. Hence, in these grades stress is laid on comprehension of the holy books.[25]

In the middle or intermediate classes, along with comprehension of the holy books, such topics are also studied which may be essential for broadening the students' minds and for elevating their mental standard.

The method of teaching at the *Darul Uloom* is such that the student first reads the textual passage. Now, it is the duty of the teacher to lecture comprehensively on the read out passage that light may be thrown on every aspect and every question of the concerned passage. The teacher tries to gather all the necessary knowledge regarding the topic under discussion, and through his lecture on the passage, may satisfy the students. During the lessons, the students are quite free and unrestricted during the lesson. They are entitled to it, as long as they do not fully understand the lesson and may not get satisfactory answers to all the objections that may crop up in their minds regarding the problems under study, and they may not allow the teacher to proceed further. The result of this method is that, on one hand, the student attends the lecture fully prepared and, on the other, the teacher also 'finds himself constrained to teach with full preparation and attention'.

As a rule, during the lessons of the textbooks, the teachers' attention is concentrated on developing the student's ability to understand the lesson or topic besides also understanding the method of explanation as provided by the author.

For *Hadeeth* scholars, besides the *Mishkat-al Masabih*, the following books are included in the course:

Sahih Al-Bukhari, Sahih Al-Muslim, Jama'e Tirmizi, Sunan-e Abi Da'ud, Sunan-e Nasa'i, Sunan-e Ibn Maja, Mu'atta-e Imam Malik, Mu'atta-e Imam Mohammad, Sharh-e Ma'ani al-Athaar-e Tahawi, Shama'il-e Tirmizi.[26]

During the lectures on *Hadeeth*, discussion regarding the adaptation (*jah wa ta'dil*) of the narrators of *Hadeeth* is, wherever necessary, covered only briefly. Instead, more attention is paid to the technique of *Hadeeth* so that more and more power of deduction of propositions and the method of deducing may be developed in the students, and they may fully understand the method of education of the *Imams* of *Fiqh*. However, if the *Imams* of the practical methods of *Shariah* (personal law) have at any time stressed to pay special attention to any authority or narrator, it becomes obligatory to bring it under discussion during the course of the lesson.

In addition, the arguments of the four *Imams*, their principles of the deduction of propositions and the answers on behalf of the *Hanafis,* to the arguments of the three *Imams* are brought home to the students in such a sober and academic manner that nothing is detracted from the weightiness and glory of any one of the four *Imams*. Rather, the arguments and proofs of the three *Imams* are presented before the students with broad-mindedness. Since most of the books of *Hadeeth* and *Tafseer* that are included in the syllabus of the *Darul Uloom* have been compiled by the *Shafi'ite* and *Malekite Imams*, their arguments inevitably come before the students. Hence, it becomes necessary for the teachers that they establish the *Hanafis* method to be preferable in the light of arguments and evidences in such a way that the casuistic greatness of the three *Imams* may remain intact, admitting no distinction.

The enthusiastic students of higher classes, in accordance with the style of the predecessors, consider it necessary to jot down the teacher's lecture. As such, *Hazrat* Gangohi's and *Hazrat Sheikh-Ul Hind's* lectures on *Tirmizi*, entitled *Nafh Al-Shazzi* and *AI-Wird Al-Shazzi*, and Hazrat Sayyed Anwar Shah Kashmiri's lecture on the *Sahih-e Bukhari*, entitled *Al-Arf Al-Shazzi* and *Fayz Al-Bari* (which is in four bulky volumes) are the result of the same zest for jotting down. These are only a few examples of such accumulated lectures, which have been published; otherwise those that are still awaiting publication are too many to be counted. These gems of scholarly work are available for the graduates of the *Darul Uloom* to attain a better understanding of the subject matter.

The teacher's medium of expression while lecturing is Urdu—the language, which is spoken and understood throughout India. However, other languages like Arabic are also used for those students who may not understand Urdu.[27]

Educational Features of the Darul Uloom

As much as the word 'education' is simple and brief, to the same extent it is important, affecting the deepest recesses of the soul. Education is not merely the name of pictures of letters, phonetic lines, dialects and big and small textbooks. On the contrary, it is the name of such an intellectual, mental and academic training through which the latent faculties and talents of a man are developed to be adorned and organised, and human sentiments and feelings are civilised and polished by bringing them under an excellent and lofty ideal, so that useful fruits and consequences thereof may be brought into play for mankind. It is a difficult task to teach a man to use his talents correctly, but it is as much necessary as it is difficult.[28]

In other words, if education is limited to merely knowing the unknown things, then it is not something extraordinary, but if it is employed for action, then its difficulties are increased manifold. Although every community of the world appreciates the value of knowledge, the Muslims' view of knowledge is quite different from that of other communities. For Muslims, the attainment of knowledge is not just to attain it to secure a better means of livelihood, but it is also seen as an endeavour to achieve a better understanding of the world, its hidden literary gems, God's message and to spread it amongst others as a form of continued good deed (*Sadqah-e Jariah*).

According to Muslims, the acquisition of knowledge is a duty, by obeying it a Muslim, besides worldly attainments, also gains forgiveness in the afterlife. A saying of the Holy Prophet (PBUH) is:

'It is an obligation upon every Muslim man and Muslim woman to acquire knowledge.'

This obligation has been made necessary to ensure action, and it is incumbent upon every person as per his needs and desires to carry it out. It is an acknowledged fact of history that no nation in the world could become great if its powers of knowledge and action remain dormant. Education alone is the means through which spiritual and moral, civilisational and cultural progress can be made, which is the *raison d'etre* for the creation of humanity. In view of such progress, it is essential that every seeker of knowledge be provided an opportunity to develop his talents in the best possible manner. In other words, it is the primary duty of society that it provides such facilities whereby every student may display his best talents. In fact, nations are made through knowledge and are weakened through ignorance. Thus, it is imperative that every person should have equal opportunities for acquiring knowledge. Islam has made it an obligation to emancipate knowledge from the monopoly of any particular strata of society.

The history of every developed nation is witness to the fact that the secret of its progress and advancement is hidden in its citizens being educated, and this is not easy until there is an arrangement for free education. In the present system of education, the weight of expenses has deprived the majority of the advantages of education. The educational experts of the twentieth century have arrived at the conclusion that education of the common people ought to be free, and as long as this system is not adopted, it is difficult for education to be universal.[29]

Darul Uloom's Old Principles for Student Welfare

Under *Darul Uloom's* original system, educational fees were not chargeable; not only this but textbooks also had to be provided for the students *gratis*. Also, no rent was charged from the students for the boarding house, and destitute and poor students were also given cash stipends by the institution for food, clothes and other necessities.[30]

Provision of Free Education

The same traditions of the old system of education are the distinguishing features of *Darul Uloom*, even now. At present also fees are not charged from the students. Food, clothes and cash stipends are given by the *Darul Uloom* to all resourceless and needy students, and text books and accommodation are provided free of charge to every affording and non-affording student. As a result, education at *Darul Uloom* has not remained a preserve of the well-heeled only but even the most impoverished man can get his children adorned with education.

However, the following conditions are necessary for obtaining a stipend:

(A) The student must have studied holy books like *Al-Nahv al-Wazeh, Sharh-e Tahzeeb*, etc. (which are being taught in the second year).

(B) He must have obtained at least 37 out of 50 marks, which are the minimum marks for success.

Maulana Abdul Khaliq Madrasi, the Registrar of *Darul Uloom* says that;

> 'Education including tutorial fees and boarding and lodging costs at *Darul Uloom* are absolutely free for all students of the institution. They are also given Rs. 200 per month to meet sundry expenses. In addition, based on their performance PG students also get monthly stipends, which vary from Rs. 500 to Rs. 2,000.'

The stipend is of two kinds: food and cash. In the terminology of the *Darul Uloom*, both these kinds of stipends are called *imdad* (aid). Those students, to whom *imdad* is given, are also given four pairs of clothes, two pairs of shoes in one year and a quilt in the winter season.

All the students admitted in *Darul Uloom* are given textbooks on loan from the library for one year without any charge. Whether or not a student gets financial aid, he is not charged rent for the hostel-room also.

The *Darul Uloom*, Deoband, is perhaps the pioneer educational institution in India, established on the principle of free education and it has been running this free system of education with enviable success for more than a century-and-a-half.[31]

Educational Autonomy

The *Darul Uloom,* Deoband, is also the first educational institution that presented the concept of 'Autonomous System of Education' during the British regime in India and assiduously endeavoured to maintain intellectual liberty of the nation in an atmosphere of political slavery. The *Darul Uloom*, Deoband, never accepted any aid from the government in power; its entire resource and capital rely on public support.[32]

Current Syllabus and Education Pattern of the Darul Uloom

An impartial analysis of the syllabus of the *Darul Uloom* shows that it is far higher than the standard of the government examinations of *Maulavi, Fazil* etc. of 'the Oriental Languages'. On this account, had the *Darul Uloom* so wished, it could have easily got its *Sanad* recognised by the government equivalent to that of *Maulavi* and *Fazil;* but instead of making its *Sanad* a passport to secure jobs in government departments, it considered it more pertinent that it should try to create in its students such academic ability and merit that the moment people see its alumnus and its *Sanad,* they acknowledge it is a mark of value and that whichever task this man takes upon himself, he will be able to discharge it with competence and elegance.

On account of the extensiveness of its educational system, maturity in conformance to the *Sunnah*, and consummate firmness in arts and sciences, the *Darul Uloom*, Deoband, enjoys the position of a singular institution, particularly in the teaching of *Hadeeth* in which it commands an individual style, which makes it distinguished over all other educational institutions.[33] On the issue of syllabus and curriculum late Maulana Asrarul Haq was of the opinion:

'Hazrat Thanvi had advocated forming two groups at Deoband, one which had more religious leanings; this group was motivated to pursue higher studies in different Islamic subjects like *Fiqh, Hadeeth, Mantiq* and memorising the Holy *Qur'an*, whereas the other group was trained in certain trades also. According to him (Hazrat Thanvi), the challenge of coming days would be more on a theological basis so he insisted to constitute a band of scholars who were experts in their field besides being good orators and debaters. The other group was encouraged to join the secular education after completing elementary Islamic studies. More and more *madaris* adopted this approach and at present about 1/3rd of *madaris* in India impart secular education also up to primary or middle level.

I would also like to tell you that we have *Madrasah Boards* in 9 states, *madaris* are both aided and affiliated by these boards, but simultaneously these *madaris* are required to include secular subjects also in their curriculum. In Bihar we have *Fauqania* and *Wastania madaris*, if a student passes out of *Wastania* then on that basis he could easily take admission in 9ᵗʰ standard of the State Education Board.'

In his address to the British Parliament on 2 February 1835, Lord Macaulay stated:

'I have travelled across the length and breadth of India and I have not seen one person who is a beggar, who is a thief. Such wealth I have seen in this country, such high moral values, people of such caliber, that I do not think we would ever conquer this country, unless we break the very backbone of this nation, which is her cultural heritage and therefore, I propose that we replace her old and ancient education system, her culture. For if the Indians think that all that is foreign and English is good and greater than their own, they'll lose their self esteem, their native culture and they will become what we want them, a truly dominated nation.'[34]

This statement by Lord Macaulay gives us an insight into the mindset of the imperial rulers and how they wanted to change the Indian society, both socio-culturally and educationally to serve their purpose of dominance.

The leaders of *Darul Uloom* were intelligent enough to realise the designs of the colonial power. Moreover, after independence also, they refused to take any grant from the government of the day, though they had fought shoulder to shoulder with the Congress during the national freedom knew that if they did so they'll lose their autonomy and independence.

A Typical Day at Darul Uloom

As it is generally the practice in Arabic schools, at *Darul Uloom* too, the timetable is divided into two parts: the first part consists of four hours and the second of two. In the summer season, from 6 am to 10 am and from 3.30 pm to 5.30 pm, and in the winter season, from 8 am to 12 noon, and from 2 pm to 4 pm. Each period is of sixty minutes.

Rules of Admission at Darul Uloom

The doors of *Darul Uloom,* Deoband are open for every student who wants to acquire knowledge of the religious sciences, provided he agrees with the objectives and the educational ideals of *Darul Uloom.* At the time of admission, a fresh student is admitted to a class for which he is considered fit by virtue of his ability and performance at a written test; admission cannot be given on the basis of the *Sanad* of any other educational institution. However, those students who pass the Persian classes and join the Arabic class are exempted from the admission test. Admission in the Holy *Qur`an* class and Persian class is through separate applications.

Conduct of Yearly Examinations

In the earlier *madaris* system, there was no provision of holding yearly exams. When a student finished a holy book under the instruction of a teacher, a higher holy book used to be begun without holding a test for the previous holy book. It is evident that under this pattern there was no opportunity to assess and assay the student's ability, and very often even an undeserving student used to go on crossing the stages of progress. Perceiving this defect, the *Darul Uloom* has put an end to this system and made the quarterly, half-yearly and annual examinations compulsory.

Rules of Examinations

The examinations here are of two kinds. One is examination

for admission. It is held for those students who come from some other seminary to be admitted to the *Darul Uloom*. Usually it is held in the month of *Shawwal* (tenth month of the lunar based Islamic calendar).

The other examination is based on studies. They are held thrice in an academic year. The first quarterly examination is held in the month of *Safar al-Muzaffar* (the second month of the Islamic calendar), the second six-monthly in *Jamadi-al Ula* (fifth month of the Islamic calendar), and the last annual examination begins in the last week of *Rajab* (the seventh month of the Islamic calendar) and ends during the last ten days of the month of *Sha'ban* (the eighth month of the Islamic calendar).

Prior to the establishment of *Darul Uloom,* all Islamic educational centres in India were by and large private institutions. They had a common factor that all of them exercised neither classification, nor muster-rolls were there, nor were the students compelled to choose a subsidiary holy book and another subject with the principal holy book. There was absolute freedom; one could read whatever onc liked and read as long as one wished. There was no fixed duration for education or any particular mode of examination. *Darul Uloom* codified duration of education, maintenance of a muster-roll, holding of examinations, relevance of subjects taught and other such matters, and it is from here that these things gradually became customary in other Arabic schools, too.[35]

Annual Prize Distribution Ceremony at Darul Uloom

Darul Uloom started this practice in order to induce and motivate students towards educational activities and create a competitive spirit among them. Students considered worthy got prizes on their success in the annual examinations. A student securing the highest number of marks is awarded a special prize. Textual and non-textual holy books are given as prize, in accordance with the student's ability.

Testimonial, Sanad (Degree) and Dastarbandi (Turban Tying)

The students who, after successfully completing the course of the *Darul Uloom* in the annual examinations are awarded *Sanads* or degrees on their graduation. The title of each studied holy book is mentioned in the *Sanad,* but a holy book in the examination of which the candidate may have obtained less than 30 marks is not entered in the *Sanad*.

There are separate *Sanads* for the class of Persian, the class of Cantillation and the Department of *Tibb*. The students who drop out during the middle of the course, before completion, are also given testimonials for the holy books examination that they have passed. The *Sanad* of an *Alim* is given to one who passes the fourth year, and that of a *Fazil* to one who completes the syllabi of the eighth year.

According to the practice of the old institutions, besides the usual award of a *Sanad,* a turban is also wrapped around the head of those students who may have achieved distinctive qualifications in arts and sciences. This is done at a public function and at the hands of their own teachers. In the Arabic schools, the technical term for this turban is *Dastarbandi* (turban of proficiency).[36]

The *Ulema* of India, particularly the *Ulema* of Deoband have been blamed that by issuing a *Fatwa* against the attainment of English education, they prevented Muslims from acquiring it, wherefore the Muslims lagged behind other communities in the field of worldly progress. But this blame is baseless, because the *Ulema* were against only the kind of curriculum that might lead the Muslims towards atheism and irreligion.

This danger was felt in Aligarh too. Accordingly, to obviate it, an independent Department of Theology was established at Aligarh Muslim University (AMU), and when Maulana Mohammad Qasim Nanautavi's son-in-law, Maulana Abdullah Ansari, was invited to head it, the *Darul Uloom* promptly accepted this invitation. Maulana Abdullah Ansari graced this post till the end of his life and after him, his son, Maulana Ahmed Mian Ansari, was appointed to this post. He was also a graduate of the *Darul Uloom*. It is, therefore, obvious that in case of opposition to the English system of education, this decision might not have been possible.

Prof Wasey makes a pertinent comment in this regard, about the ability and expertise of *madrasah*-educated people:

> 'Another interesting aspect, which very few people know is that India's first Education Minister (Maulana Abul Kalaam Azad) was not a product of Oxford or Cambridge, he was also not an alumni of Allahabad or Aligarh University, he was a product of *madrasah* tutors who taught him at home, and this Maulana gave us the IITs, IIMs, Sahitya Akademi, ICCR, CSIR, UGC, Sangeet and Natak Academy, though he himself was a *madrasah* product and should have done nothing for the promotion of art and culture.'

As regards those students who, after graduating from the Arabic schools, wished to enter government schools, Hazrat Maulana Nanautavi, in his speech delivered at a function of prize-distribution held in 1290/1873, had encouraged such students in the following words: 'If the students of this *madrasah* join government schools to acquire the modern sciences, this acquirement would definitely shore up their accomplishment.'[37]

Countering the objection of certain people as to why modern sciences were not included in the syllabus of the *Darul Uloom*, Maulana Nanautavi said:

'If this thought is a stumbling block that there is no arrangement here at all for the profane sciences, its answer firstly is that there ought to be treatment of the disease. To take medicine for a disease, which is not there, is futile. If a crack in the wall is to be filled up, is it necessary to fire-up the kiln. What is it but silliness to be anxious about the brick that has not yet fallen down? What are the government schools for? If the profane sciences are not taught there, what else is done there? Had these schools been less in number than what are required, then it would not have mattered. But it is common knowledge that through the government's attention, towns and cities apart, schools have been opened even in villages. To make arrangement for the schools of secular sciences in their presence and be negligent towards the religious sciences is not the work of the longsighted wisdom.'[38]

In fact, the *Ulema* did not feel any hesitation in adopting the arts and sciences of other nations. The Muslims in the past had not only adopted the philosophy of Aristotle and Plato and other Greek philosophers but had also become masters of the medical treasures of Hippocrates and Galen. Researches on Euclid and Ptolemy had become an interesting pastime of their lives. Indian Arithmetic too had been cast in the Arabic mould.

In this very manner, foundations were laid in the Arabic

language for new literature, history, philosophy and knowledge, medicine, arithmetic, astronomy, astrology, chemistry, physics and other arts and sciences, which are a source of wealth of sciences and civilisations of the world today. Muslims adopted these sciences in such a way that instead of being felt strange they looked like Islamic sciences. In the acquirement of arts and sciences Muslims have always been open-minded. Every student of history knows that the Muslims have not only learnt the arts and sciences of Greece and India but have also developed and contributed to them.[39]

As regards to *Ulema's* aversion to learning the English language, it is a misrepresentation of the *Ulema's* approach, as learning English was never called impermissible and illegitimate by them. Rather, the *Ulema* were opposed to that culture only, which was associated with the English education and which alone was considered the singular means of advancement. It will be pertinent to ponder over this issue in the light of historical facts. It coincided with the beginning of the late Sir Sayyid Ahmed Khan's educational movement. A reputed divine of the time, Maulana Abdul Hai Lakhnavi, who belonged to the old educational centre of *Hanafi* jurisprudence at Farangi Mahal, Lucknow, had issued the following *Fatwa* regarding the English education:

'To study the English language or learn to write English is prohibited, if it be for the sake of resemblance, but if the purpose be this that we may be able to read letters written in English or the contents of their holy books, then it matters little. It says in the *Mishkat Sharif* that the Holy Prophet (PBUH) ordered Hazrat Zaid bin Thabith to learn the Jews' script (Hebrew) and he learnt it in a few days.'[40]

In Hazrat Maulana Rasheed Ahmed Gangohi's *Fatawa*[41] in reply to a query regarding the learning and teaching of the English language, it is written: 'It is correct to learn the English language, provided one does not commit a sin and there may be no impairment to religion.'

In the early period of British colonialism, Hazrat Shah Abdul Aziz Dehlavi's *Fatwa* too was to the same effect that, 'to learn the English language is permissible.' In short the respected *Ulema* never opposed the English language in itself at any time. On the contrary, for the earning of livelihood and the acquirement of knowledge and information they explicitly issued a *Fatwa* against it and its legitimacy, as is clearly evident from Hazrat Zaid bin Thabith's example in the Prophet's era. However, that form alone was declared impermissible through which, due to different reasons, the student's belief and faith were affected and which became the means of adopting un-Islamic culture, un-Islamic morals and anti-Islamic beliefs.

The reality is that there were several reasons for the Muslims' avoidance of the English language. The foremost reason was that, on one hand, there was bitterness in the Muslims' hearts against the aggressive British who had deprived them of their rule and empire; they (the Muslims) looked at everything English with aversion. On the other hand, the English too considered the Muslims as their real political rivals. Although in the war of independence of 1857, both the Hindu and the Muslim communities had participated, as per their capacity, yet in the eyes of the English, the Muslim community was seen as the real culprit. Hence, the English after gaining control, made the Muslim community the prime target of their oppression and grinding tyranny. The policy of depriving Muslims of every high place in the country and every circumstance was adopted. The idea of the English was to make the Muslims educationally backward and useless, so that the vision of sovereignty and exaltation might get out of their heads. This wound had been inflicted so deep that it was not going to be healed in a few days.

At the same time, though the Christian missionaries and priests in India were not allowed to openly preach Christianity but they did it with the backing of the British officials. The teachers in modern schools and colleges used to be largely priests and lessons of the Holy Bible were compulsory there. The *Ulema* alone were not opposed to this, as even a common Muslim, under such circumstances, was not prepared to send his children to these schools.

Maulana Fazle Haq Khairabadi, who had been sentenced for life and transported to Andaman-Nicobar Islands for the guilt of issuing a *Fatwa* for *Jihad* of 1857 on 26 June 1857, writes:

'The English prepared a scheme to Christianise all the Indian inhabitants. It was their belief that the Indians would not be able to find any helper and cooperator, and therefore, save, submit and obey they would not have the nerve to defy them. The English had thoroughly realised that the rulers' variance from the ruled on the basis of religion would be a great stumbling block in the way of domination and possession. Hence, they began to indulge in all sorts of wiles and chicanery with complete diligence and assiduity, in their wilful attempt to obliterate religion and the sense of nationhood. To teach small children and the ignorant and to inculcate their language and religion, they established schools in towns and villages and made an all out effort to wipe out the old sciences and academic attainments.'[42]

Earlier (in the pre-colonial era) the government used to be an institution, mainly concerned with administration of the country, army, police, revenue and finances. Most other walks of life were out of its gamut. The people of the country were free to organise their educational system, practice culture, observe morals and engage in social life as per their customs. As a result, it was presumed that with the change of sovereignty, a change in education and culture need not come. But the frame of the British system of governance was different its circle of operation covered all the aspects of life of the country and the nation and its jurisdiction covered all walks of life. English culture and English education had become correlative and these were considered the only means of advancement and civility. The *Ulema* were against it.

One of the reasons for Muslims to avoid modern education was due to the machinations of the British, so as to preclude Muslims from becoming rulers again, and secondly, the Muslims themselves, for fear of becoming irreligious, hesitated in admitting their children to government or Christian schools.

These were some of the causes that obstructed the Muslims from going to government schools and colleges imparting English education. Accordingly, when the missionary activities cooled down due to their own continuous failures, and the teaching of the Holy Bible was excluded from the school curriculum, and as time passed on, the Muslims' aversion against the English and English education gradually subsided, they began to show interest in English education.[43]

In fact, aversion to English education was the result of the Muslims national sense of shame and psychological reaction, including the *Ulema*. However, the *Ulema* recognised the spirit of the times and with full insight and foresight avoided issuing any *Fatwa* calling for not pursuing English education.

It will be worthwhile to note that over the years the *madrasah* fraternity in India has taken to learning English and teaching IT Skills in a big way. Even senior members of the *Darul Uloom's Majlis-e Shura* (Advisory Council) like MP-Lok Sabha Maulana Badruddin Ajmal runs *Markaz-ul Ma'arif* in several cities of India, with its headquarters in Mumbai, where diploma courses are offered in both English and IT Skills, and the Mumbai centre even publishes a monthly magazine in English, titled *Eastern Crescent*. Currently, the centre has also introduced an English teaching App on Google Play store.

Further the thrust for knowledge has always been present in the students of *Darul Uloom*. In 2008, I was instrumental in getting two English teachers of *Darul Uloom*, Deoband enrolled for the IELTS course at the British Council, New Delhi. They were able to clear the tough course with flying colours, at the first attempt. One of them is a now an Associate Professor of Arabic at the University of Delhi, whereas the second one teaches Urdu and Persian to students at SOAS, University of London, UK, in addition to performing his duties at a local *madrasah* in Blackburn, UK.

Further, the charges that *madrasahs* and *Darul Uloom*, Deoband are set against modern education also belies the fact. In 2008, I initiated a *Capacity Building Course for Madrasah Teachers and Students*, in partnership with the British High Commission, New Delhi and Faculty of Social Work, Jamia Millia Islamia. Under the initiative, 22 training programmes in 11 Indian cities across India were conducted, mostly at *madrasahs*. There was a huge demand from teachers and students to conduct the course from various *madrasahs*, as the results were there for every one to see.

After 21 days of intensive training on aspects of pedagogy, child psychology, planning lessons for different subjects in addition to personality development and English writing and speaking, the participants found themselves well prepared to counter any allegation against the *madrasah* and its products.

An impartial study of *Darul Uloom's* pattern of education and its system leads one to conclude that besides making the student a learned theologian or an Islamic scholar, stress is laid on his overall personality development also, so as to make him a better human being, who should be able to lead not only his fellow religionists but also his community and even country as time demands. And in this regard *Darul Uloom* has indeed contributed vastly during the last one-hundred-and-fifty years of its existence.

Darul Uloom's Administrative and Academic Structure

Majlis-e Shura or the Advisory Council

The administration of the *Darul Uloom ab-initio* has been based on the consultative principle of 'and whose affairs are a matter of counsel'. For this there is an authorised high council, which was formed along with the establishment of the *Darul Uloom* itself. This council is known as *Majlis-e Shura* (Advisory Council). The responsibility of the *Majlis-e Shura* is to look after and guide all the affairs of the *Darul Uloom*.

It will not be out of place here to stress that seeing the ordinary condition and limited resources with which the *Darul Uloom* had started, the adoption of a consultative pattern of administration of the *Darul Uloom* seems surprising. The people in India at that time were ordinarily not conversant and familiar with the democratic system. The *Darul Uloom* set up the *Majlis-e Shura* in the Islamic style and, running this system successfully, established an excellent example before the community. The corollary of this mode of thinking was that the democratic method was extensively established in the making of arrangements. As regards the qualities required of the counselors, Hazrat Maulana

Mohammad Qasim Nanautavi has given the following guidance in the third article of the Constitution compiled by him:

'The counselors of the *madrasah* should always bear in mind that the *madrasah* should acquire well-being and excellence, and no one should be self-partial, God forbid! If things come to such a pass that the counsellors consider opposition to their own opinion and their subscribing to the opinions of others unpalatable, then the foundation of this *madrasah* will become shaky.

Hence, it is necessary that the counsellors should on no account be hesitant in expressing their opinion and the audience always listens to them with good faith that is, it should be borne in mind that if others' opinion were convincing though it be contrary to the opinion of some of them, they would accept it with heart and soul. And moreover, it is also necessary for the same reason that the vice-chancellor, in matters requiring consultation, must consult the counsellors whether they are the regular counsellors of the *madrasah* or any intelligent, knowledgeable visitor who may be a well wisher of the *madaris*. Over and above this, for the same reason, it is also necessary that if, by chance, due to some reason, the vice-chancellor may not have chanced to consult a counsellor but may have taken counsel from a proper quorum of the counsellor the one not consulted should not feel displeased as to why he was not consulted. Indeed, if the vice chancellor may not have consulted anyone, the counsellor can take exception to it.'[1]

These were those excellent principles of the democratic system compared to which no other procedure could be better. The way of constructive criticism was opened through this proposal, which is so necessary for the progress of any institution.

The *Majlis-e Shura* of the *Darul Uloom*, on one hand, represents the contributors—it commands the status of a legal agent of the contributors—and, on the other, takes its decisions based on majority of votes with regard to the income and expenditure of the *Darul Uloom* and its important administrative affairs. The *Darul Uloom*, Deoband, has a constitution and all the procedures of the *Darul Uloom* and all necessary decisions are decided in the light of this constitution.

The *Majlis-e Shura* makes administrative rules and regulations. All the endowments and properties of the *Darul Uloom* are under its trusteeship and supervision, and the same council is responsible for the preservation of the approach of *Darul Uloom* and for the appointment and the dismissal of the employees. As per set norms, the *Majlis-e Shura* meeting at least twice a year is necessary. (List of the current members of *Darul Uloom's Majlis-e Shura* – See Annex B)

Maulana Rashid Kandhalvi commenting on *Darul Uloom's* administrative pattern says:

'I think now we lack the vision which keeps an eye on everything, now we are just continuing these things based on tradition only without any thought about the current situation and demand, furthermore there is also no will to change. I'll give you an example, previously the meetings of the *Shura* of *Darul Uloom* used to continue for 4-5 days, delegates used to arrive 2 or 3 days before the actual meeting, they used to examine each and everything related to the issues which were included in the agenda, took notes and then heated debates used to take place to consider every issue in all its perspectives, though they used to be such tall and intelligent men. What happens now is that *Shura* takes place for 2-3 hours, and even then basic challenges are not deliberated upon, the delegates arrive in the morning and leave in the evening, which shows lack of any interest in the affairs of the *Darul Uloom* or the will to change.'

The Original Members of the Majlis-e Shura

Initially, at the time of its establishment, this Majlis consisted of the following ten members:

(1)   Hazrat Maulana Mohammad Qasim Nanautavi

(2)   Hazrat Haji Abid Husain

(3)   Hazrat Maulana Mehtab Ali

(4)   Hazrat Maulana Zulfiqar Ali

(5)   Hazrat Maulana Fazlur Rahman

(6)   Haji Sayyed Fazle Haq

(7)   Sheikh Nihal Ahmed

(8)   Maulana Muhammad Yaqub Nanautawi

(9)   Maulana Rasheed Ahmad Gangohi

(10) Maulana Rafiuddin

There have been additions to the aforesaid number. At present there are 18 members of the *Shura*. The members of the *Majlis-e Shura* are selected from amongst the distinguished and influential *Ulema* of the country. According to the constitution, at least eleven members of the *Majlis* ought to be religious divines; the remaining ten members can be experts who have insight and expertise in administrative and educational matters. The vice-chancellor and the principal are ex-officio members of the *Majlis-e Shura*. To form the quorum at least one-third of the members should be present for the meeting.

The names of the current members of the *Majlis-e Shura* are available in Annex B.

Majlis-e A'mila or The Executive Council

A council called *Majlis-e A'mila* (Executive Council) has been in existence since 1345/1927, under the *Majlis-e Shura*. This has nine members. Its meeting is held every third month. The function of this council is to give cooperation and help in the works of the *Majlis-e Shura* and to put the administrative affairs of the *Darul Uloom* into practice, in accordance with the authorities delegated to it by the *Majlis-e Shura*.

An important feature of the *Majlis-e Shura* and the *Majlis-e A'mila* of the *Darul Uloom* is that though its regulations mandate a majority of votes for decision making, they are usually taken by consensus of opinion. The incidents of not having a consensus of opinion are very rare.

The current nine members of the Majlis-e A'mila are:

Mufti Abu Qasim Nomani, Maulana Arshad Madani, Maulana Badruddin Ajmal, Maulana Ibrahim Madrasi, Maulana Abdul Aleem Farooqui, Maulana Ismail, Maulana Rehmatullah Kashmiri, Maulana Mehmood of Khirwa, and Maulana Anwarul Rehman.

Departments of the Darul Uloom

The vast educational and official organisation of the *Darul Uloom* is divided into 32 departments. Every department commands the position of a separate institution which is headed by a manager who, remaining within the circle of his limits and jurisdiction, discharges, under the supervision of the management of the *Darul Uloom*, his entrusted functions. These departments, as regards their specialty, are divided into three parts: Educational Departments, Financial Departments, and Administrative Departments.

(A) Education, *Dar-al Ifta, Ma'arif Al-Qur`an, Jamia-e Tibbia,*

Tabligh, Craft & Industry, Calligraphy, Health and Publications are various non-academic and academic departments.

(B) Accounts, Organisation & Development and Endowments are financial departments.

The Accounts Department is concerned with income and expenditure, while the Organisation & Development and Endowments departments focus on income generation.

(C) Departments concerning administration are the following:

Ihtemam (Management), Record Office, Library, Reading Room, Kitchen, Buildings, Centenary Celebrations, Electricity, Sanitation and Water supply, External Affairs, Hostels, and Publications & Press.

The Education Department

By virtue of it being an educational institution the main objective of the *Darul Uloom* is teaching and education. This department had begun with only one teacher and one student. But every step of the *Darul Uloom*, compared to the previous one, has moved forward, and now this department has been sub-divided into the following departments:

(1) The Arabic Department: This is for the eight-year course of Arabic.

(2) The Persian Department: Persian literature, Mathematics, History, Geography and Hindi are taught.

(3) The Department of Cantillation: In this department, besides the complete education in cantillation and speech therapy, all the students of the Arabic classes are compulsorily exercised in reading the *Para-e Amm* with cantillation.

(4) The Department of the Holy *Qur`an:* As is evident from its name this department teaches small children to read and memorise the Holy *Qur`an.*

(5) The Department of Urdu Theology: In this department,

besides the teaching of Theology in the Urdu language, History, Geography, Arithmetic, Hindi etc. are also taught.

(6) Jamia-e Tibbia: It is for medical education in the Unani System.

(7) The Department of Ifta: It is meant for creating the ability of fatwa writing.

(8) The Department of Calligraphy: This department, along with chirography, teaches the art of copying written material in page form for printing purposes (kitabat).

(9) The Department of Craft & Industry: It is for imparting skills in light trades, such as, bookbinding, tailoring, carpentry etc.

There are 150 teachers in these departments and the non-teaching staff numbers 350. The strength of students every year varies from 1500 to 1750.

Mastery in speech and writing, oratory, practice of the style of expression and advancement in academic information in the students are an important means of Islamic *Tabligh* (preaching) and the dissemination of the message of truth and sincerity. Hence, like teaching, lecturing, instructing, and learning, writing and speech have also been made the most important part of learning. Besides this, it is also necessary that the students may have a special knack of organising assemblies and gatherings so that they may prove capable of methodically presenting their duties of religious call and guidance before the audience. In this connection there have been established a number of students' societies. There are usually four sections of such societies:

(1) Society for speeches in Arabic, Urdu and other languages,

(2) Society for writing in Arabic, Urdu and other languages,

(3) Society for enhancing debate skills,

(4) Society for reading/recitation.

But this system has been constructed such, that it may not cause any hindrance to the real objective of education. Assemblies of students are held every Thursday night in which, besides religious and reformative problems, students take part in academic and disquisitional manner on national, historical, political and social topics, and exercise in speech making and writing, and publish hand-written monthly journals. These journals are in Urdu, Persian, Arabic, Gujarati, English, Bengali, Tamil and other languages. Students put these journals on display boards outside every department and other key places. All the articles and dissertations are written by the students, and adorned with graceful calligraphy and floral designs. Besides the teachers in the Education Department, nine clerks also work in this department to do the clerical and administration work. The Education Council manages the Education Department.

Dar-al Ifta or the Fatwa Section

At the time the *Darul Uloom* was established, the teaching institutions of the old *Ulema* had become desolate and their *masnads* (seats) were vacant. The *Ulema* were few and far between and matters had come to a sorry pass in regard to the availability of reputed *Ulema* or *Muftis*. Hence, as soon as the *Darul Uloom* came into existence, the people's attention was diverted towards it, and a long chain of legal queries (*fatwa-seeking*) from all over the country started pouring in. As it happens ordinarily at the incipience of every work, instead of the establishment of a separate department for it, this work was initially entrusted to the learned teachers.

As such, Maulana Mohammad Yaqub, over and above his duties as the Principal, discharged the duties of *Fatwa-*

writing also. But when the number of legal queries increased extraordinarily, a separate department under the name of *Dar-al Ifta* was started in 1310/1892, and Maulana Azizur Rahman Usmani was selected for this important position. The lauded Maulana, besides being a matchless divine of the time and a great jurist, also commanded a distinct position in abstinence and piety and was considered a holy saint. Since then, such learned gentlemen who have had more profound insight in jurisprudence than others have been appointed to this post.[2]

Among the *Fatwas* that were sought from the *Darul Uloom*, there were, besides ordinary propositions of everyday use, important, complex and ponderable propositions, decisions of *panchayats* (councils of village elders usually consisting of five or more members), court-appeals, and *fatwas* on other divergent rulings. It is the duty of a *Dar-al Ifta* to show legal propositions to the supplicant with complete disquisition and soundness. Besides the common people, even *Ulema* often refer to it for many propositions. Despite this importance and delicacy, the work of the *Dar-al Ifta* at *Darul Uloom* has always been looked upon with satisfaction and esteem amongst the common as well as the high-ranking Muslims. The number of *fatawas* (plural of *fatwa*) issued from the *Dar-al Ifta* from 1866 to 2017 is more than 900,000 (app).

So far 18 volumes of these *fatawas*, entitled *Fatawa-e Darul Uloom*, have been published and many more are still being arranged. No fees are charged for the *fatwas*.

The building of the *Dar-al Ifta* consisting of three large rooms is situated on the upper floor on the eastern side of the complex. It was built in 1368/1949.

The *Ifta* Department also manages a website which is

owned by *Darul Uloom* Deoband, India (www.darululoom-deoband.com) and is specially meant for Islamic queries and *fatawas*. This website is maintained and managed under the Department of Internet & Online *Fatwa, Darul Uloom,* Deoband. All the translations (from English to Urdu and from Urdu to English) are carried out by this Department. All the *fatawas* published on the website are issued by the *Dar-al Ifta Darul Uloom* Deoband. Currently, the department employs nine Muftis to deliver this onerous task.

Majlis-e Ma'arif Al Qur`an

This department is tasked to publish disquisitional books on the Holy *Qur`anic* sciences.

Jamia-e Tibbia

There is a famous proverb of the Arabic language that 'sciences are only two, one concerning the soul and purification of morals and the other of human body pertaining to health and disease'. It is evident that both these sciences are important in themselves. And then ordinarily too, the science of medicine is a respectable means of livelihood and a beneficial human service. Like the religious arts and sciences there is a permanent department for imparting medical education at *Darul Uloom* for *Unani Hakeems*.

This department is tasked with teaching of medical science to the students and medical treatment of sick students. In this department, which runs under the name *Jamia-e Tibbia*, six able teachers teach the medical sciences. Its course is of four years' duration. For medical treatment, it has a clinic where students and non-students all are treated gratis.

Department of Preaching

In 1342/1934 when the organised movements of *Shuddhi* (purification*)* and *Sanghtan* (organisation*)* were started by Arya Samaj and Hindu Mahasabha in the country, this department of preaching was established at *Darul Uloom* to save the Muslims from apostasy.

Accordingly, with the untiring efforts of this department, besides securing millions of Muslims from apostasy, help was obtained at that time in awakening religious ardour and Islamic spirit amongst Muslims. The preachers acquainted the Muslims with the Islamic teachings and today there is no corner of India, Pakistan and Bangladesh where the preachers of the *Darul Uloom* may not have reached to spread the Word of Truth. *Siyasat Daily* of Lahore in its edition dated 27 June 1923 wrote: 'As far as the protection of religion, repudiation of the antagonists and reformation of the Muslims are concerned, the part of the teachers and preachers of the *Darul Uloom*, Deoband, far exceeds that of the whole of India.'[3]

In short, there is no comparable example of the *Darul Uloom* in India, especially in the history of the education of religious sciences. Similarly, in the extensiveness and abundance of preaching services also, it is *sui generis* in the history of this country. As such, wherever such functions relating to religions or religious debate are held in the country, the *Ulema* from *Darul Uloom* are particularly invited to attend them. The Department of Preaching makes arrangements to send the *Ulema* to different parts of the country on the invitation of the organisers thereof. The preachers, in such functions and gatherings, deliver lectures and sermons on different religious topics pertaining to Islam.[4]

Department of Calligraphy

Calligraphy is in fact, a branch of the fine arts. At *Darul Uloom* it is divided into two grades and hence it is considered a separate department. The first grade is for those students who may wish to improve their handwriting and defects of writing into a beautiful handwriting. In the second grade, the art of chirography is taught as a fine art, so that the student becomes an accomplished Calligrapher, who can write *Qur`anic* verses and other religious texts in a beautiful and artistic manner.

Under the old system of education correct and beautiful handwriting commanded special importance. The handwriting is half the knowledge' is a famous dictum, in which handwriting has been interpreted to be equal to half the knowledge gained. Along with reading and comprehension, a good handwriting was also considered very necessary. The educated apart, even kings used to acquire skill and expertise in this art form.

As such, in India itself, Sultan Nasir al-Din Mahmud and Emperor Aurangzeb Alamgeer were most accomplished calligraphers. Now, as many old concepts are gradually vanishing, indifference towards excellence and beauty of handwriting is also increasing day by day, particularly among most of the *madaris* it has almost become extinct.

In view of the importance of this art, both the *Nasta'liq* and the *Naskh* scripts were taught and improved at the *Darul Uloom*, and the students had to take an examination annually to pass in the practice of handwriting and calligraphy.

Department of Craft and Skills

Barbara D Metcalf (2004) writes that an abortive innovation on the part of the school was the inclusion of training in crafts and trades. There was hope that students thus trained, could support themselves in villages and small towns, and simultaneously share the benefits of their religious training with their neighbours. No doubt, this was expected to further the influence of *Ulema*, but the plan came to naught because the students deemed such work beneath their dignity as religious scholars. There was also talk of teaching surveying and cartography in order to provide students with skills for jobs in the expanded public works department of the government, but there were no takers for it.[5]

However, it had become much more necessary for the teaching institutions in this period to solve the problem of the students' economic future and livelihood. In this connection, the *Darul Uloom* had started teaching many arts and crafts for earning one's living. Besides *Tibb*, training of copy writing or calligraphy, bookbinding, tailoring and such other light skills were imparted to the students.

Considering the present-day demands, the need of starting arts and crafts in the *Darul Uloom* was a novel one, to ensure that the graduates of *Darul Uloom*, could be equipped with skills to earn their livelihood, so that they may render services to the religion with freedom and contentedness.

Commenting on the current situation at *Darul Uloom* with regard to skills teaching Maulana Rashid Kandhalvi says:

'I feel that no effort is being made to modernise and make the *madaris* more purposeful by taking any novel or revolutionary step or even planning for it, and a beginning should be made in this regard to impart modern skills to the graduates of *Darul Uloom*. When we'll get committed, sincere visionaries to transform the system, only then *madaris* could flourish and at the moment I can't identify any such person.'

Explaining the original view of the founders, Prof Wasey is of the opinion that:

'The syllabus prepared by *Hujjat-ul Islam* Maulana Qasim Nanautavi, gave a fair preference to vocational studies also, now known as Skills Management. He included the medicine system, Holy bookbinding, leather craft, calligraphy and other trades because he wanted the graduates of *Darul Uloom* not to be dependent on any one for their livelihood. His main idea was that after graduating from *Darul Uloom*, they'd start their own businesses and in spare time propagate Islam. And in reality, wanted them to be molded into self-reliant individuals.'

But at the same time it was also conscientiously decided that only those skills may be taught at *Darul Uloom* which would be appropriate for the students' and the *Ulema's* stature, and along with physical activities, mentally and intellectually stimulating activities and training may also be imparted in the learning process. Moreover, they may also fulfill on the whole, the day-to-day human needs.[6]

Accordingly, from 1365/1946 the training in useful and employable trades was started first with the bookbinding trade. In this department bookbinding, tailoring and manufacturing of holdalls, suitcases, etc., were taught. It was thought that in future this department, due to its utility, would become a respectable means for the students' economic future. But the reality is completely different.

However, the art of Calligraphy found many learners, as it was considered to be a white-collared job, coupled with possession of education and artistic leanings, resulting in creativity.

Publications Division

Publication Division of the *Darul Uloom* publishes the monthly Urdu magazine *Darul Uloom - Deoband,* and the fortnightly newspaper in Arabic, *AI Daie*. The academic and religious articles of both these journals are popular within and outside the country. Through these journals the *Darul Uloom's* point of view on various Islamic, academic and other current issues is presented and the articles and dissertations of *Ulema* are included.

The Accounts Department

Due to its specialty this department is very important. Its formation had taken place in the very next year of the establishment of the *Darul Uloom*. One of its functions is to keep details of department-wise income and expenditure. The paltriest sum and the most ordinary thing are not entered without a proper receipt; similarly, no expenditure is made without a voucher. Through this department the treasury of the *Darul Uloom* remains under the charge of the vice-chancellor. The entries of accounts, according to the current methods of accounting, are kept very neat and clear, and for auditing its door remains open to every man. Despite this, by way of scrupulous care, professional registered auditors audit the annual accounts. The distribution of the student's stipends is also connected with this department. To audit the expenses incurred by other departments is also included in the functions of this department.

Tanzim-o-Taraqqi (Management and Development Department)

This department also serves as the public relations centre

of the *Darul Uloom*. Additionally, the department also collects donations and grants for *Darul Uloom*. Presently, the department has 38 *Safeers* (ambassadors to collect donations), who tour every nook and corner of the country to collect donations for the *Darul Uloom*, besides two Public Relations Officers, to manage its public relations and media activities. This department was established in 1355 H (1936).

Tanzim-o-Traqqi's Mumbai Branch: This office works as a branch of the *Tanzim-o-Traqqi* in Mumbai, the commercial capital of India. It aims to maintain public relations and collect donations for the *Darul Uloom*.

The department also manages the collection of wheat and other cereals for *Darul Uloom's* hostel and mess.

The Department of Endowments (Waqf)

The mode of endowments or *Waqf* had begun with the construction of the buildings of the *Darul Uloom*. From time to time the charitable Muslims continue to endow their small properties for the *Darul Uloom*. However, this trend has died down in recent times.

The Management Section

Constitutionally, the section of management is the central point of the *Darul Uloom*. The management of all the departments and divisions, their supervision and the auditing of their expenses appertain to this section. The resolutions and decisions of the *Majlis-e Shura* and the *Majlis-e A'mila* are enforced through this very section. Besides the internal supervision of the departments, it is through the same section that external relations within the country are maintained. Hence, this section commands a certain importance. For major appointments of this section, such personalities may be selected who, besides having knowledge and learning, integrity and piety, possess special capabilities in administrative affairs, and may also command special influence and dignity within the country and outside.

The building of the management section is situated above the main gate and had been constructed in 1315/1896.

Record Office

The Record Office has been interpreted as 'the soul of administration' in the reports of the *Darul Uloom*. This office documents the entire historical record i.e. literary wealth of the *Darul Uloom*. The Record Office is situated in a two-storied room, adjacent to the management office. The papers and documents of all the departments and divisions of the *Darul Uloom* are preserved in this office. A particular colour has been fixed for the papers of each department, so they can be easily recognised and bundled together.

Darul Uloom's Library

In order to evolve a high standard of education that was envisioned by the elders of the *Darul Uloom* and to acquit themselves of the important responsibilities concerning the student's study, research and the writing and compilation of holy books, it was necessary to have a well-equipped library, without which a high standard of teaching, learning and research cannot be maintained. With this object in view, efforts had been started with the establishment of the *Darul Uloom* itself.

The *Darul Uloom*, Deoband, was established in 1285/1866. This is the first-ever national educational institution, which, instead of depending upon the government, laid the basis of its expenses on public contributions and gifts. The greatest need of the students is the supply of holy books without which the completion of education is impossible. As such, simultaneously with the collection of public contributions, the authorities of the *Darul Uloom* also started the process of supplying books to students. It was that time when the printing press had just been introduced in India. Books were scarce and were highly priced. So initially, books were borrowed for a short period from 'scholar-gentlemen' of the locality and the vicinity.[7]

These included textual as well as nontextual holy books, for the teachers' and the students' advancement in knowledge and general information. Accordingly, the *Darul Uloom* made an appeal to the country and the country responded to it whole-heartedly and holy books started coming in. The people who possessed collections of manuscripts or published books donated them and those who did not but wanted to help the library, helped with cash to buy and collect books. This mode has been in prevalence for the last 157 years. In the library, there is a great number of those books, which the Sultan of Turkey Rashad Khan, the Nizam of Hyderabad Deccan, Sultan Ibn Sa'ud of Arabia, Gamal Abdel Naser, former president of the Arab Republic of Egypt, and the kingdom of Afghanistan have donated to it. The majority of books in the library are those, which only the *Darul Uloom* has received in the form of donation.[8]

In short, in this manner a prodigious stock of books has been collected for the library of the *Darul Uloom* and to which additions are made continuously. The academic treasures of many learned families of India have been transferred to the library of the *Darul Uloom*. The number of books is more than a lakh (100,000), out of which more than fifty thousand are non-textual and the remaining are textbooks. This number is over and above those books, which are being received from the well-wishers of the *Darul Uloom* every year. In terms of numbers and distinctiveness of its collection, very few libraries in India can compare with the library of the *Darul Uloom*. As this library commands a distinct position amongst the libraries of India, the literati of India and foreign countries make use of its Islamic, Arabic, Persian and Urdu books for literary and research purposes.

Besides published books, the library possesses many rare manuscripts also, some of which are scarce and some exceptionally unique. Some are praiseworthy from the point of view of the art of calligraphy; some are worthy of attention on account of the antiquity of writing. Some of the books are in the handwriting of the original authors and some are nonpareil in respect of illumination and artistry. Some of these have adorned royal libraries and hence have historical value and some are those, which have been copied from the author's original manuscript or have been in the hands of famous *Ulema*. There are a few such books of which another copy is not extant in any library in the world. As such, different libraries of the world have taken microfilms of many manuscripts from the library of the *Darul Uloom*.

The *Darul Uloom's* library is divided into two sections: one is meant for holy textbooks and the other contains non-textual books. Both the sections are managed separately. The average of issuing and returning holy textbooks and their commentaries and *scholia* is fifteen thousand per annum.

The collection of Arabic books is the largest then comes Urdu books and a little less than them are the books in

Persian. In respect of arrangement and classification, these books have been divided under 99 heads. The details thereof are listed in Appendix C.

Maulana Khaliq Madrasi giving out details of the library currently says:

'For every educational institution, a good library should be considered as its spine. However, due to financial constraints a very big library was not built in the initial years and *Darul Uloom* continued to function with a very modest library, which currently houses 1,96,610 books, 1,389 manuscripts, 30 rare manuscripts of the Holy *Qur`an*, 857 Arabic, 438 Persian and 64 rare manuscripts in Urdu. So to accommodate more books from various religions and in various languages, *Majlis-e Shura* decided to get a new library constructed. This new library is 7-storeyed, each storey spread over 40,000 sq ft, and can house more than 2,000,000 books. Its Reading Halls at various levels can accommodate more than 3,000 students at a time. The new building also has an auditorium, which will be used for imparting the lessons of *Hadeeth*, as this course has the maximum number of students enrolled and which sometimes exceeds 1,000 could be seated here, in addition to the auditorium being used for conducting literary, social and cultural gatherings of the *Darul Uloom* and it will be able to accommodate up to 6,000 students.'

Besides this, the modern card system is used for issuing a Holy book and these cards have been prepared in alphabetical order, according to the current system in the libraries. The books are issued and returned using the latest technology such as computers and scanners, like any other modern library.

In *Darul Uloom's* library, besides holy books of Arabic, Persian and Urdu, books in different languages like English, Roman, Greek, Turkish, Indonesian, Sanskrit, Hindi, Tamil, Bengali, Gujarati, Gurmukhi, Marathi, Kannada, Pashtu and Punjabi, more or less, on different subjects, are also available.

Over and above the published holy books, a large number of manuscripts are also present. A descriptive catalogue of these manuscripts is being published. Two volumes of it have already been printed. The first volume consists of manuscripts only on *Tafseer, Hadeeth, Fiqh*, Beliefs and Scholastic Theology. The second volume gives an introduction to the manuscripts of *Sufism*, history, rhetoric, Arabic literature, lexicon, philosophy, logic, astronomy, conjugation and syntax, polemics, medicine (*Tibb*), miscellaneous topics, Persian literature and Urdu literature.

Research scholars often visit the library of the *Darul Uloom* to derive benefit from its rare and unique academic stock. In the past few years many research scholars from England, Germany, America and Japan, besides those from India, have benefitted in their research work. The *Darul Uloom* provides all possible facility to such people.

The library building is situated in the southeastern corner of the *Darul Uloom*. This magnificent building consists of eight big and small rooms and three wide halls. The present building of the library was begun in 1325/1906. Incipiently, there was only one hall and one room; thereafter additions were made to it from time to time, and now this building sprawls over a large area.

Besides books, reasonable arrangement has also been made in the library for reading newspapers and journals. Files of old issues of newspapers and journals have been bound and professionally preserved in the library. In 2019 approximately 65,360 visitors used the library of the *Darul Uloom*.

The Hostel Section

The hostels at *Darul Uloom* comprises of eight wide compounds and 210 rooms, which accommodate more or less one thousand students. The allotment of rooms to students, moral supervision over them and the settlement of their quarrels are the concern of the *Dar-al lqama* and these works are discharged through the teachers. Respect for law, obedience to the elders, mutual love, sincerity and tolerance are the special features of the ethos of the students of *Darul Uloom*.

Maulana Khaliq Madrasi giving details of the current hostels of the institution says:

'Before 1980 the facilities for students were not up to the mark, as in the initial years due to financial constraints it was not possible to provide students with very high quality facilities and most of the facilities provided were only rudimentary in nature. We had only one two-storeyed hostel for the students. And even this had only brick-paved flooring in the rooms. Most of the buildings in the campus were built with mud or mortar and bricks due to the constraints.

After 1980, a process of modernisation of the campus started and the process started with building hostels with better sanitation and access. But all these were not enough to cater to the large number of students, so a new hostel building *Vaqu-e Khalid* was built with a capacity for 1000 students, another smaller building with a capacity to accommodate 100 students was also built at the back of it, another building in front was constructed to accommodate additional 200 students. All together, these three new buildings are better constructed and equipped with all modern facilities. Another new complex called 'Assam Manzil' with a capacity to accommodate 1500 students has also been constructed.'

The Buildings of the Darul Uloom

The buildings of the *Darul Uloom*, in the northwest of Deoband city, are surrounded on all the four sides by a long wall. Due to space constraints within the compound of the *Darul Uloom*, recently some buildings have been built outside the old compound. The total area of all these buildings comes to 92,000 sq. feet. *Nau Darrah* (Nine doors), *Dar-al Hadeeth, Dar-al Tafseer*, library, management office, *Dar-al Ifta*, and the long chain of *Dar-e Jadid, Bab-al Zahir*, Guest House, Jamia-e Tibbia, and the Kitchen are the main buildings of the *Darul Uloom*.

Besides being the starting point of the buildings of the *Darul Uloom*, the *Dar-al Hadeeth*, by reason of its loftiness, extensiveness and grandeur, commands a distinctive position among all the buildings. Initially, in 1293/1876, *Dar-al Hadeeth* started functioning out of the building named *Nau Darrah*. The two-storeyed building of the *Nau Darrah* faces the East; its ground floor contains three halls, each 36 by 25 sq ft and in front of which there is a long 9-doored verandah, and that's why the name *Nau Darrah*. On the upper storey there is a wide hall the area of which is 68 by 35 sq ft. The lessons of *Daura-e Hadeeth* are given here and hence it is also known as *Fauqania Dar-al Hadeeth*. Its upper storey was constructed in 1352/1933.

At the back of the *Nau Darrah*, towards the West, is the

grand and monumental building of the *Dar-al Hadeeth*. The length of the hall of the *Dar-al Hadeeth* is 68 ft and its width is 35 ft. There are thirteen rooms around it, which are used as classrooms. The *Nau Darrah* faces East and the *Dar-al Hadeeth*, West. In this direction there is a verandah of stone pillars. In front of the *Dar-al Hadeeth* there is a garden. This building was completed in 1349/1930. Above the *Dar-al Hadeeth* is the hall of the *Dar-al Tafseer*.

In the preceding pages an elaborate account of the administrative structure, faculties and buildings of *Darul Uloom* has been provided, to acquaint the first time readers about the institute's capacity and the philosophy, which governs its day-to-day administration. After going through all these details the readers can form a very clear picture of the *Darul Uloom* and how it is managed, and how transparent its working is, so as to remove any misconceived thoughts about the institution and its administrators.

Women's Education at Madrasahs

Islam arrived as guidance for all mankind and as a catalyst in the lives of women, transforming their status overnight. Rights of women, a concept previously unheard of – or even thought about – were being upheld and protected. From being just a commodity in households, wives became a source of dignity. The Companions saw the Prophet's (PBUH)'s love for his daughters and his warm behaviour with them and were stunned at the fact that it was even possible to show such affection to females.

Zaynab Aliyah (2016) in her article *Great Women in Islamic History: A Forgotten Legacy* says that the Prophet (PBUH) taught them that there is no difference between believers on the basis of gender. Both enjoy the same rights and duties to learn and teach. Women have the same duty as men to restrain themselves and others from evil and encourage themselves and others towards good. Islam placed Paradise under their feet when they became mothers; they became the reason why fathers would enter paradise, and also such an integral part of a husband's faith that without honouring his wife, his faith remained incomplete. It was with this newly acquired status that women soared high and made their distinguishing mark in history, so as to not be left behind when the leaders of Islam were glorified.[1]

Education of Women in Islam

Commentator Moin Qazi (2018) in his article *Lost legacy of Female Scholars of Islam* opines that the Holy *Qu`ran* enshrined a new status for women and gave them rights that they could have only dreamed of before in Arabia.

On a historical level, Islam was incredibly advanced in providing revolutionary rights for women and uplifting women's status in the seventh century. Many of the revelations in the Holy *Qu`ran* were by nature reform-oriented, transforming key aspects of pre-Islamic customary laws and practices in progressive ways to eliminate injustice and ensure equality amongst the sexes.

The reforms that took place in the early years of Islam were clearly progressive, changing with the needs of society; however, the more detailed rules that were laid out by the classical jurists allowed many pre-Islamic customs to continue. These rules reflected the needs, customs and expectations of the society in which they lived, not the progressive reforms that were started during the time of Prophet Muhammad (PBUH). Hence, the trajectory of reform which began at the time of Prophet Muhammad (PBUH) was halted in the medieval period through further elaboration of *Fiqh* (Islamic jurisprudence), which was then selectively codified.[2]

In the first century of Islam, the burgeoning intellectual firmament was illuminated by a galaxy of exceptional women scholars, comprising the wives and female companions of the Prophet, on whose rigorous work and sound judgement much of the edifice of Islam was built in later centuries. They contributed significantly to the canonisation of the Holy *Qur`an* and were the transmitters of prophetic traditions *(Hadeeth)*. They were held in high esteem and were approached for instructions on religious matters even by senior companions.

Crowning this list of female achievers was Aisha, wife of the Prophet (PBUH), who was a scholar of exemplary erudition and one of the most respected intellectuals of her time. She was also a well-known authority in medicine, history and rhetoric. Others include Hafsah, Umm Habeebah, Umm Salama etc. who contributed immensely to the proliferation of *Hadeeth* collection, by readily dispensing their rich knowledge. Umm Waraqah was appointed by the Prophet (PBUH) as an *Imam* over her household. Moreover, it was a woman who corrected the authoritative ruling of Caliph Umar on dowry. The credit of founding what is arguably the world's first degree-awarding educational institution goes to Fatima al-Fihri, who founded the University of Al Quaraouiyine in Fez, Morocco in 859.

Taking a critical view of the reasons ascribed to the change of view amongst Muslims on the issue of women empowerment, Moin Qazi (2016) in his article *Muslim Women: Breaking The Glass Ceiling Of Patriarchy* says that cultures that arose since that time have been characterised by customs and localised leanings more than genuine Islamic values. The lives of the first Muslim women represent valuable models, transcending time and physical boundaries; therefore, these models serve as powerful, culturally authentic tools in advancing the human rights agenda towards increased female empowerment in the political, social and economic spheres of Muslim communities. The contributions of these women to the Muslim community are undeniable and to some, they even appear almost mythical. They are mistakenly subscribing to the erroneous notion that contemporary Muslim women cannot attain such stature. However, these women are representative of many others who lived, fought, learned, worked and led during Islam's foundational period and beyond. Their male companions, the *caliphs* who assumed Muslim rule following the demise of Prophet Muhammad (PBUH), treated them with respect, admiration and appreciation, and as equals. Society needs to actively guard the progress made by the female society; otherwise, they can regress.

Even in those nascent stages, Islam sought to elevate women and define them as independent agents with a free will. Twenty-four women appear in the Holy *Qu`ran* in various forms and for various purposes; 18 of those women appear as minors, the major five being: Mary, mother of Jesus; Bilquis, the queen of Sheba; Mary's mother Hannah, Hawwa (Eve) and Umm Musa, the mother of Moses. All of them are powerful examples of the tremendous potential of women.[3]

Joynab Khatun (2016), Research scholar at the Department of Arabic, JJT University, Churlia, Rajasthan contextualising the importance of education to women given in Islam in her research paper titled *Islamic Education in India with Especial Reference to the Women Sector of India* notes that according to Islam, education is a birthright of every woman. The Holy *Qu`ran* calls both men and women to acquire knowledge. Islam puts significant emphasis on imparting knowledge to women. Islam not only gives due respect to the women but it also draws attention to their education. Both, men and women have equal educational rights. There are some verses in the Holy *Qu`ran* and *Ahadeeths*, which are related to women education, in which Prophet Muhammad (PBUH) instructs women to learn what was recited in their houses from the Holy *Qu`ran* and wisdom: whatever they directly learnt in the company of the Prophet (PBUH), they should impart it truly to the member of the Islamic Umma.[4]

Islamic scholar Tharwat Al-Batawi (2017) in his article *The Doyennes of Learning* says that Islamic scholarship has never been a bastion of male privilege. Ever since the time of Prophet Muhammad (PBUH), gifted female scholars who mastered different disciplines of traditional Islamic sciences and played pioneering roles in the transmission and dissemination of prophetic traditions and other sources of knowledge have stormed the proverbial glass ceiling from time to time.[5]

Providing exhaustive details of the women who excelled in the field of education, Zaynab Aliyah (2015) in her article says crowning this list of female achievers was Aisha, the wife of the Prophet (PBUH). Closer home in India we had Razia Sultana, the only female to sit on India's throne in Delhi for four years in the thirteenth century. Ferishta, an eighteenth century historian, writes: '...Razia, though a woman, had a man's head and heart and was better than 20 sons.'

An Indian, by the name of Rasa, was the author of a book on medical care and the treatment of women. Her book is listed among medical works available in Arabic. Mariyah al-Qibtiyyah, an Egyptian, wrote on Alchemy in the seventh century.[6]

Dr Akram Nadwi (2013), of Oxford Islamic Research Centre, UK and author of a 40-volume collection of women scholars in Islam, *Al-Muhaddithat*, has, in his research, unearthed the accounts of many such scholars whose legacy and contributions have been forgotten. According to him, the current emphasis placed on the subjugation of women in Islamic society made it important to seek the real historical records of women's place in Islam. As Dr Nadwi describes:

'Initially I thought there might be about 30 to 40 women, but as the research progressed, the accounts kept growing until I realised I had no less than 8,000 biographical accounts of Muslim women who played major roles in the preservation and development of Islamic traditions since the time of the Prophet (PBUH) himself. The women I encountered were far from mediocre when compared to men and, indeed, some excelled way beyond their male contemporaries. These were exceptional women who not only participated in society, but also actively reformed it. Most striking was their calibre for intellectual achievement and the respect and recognition they received for it.'[7]

However, subsequent centuries saw this rich legacy being masked by patriarchy and bias, with many Muslim women finding barriers to accessing Islamic knowledge. Although most centuries can point to a few notable female Islamic scholars, the number of women active in the enterprise of Islamic scholarship has sunk drastically in more recent times.

Islamic scholar and educationist Abdul Hakeem Faizy Adrisseri maintains that there is no better way of empowering Muslim women than to educate them and give them access to all streams of knowledge, including Islamic theology where they proved their mettle in the first centuries of Islam. He blames certain reactionary practices and social customs for using faith as a pretext to block women from education, reiterating that it is not religion per se, but certain ossified cultural norms masquerading as religious decrees that prevent women from scaling new heights in areas of their choice.[8]

Educational Institutes for Muslim Women in India

Joynab Khatun, based her research on the topic of women education in Muslim society in India. She opines that during the medieval period, we find traces of some rulers having taken interest in the education of girls on Islamic lines. For example, Sultan Jalaluddin of Hinawar (1433-1456) founded 23 *madrasahs* for girls in his capital. Similarly, Shahjahan had also founded a big *madrasah* for girls in Fatehpur Sikri called *Madrasah-e Banat*. Thereafter, many other *madrasahs* were established for women to impart the most necessary knowledge of the Holy *Qu`ran* and *Hadeeth*.[9]

Razia, the daughter of Sultan Iltutmish, after coming in power harmonised the affairs of the state in general and education flourished in her reign. During the Mughal rule in India, Mahim Begum, a wet nurse of Emperor Jalal Uddin Akbar, a learned and qualified lady established a big school in Delhi to propagate education known as *Khair-al Manazil*. Salma Sultana, the daughter of Gulrukh Begum (daughter of Zahiruddin Muhammad Babur) was a distinguished and eminent poetess. Nawab Zaibunnisa Begum, the daughter of Aurangzeb memorised the Holy *Qu`ran* by heart and also learned calligraphy and creative writing and studied religious text books under the guidance of Sheikh Ahmad Bin Abi Saeed Hanafi Amithawi. Nawab Zeenatun Nisa Begum, the daughter of Sultan Muhiyuddin Aurangzeb was a renowned literary woman and excelled in piousness and nobility. Arjumand Bano, better known as Mumtaz Mahal, wife of Shahjahan was highly educated with a specialisation in Persian language and literature. Gulbadan Bano, the daughter of Zahiruddin Muhammad Babur was a good poetess and an intellectual. She wrote *Humayun Nama* a book on the life and times of her father.

After India's independence many women's *madrasahs* have been opened and bold steps have been taken to educate the Muslim women Some of the prominent women *madrasahs* are *Jamiat-us Salihat*, Malegaon; Kulliya Aisha, Malegaon; *Jamiat-us Salihat*, Rampur, UP; *Jamiat-ul Banat*, Jaunpur (Azamgarh), UP; *Jamiat-ul Banat*, Hyderabad; *Jamiat-ul-Falah*, Billariyagunj (Azamgarh), UP; *Jamiat-ul-Banat Shamsul-Uloom Niswan*, Ghosi (UP) etc. Abdul Hakeem Faizy Adrisseri started the first women's college in 2008 at Valanchery, Kerala. Presently, more than 1,300 girl students are studying in 24 colleges across Kerala. Graduates from these women's colleges are known as *Wafiyyas*.

Deeni Talimi Council was established in Uttar Pradesh, with the aim of establishing *maktabs* and *Deeni madrasahs* throughout the state. It has been active ever since. Though it lays greater emphasis on religious education, yet its syllabus includes modern subjects at the primary stages. As the *Maktabs* established by the Council are better organised, both boys and girls attend them. For the first time, girls have benefited in getting some modicum of education, other than mechanically reading the Arabic *Qu'ran*. Since girls could not study in boys *madrasahs*, the need was felt for separate girls *madrasahs*, which gradually came into being. Some educated Muslim women started women's magazines and organised Muslim women's conferences, such as the *Anjuman-e Khwateen-e Islam*. The latter, of course, were attended only by the women of educated families. They fought against the Purdah system, polygamy and certain kinds of unilateral divorces. Some organisations and individuals in different areas also established school for girls, though all these changes took place very gradually. Nowadays, women *madrasahs* are present in all corners of India.[10]

Role of Education in the Upliftment of Women

The need to educate girls was felt perhaps due to the liberal and transformative winds in the western world and its effect on the Indian educated class. It was felt that a girl educated at a girls' *madrasah* will be able to play an important role in social reform and in improving the conditions of her family. Joynab Khatun comments that the *madrasahs* offered an education which exposed Muslim girls to the correct understanding of Islam, and who can later go on to play a key role in the reform of Muslim society based on 'Islamic' lines and combat what are seen as 'un-Islamic' ways of life. It is claimed that if girls are taught in Islamic *madrasahs* according to the correct Islam, they will no longer be exploited by Muslim males in any aspect. An educated Muslim woman who knows the various rights that have been provided to her by Islam, such as in the matters of inheritance and divorce, would be able to argue and challenge her husband if he acts in violation of the *Shariah* in these matters. As educated mothers and wives, Muslim women might be able to play new roles and earn added respect within the household.[11]

In a nutshell, it can be seen that the *madrasahs* fulfilled both religious and secular needs of human beings and taught what was necessary for a secular as well as a religious life. Stress is placed on the Holy books and on *Hadeeth* in the women's *madrasahs*. Syllabi of women *madrasahs* have been made shorter keeping in view the needs of women students. Since the girls in Indian society are burdened with domestic responsibilities from an early stage of their lives, they cannot spend much time for education, so the texts have been prepared in accordance with their social problems having necessary ingredients, which can be finished within five years. After that a woman can start a matured practical life. Books have been compiled in accordance to women's individual and social requirements. As women are usually forced to run families, and as they cannot spend much time, the women's *madrasahs* have prepared a short course for Arabic and Islamic studies. If one is interested, then one can go in for higher studies.

Nowadays the curriculum of many women's *madrasahs*, also include teaching, cooking, sewing and embroidery. Some *madrasahs* also manage to give training and knowledge of nursing, general medicine and gyanecology to the students.

Theological precedents aside, the equality of men and women has come late in the day to Western Europe, with the status of women as "human" being debated in the sixteenth century and equal legal rights to men only being established by the nineteenth and twentieth centuries. Misogynism was internationalised, as Aisha Bewley (1999), translator of the Holy *Qur`an* in English, opines that the Western colonial authorities often excluded women from teaching in mosques and assuming political roles in the Muslim societies they colonised. 'The lens through which the West viewed Muslim women was already a distorted one — and once imposed or implanted among the Muslims, this viewpoint gradually became an established norm. As the technologically and scientifically superior Western culture impressed Muslim intellectuals, they grew more open to the values that these cultures brought with them,' she wrote.'[12]

Darul Uloom was established at a time when the Muslim community across India was facing insurmountable problems at virtually every turn of life. The aim of the *Ulema* who established the *Darul Uloom* was to establish such an institute, which would be able to guide the community both, religiously, spiritually and politically across the country, besides becoming a centre of excellence for the Muslim *Ulema*. Thus, this institute was purported to lead the way both academically and politically.

In this background, the primary purpose was to educate and prepare a band of such committed and well-equipped individuals who could be torchbearers for the whole community. So in this scheme of things, initially the leaders might have decided to focus on Islamic education of Muslim men but as the events afterwards proved, they focussed on women's education too, and many women-centric institutes were established separately all across the country later on and even in Deoband. But as *Darul Uloom* was established as an all-boys institute, they did not labour enough towards establishing any separate wing for women education but gave their blessings and support to such institutes which were established elsewhere.

In fact, the number of women *madrasahs* across India has increased steadly and an idea of their popularity can be gauged from a report carried by *Al Jazeera* in 2013, which reported that about 15 per cent of the students in West Bengal's modernised *madrasahs* are non-Muslims, besides a substantial number of non-Muslim teachers also.[13]

Darul Uloom's Role in India's Freedom Struggle

The division of the subcontinent into India and Pakistan had a very long-lasting impact on the political, social, cultural and economic development of the two countries. Partition, hatched by the colonial rulers through their policy of divide and rule, widened the rift between the Hindus and Muslims in the subcontinent. The new narrative painted one as the aggressor, and the other as the persecuted.

The new history written under the patronage of the erstwhile colonial rulers and to a certain extent under the patronage of the new government in India, tried to overlook or hide the role played by the Muslim leaders and the difficulties faced by the minority community, besides the immense sacrifices that they made, were all either forgotten or scuffed up.

It would not be wrong to say that the biggest sufferer of this campaign was *Darul Uloom*, as the new narrative, talked about the freedom struggle of the country, minus the role and importance of the *Ulema* and *Darul Uloom*, which were completely ignored.

As a result, the present generation is totally ignorant of the role played by the *Ulema* of this premier Islamic institution in India's freedom struggle and its opposition to the creation of Pakistan. In fact, not more than five per cent Muslims voted for Muslim League in 1946, on the basis of which the decision for partition was taken.

In this regard *The Princeton Encyclopaedia of Islamic Political Thought* opines that as British rule was regarded as an obstacle to proper Islamic practice and life, many *Deobandis* viewed colonial India as *Dar Al Harb*—the land of war, as opposed to being the land of Islam—*Dar Al Islam*. This theological opposition led the *Deobandis* to cooperate with nationalists from the Indian National Congress under Gandhi. The Silk Letter Conspiracy of 1916 revealed the extent to which *Deobandi* scholars had become involved in covert efforts against the British. The *Deobandis* soon dominated *Jamiat Ulema-i-Hind* after its foundation in 1919, which was the first public organisation of Muslim religious scholars of India.[1]

Today, it is largely unknown that the *Ulema* of the period were actively involved in the struggle against the British. Dr DR Goyal, biographer of Maulana Husain Ahmad Madani, one of the most politically active of the *Deobandi Ulema*, in *Maulana Husain Ahmad Madani: A Biographical Study's* preface says:

'The Ulema were the first to give warning against the threat to India's political power and cultural life from the British who came seeking trade facilities and, through cunning manipulation of contradictions among local rulers and chieftains, became the rulers over this rich country. It was their inspiration in the main that resulted in the first great uprising in 1857 AD which the British called the Mutiny and patriotic Indians termed as the First War of Independence.'[2]

Soon after his return to India upon his release from Malta, Maulana Mahmood Hasan was was conferred the title of *Sheikh-ul Hind*, meaning leader of all *Sheikhs* of India. Maulana Mahmood Hasan issued a *Fatwa* making it a duty of all Indian Muslims to support and participate with Mahatma Gandhi and the Indian National Congress, who had prescribed a policy of non-cooperation and mass civil disobedience through non-violence.

It was Maulana Husain Ahmad Madani who dared to issue a *Fatwa* in July 1921 at the meeting of *Jamiat Ulema-e-Hind* at its Bareilly session held from 24-26 March 1921 reiterating that: 'All Government services by which the government is helped are forbidden; specially serving in the police and the army is a great sin because they have to open fire upon their brethren.'[3]

After this *Fatwa*, he was awarded two years rigorous imprisonment. Yet, he never haltered in his efforts of bolstering the freedom struggle, till India got freedom.

Maulana Husain Ahmad Madani opposed the Two Nation theory and expounded with great intellect, vigour and moral force the need for a united nationalism in India prior to partition. He wrote a book in rebuttal to his ideological opponents, including Allama Iqbal and Abu Ala Maududi, *Muttahida Qaumiyyat Aur Islam* (Composite Nationalism and Islam). In this book he expatiated support for nationalism. He argued that Islam is not opposed to a United Nationalism based on a common motherland, language, ethnicity or colour, which brings together Muslims and non-Muslims sharing one or more of these attributes in common.[4]

In her introductory remarks to *Muttahida Qaumiyyat Aur Islam,* Barbara D Metcalf (2005) writes that:

'Maulana Husain Ahmad Madani may well have been the most influential and significant intervention in religious thought of any Islamic scholar of twentieth century India. The importance of his writing lies in the fact that they laid out in uncompromising terms, the Islamic sanction for Muslims to work and live with non-Muslims in a shared polity, and specifically, to embrace the secular democracy of a state like India.'[5]

At the time of independence, the Muslim League and the Indian National Congress were at loggerheads on partition of united India. Maulana Husain Ahmad Madani opposing the partition journeyed the different provinces of India along with Maulana Abul Kalaam Azad and Mahatma Gandhi to ensure the safety and security of the masses and tried his level best to stop them migrating from India to Pakistan. Many people targeted him, but he never warmed up to the opinion of the partition.

After Independence, he was offered a ministry, but he refused and restricted himself within the confines of *Darul Uloom* and *Jamiat Ulema-e-Hind* for teaching and social work. Perhaps this was the biggest mistake of the *Ulema*, that after achieving their goal of independence, they withdrew completely from all political activities in the country.

Sheikh-ul Islam Maulana Husain Ahmad Madani was also one of *Sheikh-ul Hind* Mahmood Hasan's students and later Professor of *Hadeeth* at *Darul Uloom,* Deoband. Though he had not been convicted in the *Silk Letters Conspiracy case*, he voluntarily accompanied *Sheikh-ul Hind* to Malta to help him.

Maulana Husain Ahmad Madani stayed in Malta for three years till the release of *Sheikh-ul Hind*. On his return to India, he was actively involved in the freedom struggle. He was imprisoned several times by the British authorities for his participation in the freedom movement.

Like Madani and Sindhi, there were hundreds of *Darul Uloom's Ulema* and students, who actively took part in the freedom struggle of India. It's lamentable that historians of modern India have completely ignored the role played and efforts made by the *Ulema* of *Darul Uloom* for India's freedom struggle.

Maulana Ubaidullah Sindhi (1872-1944), an 1891 graduate of *Darul Uloom*, is also among those forgotten. He was the most active and prominent member of India's freedom movement. He left India, following the commandment of *Sheikh-ul Hind*, during World War I, to get support of the anti-British central powers for an armed revolution against the British rule.

Silk Letter Movement
(*Tehreek-e Reshmi Rumal*)

The Silk Letter Movement was a well-conceived plan for complete freedom of India. However, it was leaked before execution and resulted in the arrest of hundreds of Muslim scholars and freedom fighters including the leader *Sheikh-ul Hind* Maulana Mahmood Hasan, himself.

In 1877, *Sheikh-ul Hind* Maulana Mahmood Hasan started his political movement and set up an organisation called *Samratut Tarbiyat* (result of the training). The aim of the organisation was to prepare for armed insurrection against the British. This movement continued for at least 30 years.

In 1909, *Sheikh-ul Hind* re-organised his devotees under a new banner *Jamiat-ul Ansaar,* which was later banned by the colonial rulers. Soon after in 1913, the freedom seekers appeared in Delhi with a new name *Nizzarat-ul Tahreek-e Sheikh-ul Hind.*

Maulana Ubaidullah Sindhi and *Sheikh-ul Hind* were the leading figures behind this new setup. The zeal, spirit and purpose of the new setup were none other than the freedom of India.

Maulana Ubaidullah Sindhi wrote a letter from Afghanistan to *Sheikh-ul Hind,* who was in Saudi Arabia, with details of his activities in Kabul along with the blueprint to form a government-in-exile and names of those who would lead the armed struggle against the British from within India. It was planned to start a massive armed campaign from all corners of the country coupled with mass agitation.

Maulana Mohammad Miyan Mansoor Ansari also enclosed a long letter detailing the names of the office bearers of the government-in-exile and a blueprint of the plans against the Britishers. The letter was written on a piece of silk cloth – because of which the English gave it the title of Silk Letter Conspiracy.

These letters were to be dispatched to Madinah through *Sheikh* Abdur Rahim Sindhi. However, on the way, when these letters reached Rab Nawaz, Honorary Magistrate of Multan, he immediately passed them on to the British Commissioner in Multan.

The date inscribed on the Silk Letters was 8/9 Ramadhan 1334 *Hijri,* corresponding to 9/10 July 1916, which reached the hands of the commissioner in the first week of August 1916. How such a significant blunder occurred and what followed this letter leak is beyond comprehension. [6]

The provisional government-in-exile, as detailed in the Silk Letters was very secular in nature, despite being led by the *Ulema*.

Ursula Sims-Williams (1980), in a paper for the *British Society for Middle Eastern Studies*, giving a detailed account of the Indian Government-in-exile writes that:

'The Provisional Government of India was a provisional government-in-exile established in Kabul, Afghanistan on December 1 1915 (sic) by the Indian Independence Committee during World War I with support from the Central Powers. Its purpose was to enroll support from the Afghan Emir as well as Tsarist (and later Bolshevik) Russia, China, and Japan for the Indian Movement. Established at the conclusion of the Kabul Mission composed of members of the Berlin Committee, German and Turkish delegates, the provisional government was composed of Mahendra Pratap as President, Maulana Barkatullah as Prime Minister, *Deobandi* Maulavi Ubaidullah Sindhi as Home Minister, *Deobandi* Maulavi Bashir as War Minister, and Champakraman Pillai as Foreign Affairs Minister. The provisional government found significant support from the internal administration of the Afghan government, although the Emir refused to declare open support, and ultimately, under British pressure it was forced to withdraw from Afghanistan in 1919.'[7]

Indo-German Collaboration

During World War I, Indian nationalists in Germany and United States, as well as the underground Indian revolutionaries and Pan-Islamists from India attempted to further the Indian cause with German finance and aid. The Berlin-Indian committee (which became the Indian

Independence Committee after 1915) sent an Indo-German-Turkish mission to the Indo-Iranian border to encourage the tribes to strike against British interests. At this time, the Berlin committee was also in touch with the Khairi brothers (Abdul Jabbar Khairi and Abdul Sattar Khairi), who had at the onset of the war, settled at Constantinople and later in 1917 proposed to the Kaiser a plan to lead tribes in Kashmir and North-West Frontier Province against British interests. Another group led by the *Deobandi* Maulana Ubaidullah Sindhi and Mahmud al Hasan (principle of the *Darul Uloom* Deoband) had proceeded to Kabul in October 1915 with plans to initiate a Muslim insurrection in the tribal belt of India. For this purpose, Ubaidullah was to propose that the Amir of Afghanistan declare war against Britain while Mahmud al Hasan sought German and Turkish help. Hasan proceeded to Hijaz. Ubaidullah, in the meantime, was able to establish friendly relations with Amir. At Kabul, Ubaidullah, along with some students who had preceded him to make way to Turkey to join the Caliph's *Jihad* against Britain, decided that the pan-Islamic cause was to be best served by focussing on the Indian Freedom Movement.

The Indo-German-Turkish mission to Kabul met Ubaidullah's group in December 1915. Led by Oskar von Niedermayer and nominally headed by Raja Mahendra Pratap, it included in its members Werner Otto von Hentig, the German diplomatic representative to Kabul, as well as, Barkatullah, Champakraman Pillai and other prominent nationalists from the Berlin group. The mission, along with bringing members of the Indian movement right to India's border, also brought messages from the Kaiser, Enver Pasha and the displaced Khedive of Egypt, Abbas Hilmi expressing support for Pratap's mission and inviting the Amir to move against India. The mission's immediate aim was to rally the Amir against British India and to obtain from the Afghan Government a right of free passage.

Although the Amir refused to commit for or against the proposals at the time, it found support amongst the Amir's immediate and close political and religious advisory group, including his brother Nasrullah Khan, his sons Inayatullah Khan and Amanullah Khan, religious leaders and tribesmen. It also found support in one of Afghanistan's then most influential newspaper, the *Siraj-ul Akhbar*, whose editor Mahmud Tarzi engaged Barkatullah as an officiating editor in early 1916. In a series of articles, Tarzi published a number of inflammatory articles by Raja Mahendra Pratap, as well as publishing increasingly anti-British and pro-Central articles and propaganda. By May 1916, the tone in the paper was deemed serious enough for the Raj to intercept the copies. A further effort resulted in the establishment in 1916 of the Provisional Government of India in Kabul.[8]

Formation of the Provisional Government of India

Although hopes of the Amir's support were more or less non-existent, the Provisional Government of India was formed in early 1916 to emphasise the seriousness of intention and purpose. The government had Raja Mahendra Pratap as President, Barkatullah as Prime Minister and Sibnath Banerjee, Ubaidullah Sindhi as the Ministers for India, Maulavi Bashir as War Minister and Champakaran Pillai as Foreign Minister. It attempted to obtain support from Tsarist Russia, Republican China, Japan. Support was also obtained from Galib Pasha, proclaiming *Jihad* against Britain.

Following the February Revolution in Russia in 1917, Pratap's Government is known to have corresponded with the nascent Soviet Government. In 1918, Mahendra Pratap had met Trotsky in Petrograd before meeting the Kaiser in Berlin, urging both to mobilise against British India. Under pressure from the British, Afghan cooperation was withdrawn and the mission closed down. However, the mission, and the offers and liaisons of the German mission at the time had profound impact on the political and social situation of the country, starting a process of political change that ended with the assassination of Habibullah in 1919 and the transfer of power to Nasrullah and subsequently Amanullah and precipitating the Third Anglo-Afghan War that led to Afghan Independence.

In Kabul, the newspaper *Siraj-ul Akhbar* in its issue of 4 May 1916 published Raja Mahendra Pratap's version of the Mission and its objective. He mentioned:

'…His Imperial Majesty the Kaiser himself granted me an audience. Subsequently, having set right the problem of India and Asia with the Imperial German Government, and having received the necessary credentials, I started towards the East. I had interviews with the Khedive of Egypt and with the Princes and Ministers of Turkey, as well as with the renowned Enver Pasha and His Imperial Majesty the Holy Khalif, Sultan-ul-Muazzim. I settled the problem of India and the East with the Imperial Ottoman Government, and received the necessary credentials from them as well. German and Turkish officers and Maulvi Barakatullah Sahib were going with me to help me; they are still with me.'

The provisional government-in-exile lasted for about three years. Meanwhile, in a span of just a few months, the colonial offices produced over a thousand pages of analysis from mere three letters. Two of the letters written by Ubaidullah Sindhi detailed his activities in Kabul in gathering financial support from Britain's enemies and securing arm supplies.

Having intercepted the letters, the British made swift arrest of many key plotters. About 222 leaders were arrested and faced tough interrogations, intimidation and torture.

Sheikh-ul Hind Maulana Mahmood Hassan was moved from Makkah to Cairo and after interrogation was sent to Malta. Officials avoided his imprisonment in India fearing arousal of anti-British sentiments. When *Sheikh-ul Hind* returned to India from Malta, he received a rousing welcome in the country. Later he joined hands with the Indian National Congress (INC) to fight against the colonial masters.

The Silk Letter Movement was perhaps deliberately forgotten and buried in heaps of prejudice. Currently, it finds no place in school's history textbooks and appears sometimes as a tricky question in various UPSC exams.

On 11 January 2013, former President of India, Shree Pranab Mukherjee released a commemorative stamp on Silk Letter Movement. Speaking on the occasion, the President said that the sacrifices of individuals and groups, such as those associated with the Silk Letter Movement constitute a glorious chapter of India's history of freedom struggle and need to be acknowledged and appreciated. The President said that he was happy that the Department of Posts has done its bit over the years and has issued postage stamps to acknowledge the contribution of various groups and movements, which in their own ways contributed to the overall effort to liberate

India as it truly reflects the multi-cultural and multi-faceted dimension of the freedom struggle.[9]

When the First World War (1914) began between Germany and Britain, the freedom fighters changed their action plan. They minimised domestic activities and fully concentrated on supporting Germany.[10] The freedom fighters saw the war as a golden opportunity to strike at the roots of the British interests. Armed insurrections were planned against the British forces.

Sheikh-ul Hind Maulana Mahmood Hasan dispatched his deputy, Maulana Ubaidullah Sindhi, to Kabul and he himself left for Arabia. The purpose of the visits was to solicit support from the Muslim countries, as without weaponry and their military support it was utterly impossible to achieve the goal. *Sheikh-ul Hind* reached Makkah on 9 October 1915 (1333 *Hijri*) and met the Turk Governor, Ghalib Pasha. On his request the powerful governor of the Ottoman Caliphate (Turkey) agreed to extend support against the British government.

However, as a consequence of the defeat at the hands of allied forces with full connivance of the United States of America, the Usmani Caliphate of Turkey was destroyed. The dream of *Sheikh-ul Hind* and his lieutenants to drive away the colonialists, by waging war against them on Indian soil, became difficult.

Partition of India

It should be remembered that the concept of adult franchise did not exist prior to India's independence. Adult franchise came into force only after independence when our Constitution was promulgated in 1950. But before independence the franchise was limited to not more than 10 per cent of the Indian population and it was these enfranchised people who voted in all elections before 1950. Of the 10 per cent Muslim population enfranchised about 60 per cent took part in voting and of which 60 per cent voted for Muslim League and 40 per cent voted for the Congress and other parties. Thus, not more than 3.6 per cent Muslims voted for Muslim League in 1946.[11]

Thus, few elite Muslims – *zamindars* (land owners), top civil servants, high-ranking police and military officials backed the Pakistan movement. The vast number of Muslim masses, who had no voting right and had no interest in creation of Pakistan, could not influence the decision in any which way. Similar was the case with the Hindu masses. They too had no voting right and remained mere spectators. If the Indian masses – both Hindus and Muslims – had a right to vote, perhaps Pakistan would not have come into existence.

It should be clearly remembered that the power elite brought about partition from both sides. It was failure of the power sharing arrangement between the elite of two communities, which brought about partition, not religion. Thus, Pakistan was not the creation of Islam but of vested interests of Muslim elite. Had Pakistan been the creation of Islam, the movement for Pakistan would have been led by *Ulema* like Maulana Abul Kalaam Azad, Maulana Husain Ahmad Madani and others and not by Jinnah. But we find that Maulana Azad and Maulana Husain Ahmad Madani were staunch opponents of Pakistan and a modern educated and highly Westernised person like Jinnah led the Pakistan movement.

It is interesting to note that Jinnah found it very difficult to enlist support of Muslim *Ulema* of great repute. They were all for composite nationalism. Maulana Husain Ahmed Madani, a great *Alim* of his time and *Nazim-al Umur* (Rector) of *Darul Uloom* Deoband, was strongly opposed to the Pakistan movement.

In fact, there is a long history of the *Ulema* making great sacrifices for the cause of Indian freedom since the British rule was established in India. They were also in the forefront of the 1857 war of independence and many of them were exiled to Andaman-Nicobar (then known as *kalapani*). Most of them could never return and died there. They never apologised to the British rulers. The British rulers executed hundreds of them after the 1857 mutiny.

Maulana Qasim Ahmad Nanautavi issued a *fatwa* urging Muslims to join the Indian National Congress when it was formed in 1885 and said it was their religious duty to drive out Britishers from India. He also collected about 100 *fatwas* from other prominent *Ulema* of his time to this effect and published them under the title of *Nusrat-ul Ahrar* (for helping the freedom fighters). Commenting on the *Fatwa* Asghar Ali Engineer wrote, 'The *Ulema* were convinced of the all inclusive character of the Congress Party and enthusiastically cooperated with it for throwing out British imperialists from India.'[12]

Darul Uloom became not only the centre of Islamic learning but also a centre of activities for the freedom movement. It is these *Ulema* who supported the *Khilafat* Movement and came very close to the Indian National Congress. Even after the failure of the *Khilafat* movement (in fact Kamal Pasha of Turkey abolished *Khilafat* itself) these *Ulema* continued to support the Indian National Congress and secular nationalism and do so even today.

Farhat Tabassum (2006) in her book *Deoband Ulema's Movement For The Freedom Of India* says that it is this glorious history of *Darul Uloom*, which, has to be kept in mind. It is absurd to criticise this important institution, which played such a key role in the freedom struggle. It is unfortunate that those who do not believe in composite and secular nationalism and want to create a majoritarian state are attacking it today. These *Ulema* never supported a theocratic state and vehemently opposed creation of an Islamic nation. They supported and continue to support secular nationalism till today.[13]

Expressing his views on the contribution of *Ulema* of *Darul Uloom* in India's freedom struggle Late Maulana Asrar-ul Haq reminiscenced:

'When *Darul Uloom* was established, its first task was to revitalise Islamic education, second the Muslims themselves should study Holy *Qur'an* and *Hadeeth* in depth, so they could explain the religion through reasoning and moderation *(istidlal)*. That is why our predecessors worked shoulder to shoulder with other religionists to get India free from the colonial yolk, as they were guided by these principles of equality and tolerance. And that's the reason that *Sheikh-ul Hind* supported Gandhian philosophy not the revolutionary ideals of Netaji Subhas Chand Bose. Our forbearers didn't adopt violence even during the freedom struggle; this is a unique style of *Darul Uloom's* leaders.'

Commenting on *Darul Uloom's* role in the freedom struggle Maulana Arshad Madani says:

'The people who established', they were followers of a special ideology, they were not just teachers confined to imparting knowledge inside a *madrasah,* neither they were those who would prefer to sit in a *khanqah* (shrine) and read *tasbih* (rosary). They had a set purpose, which was to get the country independent. They utilised all their energies to formulate a plan, which called for raising oneself above religious affiliations, and to bind them together on human grounds, to make the foreign power ineffective in its nefarious designs to continue to rule the country. This was the salient feature of what could be described as *Deobandi* Thought.

Even before the establishment of the Congress party and even after it came into existence, these *Deobandi* leaders continued to strive for religious unity and tolerance. They were instrumental in getting Gandhiji the title of Mahatma. Maulana Abdul Bari, took him all across India and introduced him to all parties, groups or factions involved in the freedom movement, all the expenses for which were borne by *Jamiat Ulema-e Hind* (JUH).'

Contextualising the whole issue Maulana Mahmood Madani says:

'*Ulema* played a leading role in the freedom struggle. After 1857 there came a time when orders were issued to capture and kill every *Alim* whom police could capture, as a result, thousands of *Ulema* were killed. Some of those lucky enough to have survived in northern India took unto themselves to restart the education of Muslims, the first such school started with just one teacher and one student, under a pomegranate tree. But in a very short time the fame of this school spread so wide that it turned into a mission or a movement. The first and foremost ideal of this movement was to reawaken the religious soul of the Muslim *ummah*. *Alhamdulillah*, Deoband was a success in this endeavor; it became the mother of all *madaris* in India. Secondly, the *Ulema* who were lucky enough to have survived the tyranny had the spirit to get their nation independent in their veins. They didn't compromise their goal but instead of an armed struggle they got involved with the mainstream of the freedom struggle.'

Summing up he said, 'That's why I always say that we are not Indians by chance but by choice,

Isi gali key hain khak sey, yahin khak apni milaeyngey,

Na bulaey aapkey aayen hain, na nikaley aapkey jayengey.'

After Maulana Mahmood-ul Hasan's death, *Sheikh-ul Islam* Maulana Husain Ahmad Madani took his place at *Darul Uloom* and as President of *Jamiat*. During his time when the nation was close to attaining independence, the two-nation theory started taking shape. But against the winds of the time *Sheikh-ul Islam* Maulana Husain Ahmad Madani and his followers including *Jamiat* as a whole canvassed for one nation, though unfortunately *Darul Uloom* was divided in two parts, one in favour of a unified India led by Maulana Husain Ahmed Madani, and one in favour of Pakistan, led by Maulana Ashraf Ali Thanvi. But Maulana Husain Ahmad Madani opposed this two-nation theory not on the basis of religion but nationalist politics.

Late Maulana Wahiduddin Khan on the contribution of *Ulema* in the country's freedom struggle said:

'In the freedom struggle of India many *Ulema* were actively involved. The founder of *Darul Uloom* Maulana Qasim Nanautavi had said (quoted in *Sawanh-e Qasmi* by Maulvi Asrar Girani) 'that we wanted to create a cantonment against the Britishers at this institution'. On the basis of this statement many people feel that *Darul Uloom* was associated with militancy, which is not correct at all. This was just a sentiment expressed without any misintention. In fact, *Darul Uloom* was the revival of Shah Waliullah's movement. If you could describe participation by *Ulema* of *Darul Uloom* in the freedom struggle of the country as militancy, then that is completely wrong, during the freedom struggle every Indian desirous of attaining independence took part in different programmes of the struggle, so should every Indian be clubbed as a militant? This approach continued till the independence of India, after that nobody could point a finger at *Darul Uloom's Alims* that they have ever participated in any militant or terrorist activity; this is all just pure fabrication.'

Maulana Wahiduddin further added that after the death of Maulana Qasim Nanautavi, two schools of thought emerged at *Darul Uloom*. One was in favour of participating in the freedom struggle of the country, whereas the second one felt that its core responsibility was to propagate the religious education. This school was led by Maulana Qari Tayyab Saheb, whereas the first group was led by Maulana Husain Ahmad Madani, who was a firm believer in saying that *Darul Uloom* also has to play a political role. Second important fact to note is that *Darul Uloom* was never influenced by the Muslim League movement, except some, like Maulana Shabbir Usmani who migrated to Pakistan. Overall *Darul Uloom* stood steadfastly with the Congress party.

Examining the reasons for *Ulema* of *Darul Uloom* to participate in the country's freedom struggle Prof Akhtar-ul Wasey says:

'If you try to analyse the real aim of establishing *Darul Uloom*, then first it was to strengthen the religious belief and convictions of the Indian Muslims and secondly to challenge the imperialist or colonialist forces in the country with other sections of the society. Furthermore, since the alumni of *Darul Uloom* were not just confined to India they not only learned the religious concepts but the concepts of nationalism and independence also, and implemented them in their countries on their return.'

Prof Wasey asserts that, 'they condemned imperialism or slavery of nations. They were the people who made Mahatma Gandhi a Mahatma. *Ulema* of *Darul Uloom*, Deoband advocated the fact very fearlessly that nationalities are not formed on the basis of religion but by nation. *Darul Uloom* has never preached violence and was always a part of the non-violent struggle for independence. That's why Mahatma Gandhi became a natural ally and friend of *Jamiat Ulema-e Hind*, an organisation which was an offshoot of Deoband.'

It is an irony of India's political life that the role of the *Ulema* is almost ignored in political discourses both in politics and academics. As a result, there is lot of confusion about the relationship of religion and politics and about the role of minorities in the freedom movement. It is the duty of the government to design such books which teach the young generation the truth of India's freedom struggle. It will further pave the way for national integration and strengthen the social bonds among various communities of the country. If it is ignored consciously or by mistake it is going to inflict serious consequences on the unity and integrity of the country in the long run.[14]

Dr Farhat Tabassum (2006) laments the fact that history has rarely searched the role of *Ulema* in the nationalist movement, she writes:

'It is generally thought that *Ulema* are incapable of coming up to nationalist aspirations because there is a tendency to think that Islam and nationalism cannot be synthesised. One of the common perceptions has been that *madrasahs* are the bastions of fundamentalism and terrorism and

Ulema are the inciters of fanaticism. Muslims have largely been dubbed in the history, as supporters of separatism, and roots of their isolationist penchant are traced to the emergence of the Muslim League and its consequent victory in the birth of Pakistan. It may be noted that the above perception is off the mark.'[15]

Analysing the roles played by Maulana Qasim Nanautavi, Maulana Mahmood-ul Hasan, Maulana Ubaidullah Sindhi and Maulana Husain Ahmad Madani, Dr Tabassum writes:

'The personality of Maulana Qasim Nanautavi, the founder of *Darul Uloom*, surfaces as a link, bridging the chasm between tradition and modernity in the Muslim society. Deoband was a product of his revolutionary thinking. His personality reflected a balanced combination of a social thinker and a revolutionary.'[16]

A trusted disciple of Maulana Mahmood-ul Hasan, Maulana Ubaidullah Sindhi carried the legacy of Mahmood-ul Hasan forward and can be compared with Subhash Chandra Bose, especially in his valiant efforts i.e. challenging the British Raj by armed means.

One of the important contributions of Maulana Husain Ahmad Madani was to mobilise the masses against the British by openly supporting the Congress. He understood that it was only a mainstream party, like Congress, which could articulate the national aspirations of people in general. He pleaded with Muslims to support the Congress and relied upon the Holy *Qu'ran* for explaining to them the supreme importance that Islam accorded to the idea of rendering loyalty to the nation. Despite stringent opposition from the fellow *Ulema*, Maulana Madani continued to expound the cause of Hindu-Muslim unity.'

If an impartial research and study of historical facts and available texts is made, then it will definitely lead to a large compendium of information, attesting to the vast contributions and sacrifices made by *Ulema* of *Darul Uloom* during India's freedom struggle. Even the currently available research conducted by both Indian and foreign researchers have a mine of information attesting to this fact. What needs to be done is to include that information with the current narrative on these topics and include that in the current discourse and let the people know the vast contributions of our forbearers, lest they are buried in the historical distortion of Indian history.

Western Media's View of Darul Uloom

It has been observed that whenever the word *Deobandi* is mentioned in the Western media or even the Indian media, then a negative perception is associated with it. What is the reason behind this and who is responsible for this?

The bias in the Western media, particularly its habit of dubbing every *madrasah* as a *Deobandi madrasah*, and describing *Darul Uloom* as a front for terrorists or a *fatwa* churning factory, are issues which confound every Indian or Indian-origin cleric, and they are in complete unity to denounce the Western media for its biased and ignorant view of *Darul Uloom*. As soon as any terrorist incident happens in the Western world, its ties are linked to *Deobandi madaris*, without even questioning or researching whether they are of Indian, Pakistani or Bangladeshi origin.

Commenting on the overall approach of the Western media on this issue, Maulana Mahmood Madani believes that Western media uses tinted glasses or is mired deep in their own cooked-up theories. Thus, they are armed with a typical mindset which cannot be awakened from its stupor as it already knows the reasons, but purposely indulges continuously in *Deobandi* bashing, under a plan! This very specific and biased perception is successful in keeping the moderate individuals and movements or organisations in India and even abroad on the defensive, at the fringes of mainstream narrative and getting eliminated in due course of time. This is not a new phenomenon but an old conspiracy remodelled every time. The need of the hour is to promote moderate and unbiased thinking and approach.

Maulana Khalid Saifullah Rahmani is of the opinion that the colonial powers in India and their supremacy was opposed by Muslim leaders and most vehemently by the *Ulema* of Deoband leading to the genesis of a negative relationship between the Western world and *Darul Uloom*. And it is this negative and vengeful attitude towards *Darul Uloom* that persists till today. This this is the main reason behind Western media painting an extremist picture of *madaris* to instigate their citizens instead of introducing them with a humanist or moderate face of the *madaris*.

Leading commentator in Urdu and alumnus of *Darul Uloom*, Maulana Nadeem-ul Wajedi believes that Taliban's erroneous claim to be *Deobandi*, rests on their schools following *Deobandi* syllabi and families following the *Deobandi* principles of *Hanafi* Islam, so they call themselves *Deobandi*. However, an ignorant Western media labels Pakistani and even Afghanistani *madrasahs* as *Deobandi* and links them to *Darul Uloom*, Deoband merely due to them following the *nisab* (syllabus) and *nizam* (administrative structure) of Deoband.

Prof Ebrahim Moosa is of the view that in Euro-America's war against the Taliban, *madrasahs (Deobandi)* have been turned into scapegoats by the Western governments with the aid of despotic Muslim governments in order to sustain a narrative of Muslim weirdness. Western public and institutions of civil society with few exceptions follow this viewpoint uncritically.

He goes on to add that *Deobandi madrasahs* fit nicely with attempts to raise the specter of Islam as a dangerous ideology, not a faith, to Western political interest. Self-appointed analysts often sound half-intelligent at cocktail parties in Washington and Whitehall if they sprinkle their conversations with reference to the dangers posed by *madrasahs*.

Particularly after 9/11, Islam is frequently painted in extremist colours as a religion that must be treated as an exception. Almost instantly the word *Deobandi Madrasah* together with 'Taliban' became synonymous with the West's fears of scary Muslim actors, trafficking in terror, who look as if they stepped out of a medieval time capsule. As a result, all *madrasahs*, in a post 9-11 world, have suffered whiplash at the hands of media campaigns fomented by a diverse range of actors. This has also helped Western leaders in altering the narrative and blaming a villain, which to a large extent has been a creation of their own.

Prof Moosa further says that it is fashionable to brush the Taliban in dark colours. Yet it is important to recall that once these rustic clerics were held out as the best hope for Afghanistan after Mujahideen, the group of fighters who expelled the Soviets but later brutally turned on each other.[1]

Most authorities on the subject acknowledge that a little more than a third of the Taliban's fighting force came out of the makeshift *madrasahs* in Pakistan's NWFP (North West Frontier Province), alleged to be affiliated to the *Deobandi* thought or school. To call these institutions '*madrasahs*' is to mutate the term. There is very little reason to persist with the libel that all *madrasahs* are hot beds of terror and conduits for militant Islam. Few observers are even aware that *madrasahs* affiliated with the *Barelawi, Ahl-e Hadeeth, Shia* and even some *Deobandi* theological orientations among the orthodox groups despised the Taliban and did so vocally and publicly. But, the story linking *madrasah* to terror is simply more sensational.[2]

Senior Journalist and former MP – Rajya Sabha, Shahid Siddiqui maintains that the Indian Islam is very different, due to the positive influence of the *Deobandi* movement. *Darul Uloom* imbibed accommodation, working together and respecting other communities and religions as components learnt and imbibed from traditional Islam, and the Holy *Qur`an*. And this was amply evident during the freedom struggle of India.

Pakistan and Afghanistan were beset by aggression and conflict firstly because of the Soviet invasion, which in turn was replaced by home grown despots. The skewed vision of the West while looking at Deoband arises from the fact that they have been only partially exposed to Deoband via the Taliban in Afghanistan, but Taliban has never represented the *Deobandi* creed, of accommodation, tolerance and coexistence.

Shahid Siddiqui further asserts that the Western media views Muslims of the world as a single bloc; moulded with a single dye. The fact that Arabs have a different approach to Islam, society and the world, in conflict with the Western world have become synonymous with the vast majority of Muslims in non-Arab countries like Indonesia, Malaysia, India, Pakistan and Bangladesh, accounting for nearly three-fourths of the democratic, modern and educated Muslim population of the world. This population is all for peace and condemns militancy or terrorism. However, the Western media, bent on presenting an erroneous view of Islam, has never properly understood that Islam is different in different parts of the world. It is easier for Western media to demonise Islam than try to study it.

Ajay Upadhyay believes that Western media has evolved due to sound education in journalism and mass communication imparted in that part of the world. However, the bias which is absent while practising independent and truthful journalism in their own country rears its ugly head once they are out of their territories and they view the rest of the world from a different angle. The South Asia, South-west Asia and East Asia are home to most complex segments of society in the world! India taught caste system to monotheistic Islam and Christianity. You cannot expect the Western media to easily understand these societal complexities in India, as Indians themselves are yet to understand their own complex society and its various aspects.

Commenting on the issue, Late Maulana Asrar-ul Haq dubbed the misunderstanding of Islam as a historical tragedy that arose due to the arrogance of the Western civilisation. This led the eastern scholars to restrict their interaction with the Western scholars and the overall people to people interaction which existed earlier shrank and thus the absence of a dialogue gave rise to misapprehensions. The West faced with the problem of Afghanistan, was quick to infer that Taliban was connected to *Darul Uloom*, the mother of all seminaries, and the canard that *Darul Uloom* subscribes to terrorist ideology and the Holy *Qur`an* preaches terrorism found credence! But then the Holy *Qur`an* has been preached for more than 1,500 years in the Arab nations and for 1,300 years in India and during this period not even one terrorist incident could be cited in which a *madrasah* was complicit directly or indirectly. The Afghanistan problem despite its long history never had any one Indian player as part of the Taliban movement or even ISIL/ISIS, a fact accepted by all the governments, whether of the past or the present.

Providing a more balanced view, Prof Wasey argues that during the Afghan conflict with Russia, the Western media was portraying Afghan fighters as Mujahideen, and it was perceived that the West had come to realise the import and the potential of Islam. And once the West gained whatever advantage was needed, then they turned back upon the Mujahideen.

Prof Wasey also feels that Osama bin Laden or Mulla Umar and organisations like *Al Qaeda, Boko Haram* or *ISIS* were not agencies created by an Islamist world but were the stooges of the West, used conveniently by them, therefore not reported upon by the Western media in their incipient stages! Muslims did not provide the assets, training and arms and ammunition to these terrorists, these came from the West. Prof Wasey also maintains in the same vein that West is mostly hostile towards Islamic nations with a democratically elected secular government at the helm, in contrast to their benevolence towards Islamic nations with authoritarian regimes.

Prof Wasey cautions the young generation from falling prey to Google's Islam, and subscribes to the view that Islam's future is intertwined with the future of Muslims and other people. He further asserted that religious pluralism is going to stay because of the will, desire and design of God.

Refuting these negative perceptions, Maulana Abul Qasim Nomani delves deeper into the basic fabric from which a student at *Darul Uloom* is cut and says:

'There are two things *aqidah* (belief) and *maslak* (religious tradition), *Darul Uloom's* foundations are on the basis of belief and religious tradition. Political inclinations or political bargaining are not the basis of *Darul Uloom*. The thought process behind *Darul Uloom's* belief is moderation and when seen in the international perspective all *Darul Ulooms* in the world affiliated to *Darul Uloom*, Deoband will have their belief as per the *Deobandi* tradition and this is same as what was the religious tradition of the founders of *Darul Uloom*, and their *fiqhi maslak* (jurisprudent belief) will be *Hanafi*.'

Maulana Nomani asserts that Maulana Shabbir Ahmed Usmani and Maulana Ashraf Ali Thanvi were affiliated with the Muslim League whereas Maulana Husain Ahmed Madani was associated with *Jamiat* and Congress, but these affiliations or associations were their personal ones and had very little to do with *Darul Uloom*. So, affiliations or associations which are born due to the local demands or aspirations, cannot be linked with *Deobandiyat*. As far as politicised *Ulema* in Pakistan and Afghanistan are concerned, they are not functioning according to the way prescribed under *Deobandi* belief; they are just furthering their personal or political views or objectives taking advantage of the situation. In a nutshell, religious tradition, belief and jurisprudent belief, are interlinked and amongst all *Darul Ulooms* in the world they are the same, even the syllabi is the same, but the *fikr* (thought process) is different everywhere (based on local demands or aspirations), and Pakistani and Afghani *Ulema* have proved that they are not linked to or influenced by the original *Darul Uloom's fikr*, in their day-to-day or even long-term activities or planning.

According to Maulana Nomani, the *Darul Ulooms* all over the world cannot be described as simply *Deobandi*, it shows lack of interest or knowledge on part of all those who describe it as such, or better to say that it is done intentionally to misguide. He suggested that western authors or journalists should study and understand what *Darul Uloom*, Deoband is and how it differs from other *Darul Ulooms*, which are described as *Deobandi*. Any effort to describe everything as *Deobandi* without going into the specifics of its *maslak* or *fikr* is very misleading and perhaps it is done to spread mistrust and enmity.

Maulana further opined that today, the world media and mass communication is controlled by lobbies or businesses inimical to Muslim faith. Even in most of the Christian countries, the detrimental force to decide what should be part of the public discourse and in what manner, is in the hands of these forces. Historically, one of the three Abrahamic faiths has been always against Islam and it is their continued endeavour to present Islam and everything associated with Islam in a negative and misinterpreted manner.

Prof Ebrahim Moosa in his book *What is a Madrasa?* contextualising the issue rather eloquently says demonisation of Islam propagated by Media pundits and shoddy journalism have led to the growth of cultural differences and schism between the West and the Rest. The stereotypical projection of *madrasah* education in which children squatting on mats and swinging rhythmically while memorising the Holy *Qur`an* only emphasises a one-sided picture of the *madaris*. The governance in India, Pakistan and Bangladesh view *madaris* as a sign of backwardness and nuisance and the Western projection that the traditional centres of Muslim learning harms intercultural understanding and unnecessarily raises suspicion about Islam as a faith tradition.[3]

The Western media also has a task, first, to understand the real ethos or circumstances responsible for the inception of this institution and then to analyse and explore its links with its namesake institutions in other countries, and then analyse how institutions in every country differ from each other, apart from following a core syllabus or texts. They will have to study the traits, attitudes and perceptions of a graduate from *Darul Uloom,* Deoband and compare that to graduates of other seminaries, and after finding the differences between the two they will be able to appreciate the larger difference in psyche, ethos and overall mental frame-up of the graduates and elders of these different institutions. Only then they will be able to recognise the true identity of *Darul Uloom,* Deoband in the overall jumbled and complex narrative of religious coexistence instead of sustaining the idea of clashes of civilisations.

Indian Media's Portrayal of Darul Uloom

It would be pertinent to say that not just the Western media, even the Indian media seems to be anti-Deoband and anti-*madrasah*. For the Indian media, Muslims have always remained its favourite flogging horse. The community is most often branded anti-national and not contributing enough to the progress of the country. This narrative perhaps was the result of ethos perpetuated after the partition of India. As the Muslims had got Pakistan, most Hindus expected all Muslims along with their institutions to migrate to Pakistan. But this did not happen, so for all the ills afflicting the country the most vulnerable community became their pet leitmotif to be blamed.

From 1947 onwards there were just a handful of newspapers and magazines in Hindi (*Daily Pratap, Daily Jagran, Daily Aaj* etc.) and Urdu (*Daily Pratap, Daily Veer Arjun*), which started the trend of demonising the Muslim community for every ill, pampering to the psychological demands of their readers in order to increase their circulation and profits.

These newspapers also carried their campaign against the

Muslim community at the behest of their political patrons. However, this trend, which for a long period remained confined to the print or elusive circles, increased in intensity and viciousness after the emergence of private TV channels in the country.

As TV channels now had access to almost every household of the country, they became the easiest tool in the hands of political manipulators to vitiate the minds of the illiterate voters and create a completely false and fabricated narrative. Thus, the power of TV was utilised by the political players for their narrow, selfish gains.

In the beginning the favourite key words, which were used by the media in its tirade against the Muslim community, were: Pakistan and Kashmir plus the *Darul Uloom* and its *Fatwas*. There is a long list of stories on *Fatwas*[1] issued by *Darul Uloom*, which has been carried out by the Indian media over time.

This coupled with so-called pro-Muslim policies of different governments of the day, resulted in starting various welfare schemes for the community besides commissioning various research studies to know the causes of their vulnerability and under-achievement. This further led to the right-wing politicians blaming Muslims for every ill in the country and criticising the government of the day as being too pro-Muslim, besides making the Indian *madrasahs* and its students as new scapegoats.

This coupled untimely with the war in Afghanistan, which brought *Darul Uloom*, Deoband to the forefront of villains, as most key players in the Afghan struggle were shown as having studied at *Deobandi Madrasahs* by the ignorant Western media. To correct the narrative, *Darul Uloom* issued *fatwas* on terrorism and JUH also held a national conference against terrorism in

February 2009 at New Delhi. But the 9/11 attacks further muddied the waters and every *madrasah* and its alumni were referred to as a *Deobandi*, with a whole tirade against them.

By this time the strident Hindu politics in the country had also gained strength. Over the years it became a minor player in some of the coalition governments and later was able to form its own coalition government as being the largest party. These small victories resulted in tasting the blood for some samurais of the Hindu nationalists, who were able to manage and win elections in the state of Gujarat first, on the basis of polarisation of the communities.

The biggest contributors helping in this polarisation drive were the Hindi newspapers and TV channels. Now the new keywords for whipping up passion were; Islamic *Jihad*, love-jihad, *nikah halala*, triple talaq, every Muslim possessing four wives, Muslim personal law, beef eating, *Tablighi Jamaat*, nationalism, patriotism and *Bhartiyata* (as per the right wing definitions of these) besides usual ones like Kashmir and Pakistan.

This negative profiling of the Muslims was and is diligently done by a band of favourite TV anchors to create a sense of unity within the Hindu community for getting political mileage for their masters. It is being done crassly to create maximum impact on the minds of readers and viewers, in addition to propagating fake news.

The media, particularly the television channels have indulged in this, as they know that the impact of their stories, which are largely anti-Muslim negative reportage will result in getting more eyeballs, which in turn, translates into huge profits for them.

Indian media's view and its portrayal of *Darul Uloom* is

of a '*Fatwa* churning factory'[1] meaning that *Darul Uloom* just churns out *fatwas* on each and every issue. Elucidating what a *Fatwa* really is, Irfan Engineer (2014) in his article '*Fatwas and Muslim Women*' published in *Secular Perspective* opines that,

> '*Fatwa* in Arabic literally means opinion. *Fatwa* is opinion of the issuer on some issue of Shariah or the other. As there is no clergy in Islam, the opinion is not binding, howsoever learned and qualified the issuer of the fatwa may have been. A *fatwa* issued by *Dar-al Ifta* normally ends with the words "but Allah knows better" after the opinion is expressed. These words itself shows that the issuer accepts the opinion expressed in the *fatwa* to be his best judgment on the issue, but not binding, as Allah knows better than him.'[2]

Elaborating further Irfan Engineer says that a *Fatwa* is issued in response to a query about matters relating to everyday life in accordance with *Shariah*. The query may emanate from any person, even a third person unconcerned with the query. Often journalists approach a local *Imam* of a mosque with minimum training in Islamic religious affairs for his opinion on matters pertaining to a third person. The objective may not be to educate himself with the opinion of the *imam* or a *mufti* but to publish the *fatwa* later for increased TRP of his channel or increase the sale of his paper. Other media then pick up and discuss the *fatwa* for days and weeks if not months. For example, *fatwa* on Imrana was sought by a journalist and not by Imrana or her husband or Imrana's rapist father-in-law.

Engineer further asserts that only an Islamic scholar, on the basis of Islamic law, can issue a *Fatwa*. The persons authorised to give *fatwas* hold the position of a *Mufti*. The person issuing *fatwa* should have pure intention to guide the seeker of *fatwa*;

he should have deep insight, equanimity and tranquillity; he should have a firm religious background and deep knowledge and should be aware of daily life and contemporary issues. Poorly paid *imams* of mosques in rural areas often do not meet these qualifications and are not authorised to issue a *fatwa*. They are not men of vision nor understand the issues involved and just follow the rulebook mechanically. A *fatwa* encompasses every aspect of life such as creed, worship, transactions, the economy, family, politics, governance, etc.

The negative stereotype of the *madrasahs* in the Indian media continues unabated, and a reason, which could be ascribed to it, is that powers that be have manipulated the issue in order to hide their incompetency in not doing enough for the community. The Sachar Commission report of 2006 talks about the impoverishment of the Muslim community and in the same breath about the *madrasahs*. But the question arises of why is the government concerned about just 4 per cent of Muslim students attending the *madrasahs*, instead of focussing and trying to provide quality elementary education to the rest of the 96 per cent of the Muslim students at a place nearest to their abodes.

In addition to Indian media's proclivity to use hyperboles in relation to *fatwa* or describing the students at *madrasahs* as terrorists knows no bounds. Another issue which comes under its lens and on which a lot has been written and commented upon in the Indian media is the issue of following an out dated syllabus and the quality of education imparted at Indian *madrasahs* and that of the *Darul Uloom* in particular.

But the critics fail to see that the drive to modernise the *madrasahs* has been taken by *Darul Uloom*. It first established a Department of English and Computer Studies in 2000 and that served as a role model for other *madrasahs* too.

As Moin Qazi (2017) in his article, *India's Emerging Modern Madrasahs* opines:

'While the debate over the modernisation of *madrasahs* continues, there are several *madrasahs* in India initiating change to bring them in tune with modern times. Some recent reform efforts have focused on modernising the teachings on offer at *madrasahs*. This modernisation includes the addition of computer proficiency and English language classes, which strengthen employment potential for students outside of the religious sector. However, the introduction of computer skills at many Deoband-type *madrasahs* is focused only on equipping them with functional literacy and not enabling them to engage with the modern technological revolution.'[3]

Political observer and writer Zainab Sikander (2020) says that the Islamophobic wave – where there is a tendency to brand students from *madrasahs* as terrorists, for instance – is alienating Indian *madrasahs* further. She goes on to add that the Indian media is waging a holy war against Muslims. It acts like hyenas and Indian media is not doing journalism. TV channels add *jihad* to everything, which bigots on social media then use to target individual Muslims.[4]

She further notes that if anyone is waging a holy war today, it is a section of Indian media, which is waging *jihad* against Indian Muslims and Islam. She further adds that journalism is now endangered and what is masquerading in its name is business — with open display of bigotry and hate against Muslims and other minorities. It not only builds its viewership base by hook or crook to more advertising money but it also doubles up as a PR firm for the government in power.

While commenting on bigotry against Muslims on social media, Zainab says that it is more pronounced as it takes inspiration, and content, from the news channels that engage in hate 24x7. So, the question remains, why does Indian media detest Muslims so much? Why don't news anchors spewing this anti-Muslim venom ever get tired of demonising Muslims day in and day out? Is it that majority of Hindus have always hated Muslims and after 9/11, the advent of Bin Laden, Al Qaeda, ISIS, and 2014, it just became the new normal to do so publicly? Or has the persistent propaganda to reinforce fanatic beliefs about Muslims as being violent and irrational led majority of Hindus to inculcate them in their daily lives, even if they have personally never experienced any of those propagated beliefs?[5]

It is not as if this Muslim bashing is something new. Way back in 2002 the RSS acolytes like Rajendra Chaddha writes that the mushrooming of *madrasahs* and their turning into hotbeds of extremist elements is creating terrorism in the society at large. He wrote that the unrecognised *madrasahs*, which preach hatred against people professing other faiths, are detrimental to harmony of the Indian society. [6]

Shreyasi Rao (2019) in her co-authored article, *Situating the Madrasa in Modern India: Is Reform Around the Corner?* argues that of late, there has been renewed interest in *madrasahs* as emblematic of a safe space that can stem the systemic erasure of Islamic culture amidst a movement to saffronise mainstream schooling. This notion of privately guarding Islamic teachings from neo-colonial processes has catalysed resistance against calls for reforming the *madrasah* system.[7]

The misconceptions on this and various other issues related to *madaris* and Muslims fundamentally shows the triteness of the Indian media and also its non-readiness to understand what a *madrasah* really is and what is the difference between different *madaris*. As the word *Deobandi* has been made synonymous with *Darul Uloom*, it serves the purpose well to brand all *madaris* as a *Deobandi,* without taking pain to understand, analyse and then report that *madaris* in every country, apart from following a more or less common syllabus, differ completely in their ethos, spirit and character. Even Islam in every country is somewhat different in the treatment of different issues.

The Western world blindly categorises every *madrasah* in the Middle Eastern or Pakistani or Afghanistani sense. As Prof Moosa aptly advises that to overcome this misrepresentation, we should start '*Madrasah tourism*', by which he means that people claiming to be authorities on *Darul Uloom* and other *madrasahs* should go there and stay there for a week or two, this would enable them to observe the academics, the students and the administration from a close angle and also promote dialogue with them, enabling them to see firsthand what the reality is. In fact, the reality is completely different; all *Deobandi madaris* are not the same, particularly the *Darul Uloom*, Deoband is hundred per cent different from *Darul Ulooms* in Pakistan, Afghanistan and elsewhere, to which we now turn to the next chapter.

Darul Uloom in the Subcontinent

Darul Uloom which started off as a small sapling in 1866, ultimately grew into a giant tree with branches not only in every Indian city or state, but even in neighbouring countries like Pakistan, Afghanistan, Bangladesh and European countries like UK and Germany besides several South African nations, Canada, USA and most of the South American countries.

What was the reason for the expansion of this institution to spread so quickly and so far and wide? One reason could be that *Darul Uloom* preached a different version of Islam to the one preached in most Arab countries, though the basic tenets remained same, yet the approach towards interpreting them was somewhat different. Its foundations were also cemented by the Indian ethos and principles of tolerance and coexistence. Like Arab Islam, which spawned strict *Wahabi, Ahl-e Hadeeth* or *Salafi* versions, and to which most of the ill-famed characters associated with extremist activities belonged to, *Deobandi* Islam is a more tolerant and engaging version.

Further, as the teachings were steeped in local ethos, customs and traditions, they found sympathetic followers in neighbouring countries too. These followers established institutions that were modeled after the *Darul Uloom*, Deoband.

Madaris in Pakistan and Afghanistan

Most of the *madaris* linked to *Darul Uloom*, Deoband established in Pakistan, were part of undivided India when they were setup by *Deobandi Ulema*, who in turn were the alumni of the *Darul Uloom* Deoband and followed the same syllabus and thinking which were imbibed to them at the *Darul Uloom*.

In 1942, there was a split in the *Darul Uloom* and Maulana Ashraf Usmani formed *Jamiat Ulema-i Islam* and aligned with Muslim League. But even after the formation of Pakistan, the *madaris* established by the Pakistani *Ulema* continued to follow the practices and ideals of *Darul Uloom*, Deoband. The same pattern was followed in Afghanistan and Bangladesh, too, which were earlier part of erstwhile India.

Deobandis and *Barelawis* are the two major groups of Sunni Muslims in the subcontinent apart from the Shia Muslims. In Pakistan, *Barelawi Hanafis* deem *Deobandis* to be *kaafir*. Those hostile to the *Barelawis*, denounce them as the shrine and grave-worshipping, ignorant Muslims. Much smaller sects in Pakistan include the *Ahl-e Hadeeth* (also spelled as *Ahl-e Hadees*), *Ahl-e Tashee* (Shias) and *Ahmediyas* or *Qadianis*. The non-Pakhtun population of Pakistan is predominantly *Barelawi*. The stronghold of *Barelawism* remains Punjab, the largest province of Pakistan. By one estimate, in Pakistan, the Shias are 18 per cent, Ismailis 2 per cent, *Ahmediyas* 2 per cent, *Barelawis* 50 per cent, *Deobandis* 20 per cent, *Ahl-e Hadeeth* 4 per cent, and other minorities 4 per cent. The *Ahl-e Hadeeth* is a small group of Sunni Muslims in India who do not consider themselves bound by any particular school of law and claim to rely directly on the Prophet's *Sunnah*, but in the same breath they claim their leader as a Prophet and call him *Hazrat*. By another estimate, some 15 per cent of Pakistan's Sunni Muslims consider themselves *Deobandi*, and some 60 per cent are in the *Barelawi* tradition based mostly in the province of Punjab. But some 64 per cent of the total seminaries are run by *Deobandis*, 25 per cent by the *Barelawis*, 6 per cent by the *Ahl-e Hadeeth* and 3 per cent by various *Shiite* organisations.[1]

About *madaris* in Pakistan, Ajay Upadhyay is of the view that:

'...... those who went to Pakistan had to face local complexities and they tried to see themselves through that prism and as such they localised the universal system of *Darul Uloom's* education as per the demands of the local society and this resulted in it being harmed, but suffice it to say that *Darul Uloom's* representatives in Pakistan have taken a big diversion from the basic tenets of *Darul Uloom* in India, and one reason behind this could be being reactionary not being reformist.'

Explaining the historical legacy of *madaris* in Pakistan, Prof Moosa says that:

'In Pakistan *Deobandism* has become an anachronism, they embraced *Deobandism* much more after 9/11, but they have become the extreme Taliban version of *Deobandism*, which is eating up *Deobandis*. Earlier there were very few *Deobandi Madaris* which were close to Taliban, after 9/11 most of them became sympathetic to Taliban, even sympathising with Bin Laden, but after some time they came back to their old ways, there are some extremist *madrasah* but they are being marginalised.'[2]

Maulana Wahiduddin Khan said that:

'Before independence many students from Pakistan, Afghanistan and other countries used to come to *Darul Uloom* for studying and this trend continued after 1947 also. They also established many *madaris* in their respective countries, but over time due to political and other factors, some *madaris* in Pakistan and Afghanistan came under *jihadi* influence and then onwards they were guided by a *jihadi* mindset, but no such thing happened in India.'

Maulana further added that due to this umbilical link of *madaris* in Pakistan and Afghanistan with *Darul Uloom*, Deoband many people think that they are offshoot or branches of the same. No, in no way are they the offshoot or branches of *Darul Uloom*, Deoband. The only common denominator is that like *Darul Uloom*, Deoband they follow the *Dars-e Nizami* or *Darul Uloom's* syllabus but except that they have gone their separate way and have become *jihadi* factories, thus bringing ill-fame to their mother institution.

Maulana further said that the pass outs of *Darul Uloom*, Deoband have a very peaceful approach. Most of them find jobs as *Imams* at a mosque or as a teacher at a *madrasah* or a *maktab*, whereas those who pass out of *madaris* claiming to be *Deobandi* based in Pakistan and Afghanistan, they have those elements taught which ultimately leads them to militancy. Prof Wasey analysing this, says:

'One interesting aspect of *Darul Uloom*, Deoband is that it is the centre of *Sunni Hanafi* Islam and the students who came from Afghanistan, Central Asian and South Asian countries and some even from certain parts of Iran, for them *Darul Uloom* was a natural choice as they themselves belonged to the *Sunni Hanafi* sect.

Darul Uloom was and is a centre for propagation of religion and its consolidation; it was also a centre against the expansionist forces of the world, so all those nations in Asia and Africa who were victims of imperialist expansion found a common cause or a sympathiser in the form of *Darul Uloom*.'

According to Prof Wasey, the reality is that the centre of *Darul Uloom's* movement was India, and whatever is said about their leaders they were followers of old religious traditions and interpretation, but politically you'll find them very broad-minded and aware, as they were always supportive or advocated an inclusive society and a united country. Secondly, they condemned imperialism or slavery of nations. A critical study will show that only some *madaris* established by the alumni of *Darul Uloom* in different countries of Asia and Africa were not able to follow the progressive and open vision of *Darul Uloom,* Deoband and fell to divisive forces, and such *madaris* had their base in Pakistan and Afghanistan.

Before we move on to *madaris* in Afghanistan, it would be worthwhile to understand the rise of Taliban and then try to decipher the linkage between Pakistani and Afghani *madaris.* as Both, historically and presently, the linkages between the two are hard to ignore; through them, we get a better understanding of the word Jihad, as given in Islam originally and as used by extremist elements like the Taliban.

Taliban

The Taliban (meaning students, alternative spelling Taleban),[3] is an Islamic fundamentalist movement of Afghanistan. It spread into Afghanistan and formed a government, ruling as the Islamic Emirate of Afghanistan from September 1996 until December 2001, with Kandahar as the capital. While in power, it enforced its strict interpretation of *Shariah* law. Most Muslims have been highly critical of the Taliban's interpretations of Islamic law, in addition they were condemned internationally for their brutal treatment of women.[4,5] A majority of their leaders were influenced by *Deobandi* fundamentalism, while *Pashtunwali*, the Pashtun tribal code, also played a significant role in the Taliban's legislation.[6]

John Mohammed Butt says that,

'Yes we can describe most of the *madrasahs* in Afghanistan as a *Deobandi madrasah* and Taliban as having studied in those *madrasahs*, this make Taliban the inheritors of the *Deobandi maslak* or ideology, which is a wrong assertion. These *madrasahs* in Afghanistan were termed as *Deobandi* as most of them were established by the alumni of Deoband and mostly all of them taught the *Dars-e Nizami*, but you can't attribute these two factors to help the makeup of the Talibani mindset, which to some extent is based on the *Saudi Wahabism*.'

Commenting on the issue, Maulana Khalid Saifullah Rahmani says:

'The Western powers took an undue advantage of the religious feelings of the people of Afghanistan and gave weapons in their hands and the role of *madrasah* students (Taliban) in this was very crucial. The spill over of this took place in neighbouring Pakistan, where too, the religious sentiments of the people were taken undue advantage of, particularly in the border areas with Afghanistan. Another thing to be noted here is that if an unorganised or untrained group is given weapons, then its results are very catastrophic.'

Providing both a historical and contemporary perspective Shahid Siddiqui says:

'Most of the *madaris* in neighbouring countries of India have been established on the pattern of *Darul Uloom*, Deoband. The alumnus of *Darul Uloom*, Deoband, established these *madaris* but they only follow the study pattern of *Darul Uloom*, Deoband, due to which they are referred to as *Deobandi madaris*. The Talibans who were raised by the US against the Soviets studied in these *madaris* but they have no direct philosophical or psychological link except the heritage and tag of being a *Deobandi*. In India the Deoband movement, as an institution has always been the most peaceful, most rational movement. If we take the case of India, militancy has been there in Kashmir for so long but does anyone has any proof that even a single *madrasah* pass out has become a militant in Kashmir? Pakistan has stoked the fires in Kashmir for so long, but still it was unable to rope-in the religious scholars or *madrasah* alumni to its fight in Kashmir.'

Nadeem-ul Wajedi says that:

'These Talibans were schooled in either a Pakistani or a Afghanistani *Deobandi madrasah*, which has no direct link with *Darul Uloom*, Deoband except following its *nisab* and *nizam*, so branding them as *Deobandi* is a misnomer.'

Providing a critical analysis of the issue Maulana Rashid Kandhalvi says:

'Till the rise of Taliban, no signs of extremism or radicalisation were evident in any *madrasah* in Pakistan or Afghanistan. And even afterwards, greater participation was by those who were from the border areas of Pakistan and Baluchistan. Mullah Umar was from *Binnori Town Madrasah* but not all the pass outs of *Binnor Madrasah* were ever part of the Taliban movement.'

According to Maulana Rashid if we examine deeply then we'll find that *Ulema* of *madaris* based in border areas of Pakistan and from Baluchistan and Afghanistan differ from *Darul Uloom* in their approach on many religious issues. For example, the moderate people in Pakistan, Afghanistan and elsewhere are of the view that *Jihad* is one of the key responsibilities entrusted to Muslims but it (*Jihad*) has its own rules and laws and parameters. if they are not followed then it will not be *Jihad* in the true sense. Prophet Mohammed (PBUH) enunciated four rules of *Jihad* and for every battle they are:

i)   Do not harm the person who has laid down his arms or has surrendered,

ii) Do not target an old person,

iii) Do not attack women and children

iv) Do not cut down any green tree.

Maulana Rashid stresses that these are the Islamic rules, not those that were followed by the Taliban.

Maulana goes on to add that the *Darul Uloom* was not responsible for Taliban's activities, but they were created, nurtured, patronised, financed and supported by America, with the help of Saudi Arabia and Pakistan. First, in the garb of making Afghanistan free of Russians, they trained mercenaries in *madaris,* and when they tasted success in their planning they made Taliban the rulers. The government, which was replaced by Taliban, was a government of moderate Islamic leaders headed by Burhanuddin Rabbani, Sibghatullah Mujaddadi, Maulvi Yunus Khalis and the company. Since, both America and Pakistan were not comfortable with them, therefore, they sent not *madrasah* boys and girls but mercenaries to defeat them.

Moreover, moderate leaders in Pakistan like Maulana Fazlur Rehman were not just isolated in Pakistan but they were targeted, and every moderate voice, every sane person was eliminated, from Hakeem Saeed to different religious leaders or otherwise they were forced to leave the country. Summing up the argument, Prof Wasey said:

'As far as *Jihad* is concerned, it's a completely different thing; similarly, *Fisad* (a dispute) is also different. Those who kill or target the innocents, worshippers in the mosques, attendees at *dargahs*, students in schools, they are not *jihadists* (liberators), they are *fasadees* (trouble makers). Those who quote Holy Qur`an wrongly or out of context they are benefitting neither themselves nor Islam. To establish '*haq*' (right) and destroy the '*baatil*' (wrong), '*insaf ki bahaali key liye or zulm ko mitaney key liye*' use of force is not banned in any religion.'

Maulana Mahmood Madani giving a more precise analysis of the issue, says:

'When you talk about the *Darul Ulooms* in Pakistan or

Afghanistan, then a lot depends on the socio-political situation there. As far as the syllabus is concerned, it is in no way different from the *Dars-i Nizami*, which we follow at *Darul Uloom*, Deoband. Bigger powers in order to challenge Russia promoted these forces (Taliban) and trained them, supplied them arms and ammunitions and allured them to fight in the name of *Jihad*. So we should not try to connect them with religion or with a particular sect or with the system of education. This is 100 per cent political maneouvering; over time and even now religion has been used politically.'

The umbilical link between the *madaris* of Pakistan and Afghanistan besides the *Ulema* and political figures is very well explained by LD Hayes (1987) in *The Crisis of Education in Pakistan*. According to him, Afghanistan and Pakistan are among the few countries in the contemporary Muslim world where an active development of rural *madrasahs* took place during the 20th century. These *madrasahs* were not organised into a hierarchical teaching system. Their importance often depended on their director and on the money he could attract. These networks ignored national borders. Some of these *madrasahs* were linked with small fundamentalist groups, like the *Ahl-i Hadeeth* movement, but the majority are linked with the *Deobandi* school of thought, which is dominant in northern Pakistan.[7]

In Afghanistan the reason for the development of the *madrasahs* was probably due to the reluctance of traditional folks to send their wards to government schools. Historically, Afghanistan never had any high-level *madrasahs*. The *Ulema* used to go to Bukhara (till 1917), but more often to India.

However, they stopped sending their students to India, which, for them, became an 'infidel' state after 1947, and preferred Pakistan. Linguistic ties between the Pashtuns on both sides of the border strengthened the links, although teaching took place in Persian, Urdu and Arabic as well as Pashto.

In Pakistan, the largest *madrasahs* are probably the *Haqqaniya Madrasah* near Peshawar in Akora Khattak, and the *madrasah* of Binnori Town in Karachi. After years of studies, graduate students used to come back to their place of origin, either joining an already existing *madrasah* or founding their own. In Afghanistan these *madrasah* networks were strong in the area between Ghazni and Kandahar, the cradle of the Taliban. Some were to be found in the northern area (Northern Badakhshan). Trans-frontier connections were increased by the influx of Afghan refugees into Pakistan after the Soviet invasion. Tens of thousands of young uprooted Afghans, mainly Pashtuns, were enlisted in these *madrasahs* inside Pakistan and did provided rank and file to the Taliban.

In Pakistan, the crisis of the government educational system also led to a considerable increase in attendance at religious schools.[8] But the main reason for the politicisation and radicalisation of traditional clerical networks in both countries has been the resistance war against the Soviet troops in Afghanistan and the policy of Islamisation led by General Zia after his take-over in 1977. The two events fuelled each other. The *Jihad* against the communists gave not only a religious legitimacy to the Zia regime but also entailed important support from the West, specially the Americans. On the other hand, the same Jihad transformed the different Islamic movements in Pakistan into patrons and channels of support for their Afghan counterparts.

The war strengthened the already existing connections and accentuated the ideological dimension of the trans-frontier solidarities, albeit that these were also favoured by other kinds of connections (ethnic ties, or even business connections).

Mumtaz Ahmad (2004) commenting on the radicalisation of Afghanistan's clerical networks in his paper on *Madrasah Education in Pakistan and Bangladesh* says that in Afghanistan, prior to the war against the Soviet occupation, a movement of politicisation arose among *madrasah* students and teachers in protest against the perceived leniency of the monarchy towards the rising Communist movement. The war against the Soviets had three consequences: politicisation, 'Wahhabisation', and the enlisting of a second generation of refugees in Pakistani *madrasahs*. Most of the *madrasahs* situated in rural areas between Ghazni and Kandahar turned into military 'fronts', often called *Jebhe-ye Tolaba* (Taliban front). They usually joined traditional Pashtun fundamentalist parties: *Harakat-i Inqelab-i Islami* of Mohammed Nabi Mohammedi and *Hizb-i Islami* of Yunus Khales. Sometimes, they moved to more remote areas to avoid Soviet ground offensives. The ties with their Pakistani counterparts were maintained for the sake of getting money and weapons. Usually the Pakistani intelligence services (ISI), which were in charge of dispatching weapons, used the 'clerical' networks to identify recipients and to establish links with them. But the war also carried with it an influx of Arab specifically Saudi money.[9]

The Saudis were eager to help the Mujaheedin for two reasons: to fight Communism, but also to undercut the Iranian influence among fundamentalist circles, playing on the traditional *anti-Shi'a, Deobandi* bias. The Saudis also introduced a stronger *Salafi* (strict fundamentalist) attitude, for example, by campaigning against local traditional Muslim customs (like the flags put on tombs of Mujaheedin or saints). This Wahhabisation does not mean that the *Deobandi* school adopted new ideas and beliefs.

It is more a question of attitude. It should be noted that perhaps the term *Wahhabi* had been used by the British to apply to any Islamic reformist coming back from Makkah in the nineteenth century, at a time when the *Wahhabis* in the strict sense of the term were not established in the Holy City. But this emphasis on 'true Islam' and criticism of local customs, *Shi'a* beliefs, Western influence etc., played a role in radicalising an already strict fundamentalist *Shi'a* and *Deobandi* bias.

Madaris in Bangladesh

Bangladesh has two kinds of *madrasahs*: *Quomi Madrasah*s - estimated at more than 6,500 at the secondary, intermediate, and higher levels with about 1,462,500 students and 130,000 teachers. These *Quomi Madrasahs* in Bangladesh, are predominantly of *Deobandi* orientation, and teach the standard *Dars-i Nizami* that is prevalent in all South Asian *madrasahs*. The *Quomi Madrasahs* are private, receive no financial support from the government, and are supported by religious endowments or by *zakat, sadaqa,* and donations from the faithful. This financial autonomy of the *madrasah* system has been a major source of the independent religio-political power base of the *Ulema* in Bangladesh and Pakistan. It has also enabled the *Ulema* to resist the efforts of state authorities to introduce reforms in the *madrasah* system and to bridge the gap between the traditional system of Islamic education and modern secular education.[10]

The other category of *madrasahs* in Bangladesh is the government controlled, or *Alia Madrasah* system, a unique system of Islamic religious education with few parallels in the Muslim world.

Divided into five distinct levels—*Ibtedai* (elementary), *Dakhil* (secondary), *Alim* (higher secondary), *Fazil* (BA), and *Kamil* (MA), these *madrasahs* teach all the required modern subjects such as English, Bangla, science, social studies, mathematics, geography, history, etc., along with a revised version of *Dars-i Nizami*. Although they are privately owned and managed – with the exception of five major *Alia Madrasahs* that are wholly controlled by the government – the Government of Bangladesh pays 80 per cent of salaries of their teachers and administrators as well as a considerable portion of their development expenditures.[11]

These *Alia Madrasahs* are registered with, and supervised by the government-appointed *Bangladesh Madrasah Education Board*, which also prescribes the curriculum and syllabi and conducts examinations. However, the government has approved equivalence of only *Fazil* and *Kamil* to Secondary and Higher Secondary certificates, respectively.

Unlike the graduates of *Quomi Madrasahs*, whose degrees are not recognised by the government and who pursue their career in religious establishments and private businesses, the majority of the graduates of *Alia Madrasahs* merge into the general stream of education by continuing their education in colleges and universities. It is no wonder that a recent survey found that 32 per cent of Bangladesh university teachers in the humanities and social sciences graduated from *Alia Madrasahs*.

In the case of Bangladesh, an overwhelming majority of *Quomi Madrasah* students (82 per cent) come from poor families of rural areas and small towns. Sylhet, Chittagong, and some northern districts have traditionally been the main base of enrolment for the *Quomi Madrasahs*.

The student body of the *Alia Madrasah* system is much more diverse and includes a large number of students from the lower middle classes as well. Further the Bangladeshi *Ulema* have shown remarkable flexibility in adapting to the changing social, economic, and political conditions, as is evident in the important changes in the social organisation of *madrasah* education. The *Alia Madrasah* system is a spectacular example of how modern and traditional systems of education could be combined to derive maximum and worthwhile results. But what is not widely known and appreciated are the important changes that have been introduced in *Quomi Madrasahs* during the past three decades. The following changes are worth mentioning:

1. Bangla language has replaced Urdu as the medium of instruction. This is an important step in the process of integrating local traditions and Islamic scholarship, and their de-linking from their North Indian Islamic origins.

2. Bangla has been made a compulsory subject up to the secondary level (*Marhala-i Sanvia*). It is interesting to note that *Quomi Madrasahs* did not teach Bangla at any level before 1972.

3. Subjects such as politics, economics, and history of Islam in the Indian subcontinent up to the establishment of Bangladesh have been added.

4. English has been added as a compulsory subject in the primary section, and several *madrasahs* now provide facilities for English education at higher levels as well.

5. Elementary school education has now been integrated within the *Quomi Madrasahs,* incorporating all subjects of general

education along with the usual Islamic education.

6. Comparative religion has been added to the curriculum.

7. A major breakthrough has been the standardisation of academic performance evaluation, by instituting a centralised system of curriculum, syllabi and examinations under the auspices of two major federations of *Quomi Madrasahs*: *Wafaq-ul Madaris*, which has 1,500 affiliated *madrasahs*, and *Anjumun Ittehad-ul Madaris*, which has more than 500 affiliated *madrasahs*.

9. Funding resources have been diversified. Although traditional sources—*zakat* and *sadaqa* raised from local communities—are still important, but globally, the expatriate Bangladeshi workers have now become a substantial source of funding for *Quomi Madrasahs*.[12]

Commenting on the *madaris* in Pakistan, Afghanistan and Bangladesh, Maulana Abul Qasim Nomani points out that:

'In all *Deobandi madrasahs*, globally *nisab-e taleem, nizam-e taleem, tarz-e taleem, fikr* and *manhaj* (syllabus, administration and style of imparting education, besides the thought and basic ideals) remains the same. The difference wherever it is, is due to their peculiar local conditions. And this too is not universal. In fact, in Pakistan there is the *madrasah* run by Maulana Fazlur Rehman, whose temperament and management is just like *Darul Uloom*. On the other hand, you'll find other *madaris* in Pakistan, which follow the extreme interpretation of Islamic teachings and mindset. This is applicable to Bangladesh and Afghanistan also.'

Commenting on the similarities and differences between *Darul Ulooms* in Pakistan, Afghanistan and Bangladesh with that of India, Maulana Asrarul Haq was of the view that:

'The syllabus of *Darul Uloom* is also followed by *Darul Ulooms* in Pakistan, Afghanistan and Bangladesh. But this issue is not related to the syllabus. The mindset and several other external factors also affect this. Both these countries are Islamic republics, yet like India they follow two separate systems of education, one secular and the other religious, but the religious one there got compromised somewhat, leading to a narrow mindedness, and if you are narrow minded then you'll not be open to a dialogue or understanding of other religions or sects within your own religion, which gives rise to intolerance. If you go even a little back into history, the Taliban arrived on the scene in only early 90s, so for the last approximately 50 years after the formation of Pakistan there were no Taliban. Taliban in reality were founded to drive the Communists out of Afghanistan, a movement was started that religious leaders should come forward to lead so that people who do not believe in God are replaced and are not able to lead the populace.'

As postulated by leading Indian *Ulema*, the *madaris* in Pakistan, Afghanistan and Bangladesh have an umbilical link with *Darul Uloom*, Deoband, and if, they have digressed from the teachings of the *Darul Uloom* or have adopted new innovations or have changed their functioning as per the demands of the local social and political conditions, then *Darul Uloom* can't be held responsible. These institutions in these countries are autonomous and fully empowered to present whatever image they want to project of their institutions and its leaders.

Darul Ulooms in South Africa and the United Kingdom

Before embarking on the history of *madaris* in South Africa and the UK, we have to understand that most of the *madrasahs* established in the UK were established by Gujarati-origin Indian immigrants, who had first migrated to African nations like Uganda and South Africa around 1947. So this group was responsible for first setting-up *madrasahs* on *Darul Uloom's* patron in Uganda and South Africa and then continued with the same pattern in the UK and other European countries, when it migrated to the UK and other European countries in 1970s.

Masooda Bano (2018) in her book *Modern Islamic Authority and Social Change,* Volume 2 says that the *Deobandi Madrasah* network has expanded successfully in many countries, including the UK and the USA, with a strong South Asian Muslim diaspora. This conservative South Asian scholarly tradition has also been pragmatic about the use of modern technology to advance its message.[1]

Darul Ulooms in South Africa

- *Darul Uloom* Newcastle, Newcastle, KwaZulu-Natal - The first *Deobandi Madrasah* in South Africa, was founded in 1971 by Maulana Qassim Mohammed Sema.[2]

- *Al-Madrasah Al-Arabiyyah Al-Islamiyyah*, Azaadville - One of the largest and most prominent *Deobandi madaris* in South Africa, is connected with both the teachings of Maulana Mohammad Zakariyya Kandhalwi and Maulana Ashraf Ali Thanvi.[3] Since several of its graduates are Western students especially from the UK and United States, who join it based on their familial links with South Africa, the *madrasah* plays an important role in shaping Islam in the West, too, besides just South Africa.[4] The school is also important within South Africa as a site for activities of the *Tablighi Jama'at*. Holy books in English from this *madrasah* are used in English-medium *Deobandi madaris* in the West to teach the *Dars-i Nizami* curriculum.[5]

- *Darul Uloom Zakariyya*, Zakariyya Park, Lenasia - One of the most prominent *Deobandi madaris* in South Africa, it was founded by disciples of Maulana Mohammad Zakariyya Kandhalwi, the school's namesake. The school is also important within South Africa as a site for activities of the *Tablighi Jama'at*.[6]

- *Madrasahh In'aamiyyah*, Camper Town, KwaZulu-Natal - This *madrasah* is recognised for its *Dar Al-Ifta* (Department of Fatwa Research and Training) which also runs a popular online *fatwa* service.[7]

Most of the South African *Ulema* maintain continuous and harmonious ties with their brethren in Gujarat and particularly Deoband. In fact, some of them manage *Darul Ulooms* both in Gujarat in India and also in South Africa. Thus, there is constant movement and interaction between the top leadership of these institutes and as such in most of their initiatives they are guided by the *fikr* of the *Darul Uloom*.

Darul Ulooms in the UK

According to *The Times*, about 600 of Britain's nearly 1,500 mosques are run by *Deobandi* affiliated scholars, and 17 of the country's 26 Islamic seminaries follow *Sunni Deobandi* teachings, producing 80 per cent of all domestically trained *Ulema*.

- *Darul Uloom Al-Arabiyyah Al-Islamiyyah*, Holcombe, Bury, UK - Popularly known as 'Darul Uloom Bury', is historically the first *madrasah* established in the UK in 1975. Many of the newer *madaris* are its branches, or founded by its graduates. *Darul Uloom*, Bury, together with the *Dewsbury Madrasah* have been called the 'Oxbridge of the traditional *madrasah* world' in the UK.[8]

A point to note here is that *Darul Uloom Al Arabiya Al Islamiyyah*, Bury, has received 'outstanding' in every area of school education in its latest inspection by The Office for Standards in Education, Children's Services and Skills (Ofsted), which is a non-ministerial department of the UK government, reporting to parliament. Ofsted is responsible for inspecting a range of educational institutions, including state schools and some independent schools.[9] Inspectors found the quality of teaching, achievement of pupils, sixth form provision, leadership and management and behaviour and safety, amongst the highest in the country during an inspection conducted with only a day's notice.[10]

- *Jami'at Ta'lim Ul Islam*, Dewsbury, UK - The *Dewsbury Madrasah* as it is popularly known, was established in 1981 by the *Tablighi Jamaat*.

- *Jameah Uloomul-Qur`an*, Leicester UK - This *madrasah* was established in Leicester in 1977 by *Sheikh-ul Hadeeth* Hazrat Maulana Adam Sahib. It has over 600 students studying the Exegesis and Jurisprudence courses.[11,12]

Commenting on the difference and similarities in *Darul Uloom's* of other countries and that of India, Maulana Arshad Madani said:

'All *Darul Ulooms* globally, if they claim to be a *Deobandi Madrasah*, they follow only the syllabus of *Darul Uloom*, Deoband and also adhere to *Deoband's* religious ideology and stand. If they deviate from the *Deobandi* system, then that is due to their own local conditions.'

Commenting on the *Darul Ulooms* in the UK, late Maulana Asrarul Haq commented:

'The British very well understand the differences between an Indian and a Pakistani religious institution. An example in this regard relates to your entry at the airport in the UK, when they are dealing with Indian religious leaders, then their attitude is much softer and understanding when compared to dealing with a Pakistani-origin scholar. And the fact is that the face of Islam, which has been distorted in the UK, is the doing of such Pakistani scholars. In UK there is a freedom of expression, which was misused by these Pakistani scholars, for everything negative of Islam they would collect in thousand but to portray the positive side of Islam or taking the side of a just matter you'll see nobody there.'

Maulana Khalid Saifullah Rahmani says:

'I have not been to the US, but other Western countries, which I have visited, including UK, have Islamic institutions or *madaris*, the model for whom is *Darul Uloom*. And leading religious leaders there feel that the religious leaders from India are more moderate, they know how to function in a multicultural environment and their opinion and views on most of the issues are much more liberal than their counterparts from Pakistan or Afghanistan. And most of these *Deobandi* institutions in these countries are very well connected with the society and they don't prescribe to any hard line or extremist views. As most of the teachers there are from India, so just like India they teach principles of brotherhood and how to be tolerant and coexist in a multi-cultural society.'

It can be surmised that *Darul Ulooms* in all countries differ from their alma mater i.e. *Darul Uloom*, Deoband. Though most of the *madaris* in these countries follow the syllabus of Deoband, yet they differ in their approach to the treatment of educating these subjects. When taught to students, even a nuanced change can give a completely different picture of the subject. Also, the basic ethos is based on the local conditions of these countries, which furthermore differ from country to country. So, in a sense the message being conveyed everywhere is different, just like that Islam differs in every country. Two-third followers of Islam live in non-middle eastern countries, and in countries where they are in majority like Malaysia and Indonesia, Islam .The interpretation is to a large extent moulded to local conditions, traditions, and culture.

The friendly relations between the British and *Deobandi Ulema* are a copy of the South African model, and there is a constant flow of *Ulema* between the two countries, which further helps in exchange of ideas and guidance provided by the Indian *Ulema* to their British counterparts. In addition, it also has to be stressed that *Darul Ulooms* in South Africa, the UK and other European countries have managed to hold on to the ideals and principles of the *Darul Uloom*, Deoband more steadfastly, as compared to the *Darul Ulooms* in Pakistan and Afghanistan.

Differences between Deobandi, Barelawi and Ahl-e Hadeeth Sects

The vast multitude of Muslims in the Indian subcontinent apart from being divided in two major groups of *Shia* and *Sunni* is further subdivided amongst the *Sunni* Muslims into *Deobandi, Barelawi* and *Ahl-e Hadeeth* sects. It should also be noted that both *Deobandi* and *Barelawi* sects are subsets of the *Hanafi* branch.

Deobandi

The term *Deobandi* points to the origins of the movement based in the famous seminary, *Darul Uloom* in Deoband, India. The followers of this branch adhere strictly to the *Fiqh* of Imam Abu Hanifa and his students.

One of their fundamental concepts is the practice of *Taqleed*, which means to 'follow' as opposed to using one's own or a secondary opinion. Their second hallmark is *Talfiq*, which restricts venturing into ideas other than those as codified by the *Hanafi* School. Therefore, the contemporary scholarly work based on the interpolation/extrapolation of religious text is relatively rare.

Although *Deobandi* School recognises the changing needs of the society, because of their strict adherence to an interpretation that is a millennia old, it is limited in offering solutions to many ills of society in modern times or offer explanations in a language that aids the modern mind.

Deobandis recognise the mystical form of religion that is embedded in the Islamic history of the subcontinent. With regards to the mystical-spiritual aspect of Islam, the *Deobandis* do not encourage the proliferation of esoteric knowledge or practices to masses. It maintains that such knowledge should be the preserve of those who are perched on the higher echelons of faith.

Barelawi

Ahl-e Sunnah-wal Jamàat[1] or *Sunni Barelawi* is a *Sunni* revivalist movement following the *Hanafi* and *Shafii* school of jurisprudence, with strong *Sufi* influences and with over 200 million followers in South Asia and in parts of Europe, America and Africa. It is a broad *Sufi*-oriented movement that encompasses a variety of *Sufi* orders, including the *Chishtis, Qadiris, Soharwardis* and *Naqshbandis*.

The movement drew inspiration from the *Sunni Sufi* doctrines of Shah Waliullah Dehlavi, Shah Abdul Aziz Muhaddith Dehlavi (1746-1824) and Fazl-e Haq Khairabadi (1796-1861), founder of the Khairabad School. It emphasises personal devotion to God and Prophet Muhammad (PBUH), adherence to *Shariah*, and *Sufi* practices such as veneration of saints. Ahmed Raza Khan *Barelawi* (1856-1921) who was a *Sunni Sufi* scholar in North India wrote extensively in defence of popular *Sufi* practices and became the leader of a movement called *Ahl-i Sunnah-wal Jamàat*.

Professor Usha Sanyal, an expert on *Barelawis*, refers to the movement as *Ahl-i Sunnah*. She wrote that the movement refer to themselves as *Sunnis* in their literature and prefer to be known by the title of *Ahl-i Sunnah wal Jamàat*, a reference to their perception of forming an international majority movement, although *Barelawi* is the popularly used term.[2] Barbara D Metcalf describing *Barelawis* writes,

'Barelawis held fast to *Hanafi* law, but broadly interpreted, and to a custom-laden style of *Sufism*, closely tied to the *Peers* of the medieval tombs. They placed relatively little emphasis on individual responsibility and much more on intercession of the *Ulema* and the *Sheikhs*. Nothing characterised their teaching more than hierarchy that elevated the Holy Prophet (PBUH), the saints and the *Ulema* themselves as benefactors, patrons and intercessors. The community they defined was more tied to particular shrines and fixed occasions, and tended to be rural rather than urban. True to their concept of hierarchy, they accepted the existence of the colonial authority apparently without question.'[3]

Beliefs and Theological Positions

Barelawis like other *Sunni* Muslims, base their beliefs on the Holy *Qur`an* and *Sunnah* and believe in monotheism and the prophethood of Muhammad (PBUH). In addition, most *Barelawis* in *South* Asia follow the *Hanafi Fiqh* and the *Qadri* or *Chishti Sufi* orders.[4]

Several beliefs and practices of the *Barelawi* movement differentiate them from others (particularly *Deobandis* and *Wahhabis*) including beliefs on the intercession of Prophet

Muhammad (PBUH), the knowledge of Prophet Muhammad (PBUH), the *Nur-e Muhammadiyya* (Light of Muhammad), and whether Prophet Muhammad (PBUH) views and witnesses actions of people.[5]

Maulana Khalid Saifullah Rahmani opines that:

> 'At a larger level the major points of difference are celebrating *Urs* – annual anniversaries of *sufi* saints, reading *Milad* – *naats* being sung by men in praise of Prophet Muhammed (PBUH), the knowledge of Prophet Muhammad (PBUH) as *Alim ul Ghaib* – one knowing about everything to happen till the doomsday, the *Nur-e Muhammadiyya* (Light of Muhammad), and whether Prophet Muhammad (PBUH) views and witnesses actions of people even now – *hazir o nazir*-- if he is omnipresent, by *Barelawis*. The *Deobandi Ulema* describe this as *Bidaat* – deviating from Islamic teachings. And certainly some of these beliefs even touch the boundaries of *Shirk*-unIslamic, such as describing Prophet Muhammad (PBUH) as *hazir-o nazir (omnipresent)*, being *allam-ul ghuyub* (knower of the unseen), as these characteristics are reserved for Almighty Allah only. So one cannot associate these qualities even with Prophet Muhammad (PBUH). Further, *Deobandis* are very particular to stress that we will not adopt a ritual until and unless it is proved by the *Sunnah*, even though it may come from a senior religious personality, we'll give due regard to that personality but we'll not follow all his teachings blindly.'[6]

Renowned Islamic scholar, Waris Mazhari, Associate Professor at Department of Islamic Studies at Jamia Hamdard University, New Delhi, opines:

manifold, but when the differences were dissected then it was found that these differences were mostly on contextual or literal basis not on theological basis. They were not fundamentally different, which could not be sorted out and most of the young Islamic scholars are realising that these differences are not so big which cannot be overcome.

I understand that both the groups profess their respect and love for the Holy Prophet (PBUH), but the manner in which it is expressed is different. The respect and love for his personality is part of being a Muslim, provided it should not cross the boundaries of *Shirk*. However, the manifestation of this respect and love and the words used to describe or praise him led to the genesis of misunderstanding between the two groups, and one group blamed the other that it does not respect the Holy Prophet (PBUH) as much as they do, and it borders on disrespect for the Holy Prophet (PBUH).'[8]

Ahl-e Hadeeth

It is generally believed that *Ahl-e Hadeeth* is the youngest sect in the subcontinent when compared to the other two *Hanafi* sub-schools, but Barbara D Metcalf contrary to popular belief that *Ahl-e Hadeeth* in India spread after the *Salafi* became stronger in Saudi Arabia in late 1970s writes that,

> 'The *Ahl-e Hadeeth* was one of the most visible of the Muslim intellectual movements of the late 19th century both because of its avowedly sectarian character and because of its membership from among the educated and well born. It was, like the *Deobandi,* a movement of people sensitive to the widespread political and social changes of the day, but its intensity and extremism were far greater and the range of its influence less.'[9]

Taqleed (following a particular Imam) and *Ibtibah* are fundamental to both *Deobandis* and *Barelawis*, you have to act on the basis of the Holy *Qur`an* and *Ahadeeth* only, but to get the correct meaning of the Holy *Qur`an* and *Ahadeeth*, we will have to depend on the interpretation given by Islamic scholars—*mujathideen* and even then they have the right to question the interpretation offered by the Imams. For example, Imam Abu Hanifa has allowed usury in *Dar-al Harb* but the *Deobandi Ulema* disagree on this and have thus rejected this interpretation on the basis that a fundamental Islamic principle has to be universal and could not differ based on the type of government or your place of living. On the other hand, *Ahl-e Hadeeth* followers do not feel the need to depend on any *mujtahid* to get the correct meaning of the Holy *Qur`an* and *Ahadeeth*, but give this power to every individual Muslim.'

Further, the *Ahl-e Hadeeth* are focused on a singular interpretation of religious texts. Therefore, they do not accommodate most of the regional customs and norms in their prescribed lifestyle.

In fact, *Sufism* that is popular among poor working class people in the subcontinent is considered an anathema to *Ahl-e Hadeeth* beliefs. Furthermore, articles on the faith and jurisprudence are derived from an absolute viewpoint, casting aside the needs of the community or consideration of changes in the society.

The *Ahl-e Hadeeth* focuses on a more puritanical faith. It therefore does not allow any margin for the usage of religious texts that are not from an authentic source. The followers of this school seek knowledge directly from the Holy *Qur`an* or *Ahadeeth*.

Dr Waris Mazhari, bringing out the difference between *Deobandis* and *Ahl-e Hadeeth* or *Salafis* says:

'*Ahl-e Hadeeth* are also *Muqallid* (followers or imitators) but they are very particular about proving everything from scriptures or the Holy *Qur`an* and the *Ahadeeth*. The *Deobandis* believe that we can also follow the *Sunnah* of *Sahab-e Ikram* (companions of the Holy Prophet), *tabaain* (first generation of Holy Prophet's followers), and also the sayings and practices of the Imams and *Mujtahideen* (religious scholars). *Salafi Ulema* become literalist, scripturalist to a large extent and try to contextualise every issue. Further, they maintain that Islam should be seen and practiced, as it was during the days of the Prophet Mohammed (PBUH), i.e. at the societal level, every society should try to model itself, as the Arab society was present during the days of the Prophet Mohammed (PBUH).

'As far as differences between *Ahl-e Hadeeth* and *Deobandi Ulema* is concerned, it is basically centered around *Taqleed*. *Deobandi Ulema* maintain that for ordinary Muslims *Taqleed* is necessary, meaning permission should not be granted to every person to deduce learning from the Holy *Qur`an* and the *Ahadeeth*, instead it is necessary that he should be following an Imam or a *Alim* or a *Mujtahid* (a learned scholarly person). Shah Waliullah has written that a commoner should follow the lead of an Imam. *Ahl-e Hadeeth* counter this by saying that we cannot follow just one Imam, instead we should possess the power of logical deduction, which is the basic fundamental of Islam and a privilege given by Allah to even common followers of Islam to deduce every issue directly from the Holy *Qur`an* and *Hadeeth*.

'In the Indian context however, it has been observed that Indian *Ahl-e Hadeeth Ulema*, follow the lead given by the Saudi *Ulema* and scholars on different issues. Similarly, Saudi scholars follow Imam Abu Tamiyah and Ibn-e Qayyum very strongly, but even in this following they show flexibility as on many issues they differ from other Imams and emphasise and follow the teachings of these two scholars.

In addition, *Ahl-e Hadeeth* completely reject *Tasawwuf*, whereas *Deobandi Ulemas* do not reject it outrightly and say we can follow *Tasawwuf* or Sufi practices provided it is free from *bidaat* (unIslamic practices) and should not come under the purview of *Shirk*. Similarly, they also agree that many issues which have not been banned or described as wrong in the Holy *Qur`an* and *Ahl-e Hadeeth*, they can also be followed or imbibed or practiced, if their origins are authenticated as one given by *Ulema* and religious personalities. So at a certain level they *(Deobandis)* accept certain customs also, but not to a very large extent.'

However, on the flipside, it is known that not everyone has the capacity to become an expert in Islamic theology. Therefore, one of the pitfalls of the *Ahl-e Hadeeth* followers is the formulation of conclusive opinions based on selective rather than holistic knowledge. The other problem with this approach is that wheels are constantly reinvented and a great body of scholarly work that has been built on the Holy *Qur`an* and *Sunnah* by distinguished theologians is ignored.

Dr Fahim Akhtar Nadvi opines:

'It should be clear that *Ahl-e Hadeeth* and *Salafi* are the same. But *Deobandis* and *Barelawis* differ from *Ahl-e Hadeeth* and *Salafi* on *Fiqhi* or jurist or *Shariah* basis. *Maslak-e Salafiya* does not accept any four schools or Imams of Islamic jurisprudence, so they are called *ghair-muqallid* (followers of none). This is a school of thought, which holds that we should not blindly follow a particular Imam for sanctifying our religious practices but we should deduce every ritual or practice ourselves from the Holy *Qur`an* and the *Ahadeeth*. They further call for *Ijtihaad*, but only learned scholars, not everyone, could engage in *Ijtihaad.*'

The cumulative wisdom garnered over centuries in the form of Islamic jurisprudence is cast aside which leads to regress. The *Ahl-e Hadeeth* because of their stance against unorthodoxy, are also completely at odds with *Sufism*. Note that *Sufi* saints have a huge contribution in spreading Islam in the subcontinent. *Sufi* poetry has been part of the folk culture for centuries and the saints have been revered for generations. The recognition of the work by saints has allowed room for spirituality within both the *Hanafi* sub-schools (*Deobandi* and *Barelawi*).

However, most of the scholars are hopeful of a unification or coming together of these sects. Dr Fahim Akhtar Nadvi opines: 'A satisfying development that young scholars from all these sects are trying to sort out their differences and highlight the absence of any difference or show that they are following the same path is a positive step forward.'

Summing it up Maulana Khalid Saifullah Rahmani says that the differences between *Deobandis*, *Barelawis* and *Ahl-e Hadeeth* are just 3 per cent and the rest 97 per cent are the more pronounced similarities, thus a way out is open to agree to disagree and show oneself as a united faith.

Additionally, the notable feature that binds the *Sunnis* in the subcontinent is that all three schools allow taking an atomistic approach towards understanding the Holy *Qur`an* without taking into account the context. The verses of the Holy *Qur`an* should not be looked at in isolation for understanding the true meaning of the text. This approach often leads to a very myopic and literalistic understanding of faith.

Split in Darul Uloom

In its glorious history spanning 156 years, *Darul Uloom* has been hit by several controversies, all of which apparently died down after some time, as they were found baseless. But one major incident, which had a reputational bearing on *Darul Uloom*, was its breakup in two parts in 1982.

Commenting on the event and its background Dietrich Reetz (2006) in *Islam in the Public Sphere*, comments:

> 'leadership in *Deobandi* institutions has traditionally been influenced by clan and family loyalties. Deoband shares this trait with many other public bodies and educational networks in South Asia, irrespective of religious affiliation. The long-standing grip of caste and family affinity on the social fabric is usually held responsible.'[1]

Although Islam is potentially more egalitarian in social matters, in South Asia in particular, it failed to escape the influences of tradition. Religious schools – the *Darul Uloom* and the *madrasahs* – were also affected. Over time, key positions such as that of rector, head teacher or Hadeeth teacher tended to become hereditary by default. Sons are deliberately groomed to assume the father's post at some point in time. Consequently, family factions competing for control of the school and its resources emerged.[2]

Though it's a well-known fact, it is rarely discussed openly. The Muslim public in India and beyond was therefore deeply shocked when family feuds – i.e. between the Tayyab and Madani families – broke out in the prestigious *Darul Uloom* and eventually led to a split.'[3]

Listing out the chain of events leading to the breakup, Reetz says:

'In hindsight, we can see that the centenary celebrations in 1980 and the concomitant preparations intensified the rivalry between these families for control of the seminary, especially as its long-time rector, Qari Muhammad Tayyab (1897-1983), had by that time become increasingly frail and the issue of succession had emerged. He assumed the post of *Muhtamim* or Rector of the *Darul Uloom* in 1929, a post he held until 1982. As the grandson of *Darul Uloom's* founder Qasim Nanautavi, he embodied the classical tradition of learnedness and piety and had little interest in political manoeuvring.'[4]

The official version on the school website of *Darul Uloom* holds Qari Tayyab and his advisors responsible for the debacle. It maintains that subsequent to the elaborate and highly successful centenary celebrations, Qari Tayyab allegedly requested that the *Majlis-i Shura* (Executive Council) provide assistance because his administration duties (*ihtimam*) were too much for a man of his advanced age. The *Majlis-i Shura*, as per request, elected Maulana Marghub-ur Rahman as *Muhtamim*. Thereafter, he, (Tayyab) fell victim to the insincere policies of his close advisors. In December 1980, after returning from a trip to America, he appointed Maulana Muhammad Salim Vice-Rector (*na'ib muhtamim*) and Maulana Anzar Shah Kashmiri, head teacher (*sadr-i mudarris*); all of these appointments were against school regulations.

After the *Majlis-i Shura* protested he revoked his decisions. He then undertook the radical step of convening an illegal meeting (*ijtimaa*) in which he announced the dissolution of the *Majlis-i Shura*.

This incident disrupted the entire *Darul Uloom's* administration. The political turmoil within the administration left Muslims throughout the world with a sense of sorrow. In October 1981, the sad incident of the eviction of students from the *Darul Uloom* with the help of police occurred, which led to its closure.

The years 1981 and 1982 are well known in the history of the *Darul Uloom* because, in addition to the state of emergency, the *Darul Uloom* closed its doors for five months (deprived of the sound of Allah and his prophet's words). The students retook possession of their Alma Mater on March 23-24, 1982 and the administration was resurrected under the supervision of the regular *Majlis-i Shura*.'5

This account, which has dominated the media and the official representation of the events at the time, seems to be at odds with the reflections of members of the defeated faction and the loyalist camp that remained at the school.

Prof Azam Qasmi, of the Department of Islamic Studies, AMU, Aligarh and son of Late Qari Mohammed Tayyab sahib, is perhaps the only voice from the family of Qari Tayyab sahib, who agreed to speak to the author and give their family's version of the events for the first time, says:

> 'One central and prominent character whom he could name as the main progenitor of the campaign against his father, the Late Qari Mohammed Tayyab sahib, former Rector of Darul Uloom, Deoband, then the name would be of Late Maulana Asad Madani sahib.'[6]

According to Prof Qasmi the division did not take place overnight but it was a campaign which was about ten years old, and during that period the platforms were provided by *Jamiat Ulema-e-Hind* and the *Al Jamiat* newspaper published by it. Similarly, during that period whenever the *Majlis-e Shura* of *Darul Uloom* used to take place, it became a common practice that some youngsters would raise placards and slogans demanding that sahibzada Asad Madani should be nominated as a member of the *Majlis-e Shura.*

Prof Qasmi says further:

> 'If we go back and try to dissect the real campaign, which culminated in 1980, then it would be clear that a sustained campaign was launched but Asad Madani was missing from that campaign, as he was not officially associated with *Darul Uloom*, in any capacity, till that time. He was associated with *Darul Uloom* earlier, about 15 years back, as an Honorary Teacher and as he didn't used to teach any class, he was asked either to teach and agree to a salary or resign from the honorary position, then he resigned and became actively involved in Jamiat's political activities.'[7]

Prof Qasmi says that:

> 'The anti-Qari Tayyab group planned their activities during

the three years preceding the division in 1982, during this time they mounted a barrage of letters against Qari Tayyab sahib, organised the alumni of *Darul Uloom* against my father and a sustained campaigned was operational during that period, at the end of which, Maulana Asad Madani acting in a self-appointed capacity as the representative of *Darul Uloom* met the then Prime Minister Mrs Indira Gandhi and invited her to participate in the Centenary celebrations in Deoband.

'At that time, he was not an MP, neither was he connected to *Darul Uloom,* Deoband in any official capacity. Just days before the start of the Centenary celebrations he informed the *Majlis-e Shura* about this development. Many members of the *Shura* were against this unilateral invite, as they did not want to politicise the whole event. But after due deliberations it was decided that you can't turn away the prime minister of the country, as she had already agreed to attend the function. Further, it would unduly bring out in the open the internal divisions of *Darul Uloom,* So now another official delegation of *Darul Uloom* went to meet and invite her, but it was all due to compulsion.'[8]

Disclosing the other events, Prof Qasmi went on to say:

'Ultimately the centenary celebrations started on March 20 and carried on till March 22. About 15 lakh people attended the celebrations, many of whom were lodged by even Hindu residents of Deoband city in their homes. However, Maulana Asad Madani was not involved in any of the functions, but his home was another centre of beehive activity, about which I don't know as to what was happening there, as it was within the confines of his home only. These activities culminated in the form of a news published on the front page of the daily *Al Jamiat* on March22, that a new organisation called *Ibna-e Darul Uloom* (Alumnus of *Darul Uloom)*, Deoband has been constituted under the banner of *Jamiat Ulema-e Hind*, in his capacity as the president of the Jamiat and he'll also be the president of the new organisation. This was a surprise, as it was planned to be announced from the official platform of *Darul Uloom* and Asad Madani was not even connected to it in any manner. So the main controversy started from this point onwards. After that day regular articles started appearing in the daily *Al Jamiat,* that some people at *Darul Uloom* want to throw out Asad Madani from *Darul Uloom*. This resulted in an increased chasm being created amongst the residents of Deoband and students and teachers of *Darul Uloom*.'[9]

Reetz further comments that:

'Even years after these events, these factions remain surprisingly unanimous in their criticism of the 'Madani faction',13 which consisted of the offspring of Husain Ahmad Madani. Its main protagonists were Asad Madani (1928-2006), former president of JUH, and his son Mahmood Madani, general secretary of JUH.

Respondents pointed out that Maulana Marghub was related to the Madani family and was appointed solely to wrest control of the administration from the Tayyab family, which together comprised the larger 'Qasimi faction'.[10]

They stress that during his time in office, Maulana Marghub demonstrated little scholarly inclination or capacity to enhance the administration. In 2004, he appeared frail and was on sick leave for long periods of time, during which deputy-rector Qari Usman, Maulana Arshad Madani as head of the teaching department (*Daftar-e Taalimat*), and another member of the Madani family steered the school through troubled waters.[10]

Respondents allege that more scholarly and devoted teachers had left the old school as a result of the split. However, they basically agreed that they have been replaced by other teachers who are just as able. Asad Madani presented his nominees to the *Majlis-i Shura*. When Maulana Marghub was gradually judged as having failed his duties, Maulana Asad Madani was said to have laid claim to the chairmanship of the *Shura*. He remained politically active for the Congress Party.'[11]

Refuting the version of the Asad Madani camp as regards to the steps taken by Qari Tayyab sahib to dissolve the *Majlis-e Shura* and appoint Maulana Salim as the new rector, Prof Azam says that:

'In reality Qari Tayyab sahib had himself stopped going to the meetings of *Majlis-e Shura*, both due to his failing health and the politically surcharged atmosphere. In fact when the offices and other buildings of *Darul Uloom* were occupied forcibly by Asad Madani and his younger brother Maulana Arshad Madani, which they hailed as *Fatah-e Makkah*, they unilaterally dismissed Qari Tayyab sahib from his post.'[12]

Reetz observes that:

'The 'Madani faction' still draws sharp criticism for its approach in the matter. Some of the critics claim that the scholarly tradition had been replaced by a more policy-oriented superficial activism. Numerous issues remain unresolved, such as the maintenance of school buildings and student hostels. The library and the archives (*muhafiz khana*) showed signs of decline and disorder. Staff members frequently went on leave. Debates that might have redefined the role of the seminary and Islamic teaching in today's world were avoided or deliberately stifled.'[13]

However, the current leadership portrays the period since the split as a success story marked by expansion and modernisation.

Both of the quarrelling factions insist that the differences have less to do with principles than with personal matters. In 1982, the Qasimi or Tayyab group opened a new school called the *Darul Uloom (Waqf)* at another location in Deoband.

The name is derived from the endowment (*awqaf*) land to which they had laid claim in the process of partition. The old school was associated with the 'Madani faction' and portrayed the 'Qasimi faction' as the 'defeated' party that had caused the 'split', and accused them of causing the rift by founding a new school.[14]

Reetz further observes that Maulana Salim Qasimi, Qari Tayyab's son, became rector of the new school. Maulana Anzar Shah Kashmiri was nominated head of the teaching department. He represented a separate 'sub-faction' formed by the offspring of Anwar Shah Kashmiri. He served as *Shaykh al-Hadeeth* and later head teacher of *Darul Uloom* from 1915 to 1927. At the new school, the 'Kashmiri faction' seemed to be gaining ground, as demonstrated by a small but telling detail. A major gate to the premises, previously known as *Bab-i Tayyab*, has been renamed after Anwar Shah Kashmiri.[15]

In a typical illusory manner, the 'Qasimi faction' presented its school as the only true *Deobandi* School, especially in its student recruitment flyers and brochures. In private, however, they were forced to concede that the old school was still regarded as the standard of reference, observes Reetz based on his personal interactions with people, whom he has not named in his paper.

The 'Qasimi faction' considered themselves *Deobandis* in terms of school of thought (*maslak*) and beliefs (*aaqida*) and were waiting to be invited to join the network activities of the main school, an invitation they suggested would be favourably adjudged. In the meantime, they used the increased demand for religious education to consolidate and increase their own share of the market. This expansion was mirrored in the enrolment figures, which had already reached 1,500 and represented about half of the old school figure, wrote Reetz.[16]

Commenting on the establishment of *Darul Uloom (Waqf)*, a new institution founded by Qari Tayyab, Prof Azam says that:

'After taking over the old institution of *Darul Uloom*, Asad Madani had his followers picked up those people including academics and official staff both, whom they felt had any sympathy with Qari Tayyab and terminated their services. The number of these people was around 80-90, they were not given any compensation for terminating their services unilaterally. Having lost their livelihood, they used to come and meet my father (Qari Tayyab) and urge him to start a new institution, where they could be employed and thus be able to take care of their families. Meanwhile Asad Madani faction formed a society under the Society Act and brought *Darul Uloom* under its patronage, whereas my father and others insisted that *Darul Uloom* was and is a Trust. Even the District Judge in Saharanpur District Court, who was deciding this case about the ownership, asked Asad Madani in a very belligerent tone that isn't he ashamed to declare *Darul Uloom* as a society, whereas in reality it is a Trust and has been formed to impart religious education to the Muslims, Asad Madani kept quiet, whereas my father refrained from making any other comment except that *Darul Uloom* is a Trust.'[17]

Elaborating further, Prof Azam says:

'Ultimately in 1983, a few months before the death of my father, as per his desire *Darul Uloom (Waqf)* was established, under the supervision of my eldest brother Maulana Salim Qasmi, as we also had to think about providing employment to those *Ulema* whose services were terminated from *Darul Uloom*. In this endeavour my brother got help from Maulana Anzar Shah Kashmiri. Initially the new institution was started in rented accommodation in and around the houses of Qari Tayyab sahab and his sons, and this situation continued for about 15 years. Later some land was purchased in 1990s and construction of the main buildings of the new institution *Darul Uloom (Waqf)* started.'[18]

Reetz further observes that since the new school was constructed on barren land, plans for expansion would be relatively simple. Meanwhile, the 'Kashmiri faction' (led by Maulana Anwar Shah Kashmiri) established graduate training institutes for computer science and English at *Maahad al-Anwar* here. 'On principle', however, they do not provide these courses at their own *Darul Uloom* so that students are not distracted from their religious studies.

Reetz goes on to say that the family networks that run the *Darul Ulooms* relied on traditional forms of allegiance, while also appealing to *Sufi* traditions. They presented the family as constituting a line of transmission of blessing (*barakat*), which was passed down from father to son more reliably than to unrelated disciples.[19]

This argument was used when Qari Tayyab was first appointed pro-rector in 1922 to refer to the fact that he was a member of Darul Uloom's founder Muhammad Qasim Nanautavi's family. In the 1970s, the private privilege of family rule was replaced by a more competitive game of politics at the institution. However, both the old and new school have now been placed firmly and unceremoniously in the hands of a family faction that no longer seems to advance arguments of spiritual blessing but instead exudes an attitude of sheer expediency based on political and economic survival.[20]

View of the Current Dispensation

Commenting on the controversy and its resolution, Maulana Sufiyan Qasmi, Rector of *Darul Uloom (Waqf)* in an interview with the author, says that:

> 'If we keep aside the causes and reasons, then in this world there are always two views, which usually are diametrically opposed to each other if we analyse it, then we come to the word differences, which could succinctly describe this opposition. But it is a natural fact that the whole construct of nature is based on positive and negative forces, even the Holy *Qur`an* mentions it. Therefore, differences also have two sides, one positive the other negative so the need is which position we adopt and view an issue from

which angle. So this is the fundamental issue, which was referred to even by Hazrat Qasim Nanautavi, Qari Tayyab sahab and then my father Hazrat Maulana Salim Qasmi sahab, also. Basically, the differences were of opinion and philosophy or thinking, and I feel that it was written in fate, and whatever is written in fate, happens. But we also have to see the positive side or the constructive side in every decision of Allah. So with the passage of time, my father thought that he and his contemporaries are in the last stages of their life, so they have two options, either to leave an inheritance of disagreement or leave a message of unity. He felt that whatever we leave today, the community will traverse on those very same lines in the future.

Definitely this was a very excellent and noble thought, and it received guidance from Allah too, as the subsequent events proved, as they progressed in a fruitful manner. When we received the news of Hazrat Maulana Asad Madani sahab falling ill in Madinah, Saudi Arab, then my late father telephoned him, which was a very unexpected call for Maulana Asad.

But this little humane act helped a lot in thawing of relations between the two families, as now the communication process started between the two. My father mentioned about this to me, as I was also a part of this whole issue (*sahib-e mamla*), though in presence of elders the young one can't express their opinion, but when, my father mentioned this to me I agreed with his thoughts and said this will be a historic step. But I also mentioned to him that so far 22 efforts have been made to patch up the affairs between the two families, and the main reason for their failure was that once you want to reach a consensus on any particular issue, then most of the times, the consensus isn't in your favour, as most of those who extend their good offices for the conciliation process are also guided by their own interests, so they counsel accordingly. That's why I very humbly asked my father to keep this within his heart and proceed on his own, as the two main parties (*sahib-e mamla*) to the issue are you and Hazrat Maulana Asad Madani sahab. Whenever you two agree to a certain way forward, then slowly everyone will follow both of you. He accepted my recommendation and also my desire to be a part of this endeavour as a counsel, as I have been part of the whole incident right from beginning.

I mentioned this in front of Maulana Asad sahab also, and he very affectionately said that your recommendation in this regard was very sincere and I fully agree with it, and from our side (Late) Maulana Haseeb Siddiqui sahab would be our representative.

Once the basic issue was resolved, it was not very difficult to solve the rest of the issues, and the message which went to the community was that if you have the sincerity to resolve a matter for the best of the community, putting your personal differences at the back, then you could reach an amicable resolution to any dispute.

This further shows that an issue festering for 23 years could be resolved within 23 minutes. And this really happened. The whole Deoband community, not just in India but globally too, welcomed this initiative warmly.

This also paved a new path for the associates on both sides to come together and work unitedly, besides providing a lesson of compassion and forgiveness to our future generations, too, once the guidelines to achieve them have been earmarked.

The lesson is: in case of differences, put your personal interests at the back. Whatever happened in the past, taking it as the will of God, put your best foot forward to resolve it positively. In the current times, I feel that this message itself is very important and path breaking for the community, which was and is passing through a rough patch.

Another positive feature is that both elders also ensured that this decision was carried forward by their progenies, and they were duty bound to carry it forward, as desired by their elders. And further also transfer it similarly to their future generations. *Alhamdulillah,* my generation and also my progeny, similarly Maulana Mahmood Madani are still steadfastly following the guidance of our elders. So this connection at individual level, family level, organisational level and also the community (*Milli*) level has been established and is continuing.

So *Darul Uloom (Waqf)* is known as a harbinger of promoting the unity of the community. Being sincere to find a united or consensual solution to every issue is one of the key demands of life, but it depends on our abilities how do we view and approach it, and present it. It also has a message of sacrifice within it.

Alhamdulillah, for the last 16 years, from 2006 to 2022, these relations have continued on the same lines of unity and brotherliness, as envisioned by our elders.'[21]

Maulana Mahmood Madani, President of *Jamiat Ulema-i-Hind* and son of Maulana Asad Madani views the whole chain of events as:

'The one which leads to a rather unsavoury taste.' He further adds that, 'the differences which cropped up were really regretful. And many incidents related to those differences happened which makes one rather disturbed. However, one good thing which happened was that the very same elders who had their differences over the style of working, they themselves initiated a conciliatory process and overcame all their differences. Maulana Salim sahab withdrew all court cases against *Darul Uloom*, returned all the funds, frozen in banks, back to the *Darul Uloom* and even gave it in writing that all funds in various banks should be given back to the *Darul Uloom*, Deoband. So these were very sincere and praise worthy steps and this lead to further normalising of strained relations, we meet each other, participate in each other's family functions. We have been able to restore our relationship back to the lines of mutual cooperation with each other and I don't think that anyone has any complaint against any one, any more from both sides. And this is a good and positive development, as both institutions follow a common philosophy, thinking and style.'[22]

This leads us to surmise that the current generation of the leaders at *Darul Uloom* and *Darul Uloom (Waqf)* have been able to forgive the mistakes of the past. Both institutions are ready to function along side each other, and the biggest positive result is both the institutions are prospering, the number of students have increased at the two and both carry on with the main function that is to disseminate the Islamic religious teachings as guided by their elders.

Directions of Change

Reetz further observes that since the split in 1982, the school i.e. the *Darul Uloom* has undoubtedly undergone major changes. From the multitude of school events, this book has focused on four major directions of change:

- From a family network to politics of influence,
- From a school of thought to a well-built network of schools that is becoming more formal and cohesive
- From a 'traditional' mode of operation to the Islamist notion of modernity that includes expansion and technical professionalism
- From religious instruction to the wider pursuit of ideological, political and development concerns

These changes illustrate the winding course of the *Darul Uloom*, Deoband. It faces the challenges of modernity but endeavours to tackle them in the spirit of its own largely ideological mission. It is clear that it is far from being a homogenous school of thought, because it is powerless to prevent the penetration of society's mainstream concerns and perspectives into its body politics.

Its graduates play a decisive role in the creation of new *Deobandi* institutions, which focus to a large extent on development and education issues. Girls' education, computer knowledge, and language qualifications in English and modern Arabic are among the growing demands of the students.

Its administrative operations are also undergoing adjustments. The administrative reports analysed for this book indicate that the school is becoming increasingly more professional by the year. The growth in transparency of the school's operations has been remarkable. Nevertheless, this does not mean it is becoming ideologically more flexible, as it grows more defiant in the face of what it perceives as mounting political adversity.

Looking at the *Darul Uloom*, Deoband, it is difficult

to speak of a crisis of orthodoxy in Islamic education, or of Islamic education in general. The school continues to expand at a rapid rate. At the same time, its financial resources have become more strained. Sustaining the standard of support for students in terms of hostels, food, or medical aid seems more difficult. The school is currently tapping into new private resources to upgrade its infrastructure. Income from the private sector, such as Badruddin Ajmal's contribution to the running of several departments like, Computers, English, *Sheikh-ul-Hind Academy*) could significantly alter how the school is run, if only on the technical side.

It holds fast to its ideological mission, training students in the school's narrow theological dogma and its ideological interpretation of the world. It continues to rekindle sectarianism and polarisation among Muslim groups in India and further afield. Its graduates, however, are still divided over their activist role in society. Most are guided by a contemplative mood and personal piety. The rigours of the school's training make them humble and disciplined servants of the school's cause.

Debates on the school curriculum and its teaching methods will only continue to increase, although the grip that the conservative elders have on the school's philosophy is still strong and uncompromising. The school itself is directly confronted with the problems and demands of a broader society, particularly when it comes to such practical issues as the application of Islamic law in India and other countries. These concerns will continue to stimulate debate and exert pressure on the *Darul Uloom* to adapt to changes in society.

The political and religious impact of the school in India and the rest of the Muslim world has gathered momentum since 1982. Its diversity has likewise increased. Although it became a national institution in India, with students from every Indian state, it remains firmly rooted in the northern Indian states of Uttar Pradesh and Bihar. It is highly influential in West Bengal and neighbouring Bangladesh. Pakistan is still a powerful *Deobandi* centre in its own right, with little evidence of direct influence from the *Darul Uloom* in India.

The *Darul Uloom* continues to be the focus of international attention as long as militant groups in countries such as Pakistan, Afghanistan and Bangladesh adhere to the *Deobandi* doctrine. Its networking in India is becoming increasingly formal and works through the *Association of Deobandi Madrasahs* (RMA), whereas *Deobandi* scholars and schools are linked at the international level via public conferences, youth work meetings, and missionary objectives, and also through *Tablighi Jamaat* channels.

In the academic field, efforts have multiplied to understand the character and dynamics of Islamic schools; however, much of it is politically motivated. Detailed studies that take the concept of the schools and their approach into account, without refraining from critical assessment, are required. Measured against its long history, the *Darul Uloom* is under enormous pressure and is experiencing change at a breakneck speed. Whether this will suffice to ensure its smooth adaptation to a new and radically changing world remains to be seen.[23]

Epilogue

An impartial study of the *Darul Uloom*, its founders, its institutional philosophy, its character and growth, contribution to India's freedom struggle, and service to Indian Muslims from 1886 till date, presents a lofty image of the institution and its leaders. Yet, one wonders what are the reasons for attributing a negative image to the *Darul Uloom*, Deoband.

Perhaps the *anti-Deobandi* narrative started soon after India's independence as pointed out by several scholars in their interactions for this book. The announcement of independence for the country saw Maulana Husain Ahmad Madani shifting his base to Deoband, cutting himself off from the process of being a part of the new polity in the country or sharing the spoils of a new government.

In a way, Deoband sort of barricaded or insulated itself from the outside world. On the other hand, the new political class also didn't encourage the *Deobandi* leaders to play an active role in the governance of the country, due to its adherence to the so-called secular principles. In the years to come, it conveniently used *Darul Uloom* and its leaders, as and when it suited them. Also, over the years the leaders perhaps sought to receive the state's patronage and bounty for themselves individually and not for the institution as a whole.

The absence of an intellectually, religiously and politically robust leadership among Indian Muslims, post-1947, put the community to a great vulnerability. A vacuum was created, which to a certain extent was tried to be filled by nationalist leaders like Maulana Azad, but his untimely death put an end even to that effort. It would not be wrong to say that ever since then, Muslims in India and their institutions like Deoband have had to face the vagaries of time and politics. We cannot identify a single Muslim leader who worked for the community single-mindedly without a hidden agenda.

However, to a certain extent, *Darul Uloom* can be blamed, too. First, not participating as a component of the new polity and secondly, by hiding in a cocoon and even ignoring those advances, initiatives or reforms, which were necessary for the institution for furthering its core aim i.e. education.

Education, knowledge and tradition, like any living entity, need continuous growth and updation. It can take place only when there is a serious engagement with the knowledge of the present era. And the academics at *Darul Uloom* were unable to traverse this path to a large extent. They continued to harp on their glorious past, instead of trying to integrate the past to the requirements of a new era and its demands.

However, the critics must realise that *Darul Uloom* was established to provide Islamic education to its students and they were supposed to lead the vast multitude of Muslims across India. The *Darul Uloom* is just like scores of Sanskrit *pathshalas* or monasteries, which produce Sanskrit and Vedic scholars to lead and perform various Hindu traditions or pujas as per the *Vedic* or *shastra* knowledge. So in that sense it continued singularly on its mission.

Moreover, if *Deobandi* scholars are blamed that they don't possess any knowledge of science or mathematics or language skills in English or Hindi, then it should be remembered that these students are not barred to pursue these subjects. In fact, a large percentage of scholars pursue study in these subjects to increase their chances of employability and also to gain insight into other subjects. As has been covered in the book earlier, *Darul Uloom* itself and several other institutions or organisations affiliated to *Darul Uloom* run courses in English language and computer skills for the students and graduates of *Darul Uloom*. Here it would be pertinent to point out that graduates of *Darul Uloom*, who are also *Hafiz*, possess a unique capacity and ability to recall any verse from the Holy *Qu'ran*. Can any regular school passout claim to remember what he was taught in class III or what was written on page number 89 of his English/Hindi book for that class? This amazing memory retention is possessed by passouts of *madrasahs* only. In fact, some of them after passing out of a *madrasah* have pursued studies in computer science and have become systems analysts/programmers.

In fact, a good many of them become doctors (*hakims*), lawyers and some have even cleared the civil services examinations, all based on their personal quest for knowledge and overcoming those hurdles which many viewed as insurmountable for a *madrasah* graduate. But still a dichotomy persists. In fact, in my interactions with various religious scholars, it was stressed by them that in order to understand the Holy Texts and Islamic intellectual thought, it was necessary to give the students a proficiency in contemporary issues. However, it was difficult for most to pursue this due to a lack of exposure to modern subjects, and their posture seemed to be rather self-protective supported by half-baked vague replies. This might be one of the reasons that you will find that there is no spirit for *Ijtihād* amongst Indian *Ulema*.

Though they agree that there is a need to find a middle path. Yet, few recognised that it was possible to approach the Holy *Qur`an, Hadeeth*, theology or jurisprudence in the light of a modern subjectivity, where newer understandings and meanings could play a central role. To a certain extent, the absence of *Ijtihād* in their common will to face the contemporary topics or issues is also to be blamed.

On the other hand, the West too is to be blamed. First, in being selective and secondly, treating Islam as a monolithic religion. As has been pointed out, Islam and its finer points vary from country to country, and one country where it can be really described as a 'secular' Islam, is India. And by ignoring or castigating the largest institution of Islamic education in that country, and blaming it as one responsible for all evils, is completely erroneous.

Annexure A
Darul Uloom Deoband Syllabus

First year syllabus

Subject	Books
Biography of the Prophet (Sitta)	Seerat-e-Khatimul Ambiya (By: Mufti Mohammed Shafi
Conjugation-Grammar (Sarf)	Arabic Primer; Mizanus-Sarf and Munsha'ib(complete); Panj Ganj (complete)
Syntax (Nahv)	Memorising of Nahv-e Mir (complete); Sharh-e Mi'ata A'mil (complete).
Arabic Literature	Miftahul Arabia, Part 1,2, & Al-qir'atul Waziha, Part 1
Logic	Taiseer al-Mantiq
Chirography (Khush navisi)	Correct Transcription and Dictation
Cantillation (Tajvid)	Exercise in cantillation of the Para-e Amm

Second year syllabus

Subject	Books
Conjugation-Grammar (Sarf)	Ilmus Sigha & Fusool-e-Akbari
Syntax (Nahv)	Hidaytun Nahv (complete) & Kafiya (chapters: Fail & Harf)
Arabic Literature	Al-Qir'atul Waziha (2) & Nafhatul Ab
Jurisprudence (Fiqh)	Noorul Izah & Qudoori (Till Haj chapter)
Logic (Mantiq)	A'san Mantiq & Mirqat
Chirography (Khush navisi)	Correct Transcription and Dictation
Cantillation (Tajvid)	Jamalul Q'uran & Exercise in cantillation of the Para-e Amm

Third year syllabus

Subject	Books
Qur`anic Exegesis	Tarjumatul Qur`an (From Surah Qhaf till end)
Jurisprudence (Fiqh)	Qudoori (From Kitabul Boyoo till end)
Syntax (Nahv)	Sharah Shuzuruz Zahab (complete)
Arabic Literature	Nafhatul Arab & Al-Qri'tul Waziha (3)
Hadeeth	Mishkatul A'thar
Logic	Sharah Tahzeeb (complete)
Islami Akhlaque	Talimul Muta'allim
Cantillation (Tajvid)	Exercise in Cantillation of the first Five para (volumes) of the Holy Qu`ran
Additional Study	Tareekh-e Millat (Khilafat-e-Rasheedia)

Fourth year syllabus

Subject	Books
Qur`anic Exegesis	Tarjumatul Qur`an (From Sura-e Yousuf to Qhaf)
Jurisprudence (Fiqh)	Sharah Wiqayah (Part 1 complete & part 2 up to Itaque)
Principles of Jurisprudence	Tasheelul Usool & Usool-us Shasi
Rhetoric	Darusul Balaghah (complete)
Hadeeth	Al-Fiyatul Hadeeth
Logic	Qutbi (complete)
History	Khilafat-e Bani Umayya, Abbasiya, Turkiya (By: Zamullah Shahabi)
Cantillation (Tajvid)	Exercise in Cantillation of the Five Paras
Modern Sciences	Sciences of Madaniyyat, Geography of the Arab Peninsula and other Islamic Countries

Fifth year syllabus

Subject	Books
Qur`anic Exegesis	Tarjumatul Qur`an (From beginning up to Sura-e Hud)
Jurisprudence (Fiqh)	Hidayah Part 1 (complete)
Principles of Jurisprudence	Noorul Anwar up to Sunnah & Matan Al-minar (from Kitabus Sunnah up to end)
Rhetoric	Mukhtasarul Ma'ani 1st subject & Talkhisul Miftah (2nd & 3rd Subject)
Beliefs (Aqa'id)	Aqidatut Tahavi
Logic	Sullamul Uloom (up to subject of Shartiyat)
Arabic Literature	Muqamat (up to 15 Muqama)
Cantillation (Tajvid)	Exercise in Cantillation of the Five Paras
Additional Study	History of Kingdoms in India (up to 1947 AD)

Sixth year syllabus

Subject	Books
Tafseer	Tafseer Jalalayn (complete)
Jurisprudence (Fiqh)	Hidaya Part 2 (complete with Itaq subject)
Principles of Tafseer & Jurisprudence	Alfauzul Kabeer & Husami (complete)
Arabic Literature	Deevan-e-Mutanabbi (appointed chapter) & Deewan-e-Himasa (Babul Adab)
Philosophy	Mabadiul Falsafa & Mabazi (Complete)
Cantillation (Tajvid)	Exercise in Cantillation of the Five Paras
Study of Sitta	Asahhus Siyer

Seventh year syllabus

Subject	Books
Hadeeth	Mishkat, Sharah Nukhba & Muqadma Sheikh Abdul-Haque
Jurisprudence (Fiqh)	Hidaya Part 3
Aqa'ed	Sharah Aqa'ed
Fara'iz	Sijraji
Cantillation (Tajvid)	Exercise in Cantillation of the Five Paras
Additional Study	Al-Mazahibul Islamia Urdu (Sheikh Abu Zahrara)

Eighth year syllabus (Daura-e Hadeeth)

Subject	Books
Hadeeth	Bukhari (Complete)
Hadeeth	Muslim Sharif (Complete)
Hadeeth	Tirmizi Sharif (Complete)
Hadeeth	Abu Da'ud Sharif (Complete)
Hadeeth	Nasa'i Sharif (Complete)
Hadeeth	Ibn-e Maja Sharif (Complete)
Hadeeth	Tahavi Sharif (Complete)
Hadeeth	Shama'il Tirmizi Sharif (Complete)
Hadeeth	Mu'atta Imam Malik (Complete)
Hadeeth	Mu'atta Imam Moham-mad (Complete)
Additional Study	Tajvid

Annexure B
Members of the Current Majlis-e Shura of the Darul Uloom

1. Mufti Abu Qasim Nomani, Vice-Chancellor, *Darul Uloom*, Deoband
2. Maulana Arshad Madani,
3. Maulana Syed Anzar Husain,
4. Maulana Mahmood Hasan,
5. Maulana Badruddin Ajmal Qasmi, Assam,
6. Maulana Abdul Aleem Farooqui,
7. Maulana Abdus Samad,
8. Maulana Ghulam Mohammed Vastanvi, Maharashtra,
9. Maulana Mahmood Hasan Aqil, Saharapur,
10. Maulana Habi Ahmad Bandwi,
11. Maulana Shafeeq Ahmad Banglorvi,
12. Maulana Ishtiyaque Ahmed Muzaffarpuri,
13. Mufti Mohammed Ismail Qasmi,
14. Maulana Mohammad Aqil Qasmi, Shamli,
15. Maulana Malik Mohammed Ibrahim Qasmi,
16. Maulana Mahmood A. Madani,

17. Maulana Syed Bilal Abdul Hai Hasni, Lucknow,
18. Mufti Ahmed Khanpuri,
19. Maulana Mohammed Rehmatullah Kashmiri,
20. Maulana Anwar ul Rehman Bijnori
21. MaulanaHakim Mohammed Kalimullah

1. Holy Qur`an
2. Cantillation (*Tajvid*)
3. Principles of Exegesis (*Usool-e Tafseer*)
4. Exegesis *(Tafseer)*
5. Commentaries & Scholia of Exegesis *(Shuruh wa Hawashi-e Tafseer)*
6. Commandments of the Holy Qur`an *(Ahkam-e Qur`an)*
7. Words from other languages in the Holy Qur`an *(Gharib Qur`an)*
8. Vowel Points in the Holy Qur`an *(Ira'b Qur`an)*
9. The Abrogating and the Abrogated *(Al-Nasikh wal-Mansukh)*
10. The Causes of Revelation *(Asbab al-Nazool)*
11. Accessories of the Holy Qur`an *(Mutalliqat Qur`an)*
12. The Derivation of the Holy Verses of the Qu`ran *(Istakhraj al-Aayat)*
13. The Topics of the Holy Qur`an *(Mazamin-e Qur`an)*
14. Translations of the Holy Qur`an *(Urdu)*

15. Translations of the Holy Qur`an *(Persian)*
16. Principles of Hadeeth *(Usool-e Hadeeth)*
17. *Hadeeth-e Sihah Sitta* with Commentaries & Scholia
18. *Masanid wa Sunnah* (Collections of Hadeeth)
19. Other Collections of Hadeeth
20. The Fabricated Hadeeths *(Mauzuaat)*
21. Foreign Words in Hadeeth *(Gharib al-Hadeeth)*
22. The Derivation of Hadeeth *(Istakhraj al-Hadeeth)*
23. The Art of Determining the Authenticity of the Narrators of Hadeeth *(Asma al Rijaal)*
24. Principles of the Hanafi Jurisprudence *(Usool-e Fiqh-e Hanafi)*
25. Principles of the Shafi'i Fiqh
26. Principles of the Maleki Fiqh
27. Principles of the Hanbali Fiqh
28. Principles of Fiqh of Ahl-e Hadeeth
29. The Hanafi Fiqh
30. *Fatawa-e Hanafi* (The Hanafi Fatwas)
31. The Maleki Fiqh
32. The Shafi'i Fiqh
33. The Hanbali Fiqh
34. The Externalists Fiqh *(Fiqh-e Ahle-Zahir)*
35. The Fiqh of the Followers of Hadeeth *(Fiqh-e Ahle-Hadeeth)*
36. The Duties *(Fara'iz)*
37. The Science of Beliefs & Scholastic Theology *(Ilm-e Aqa'id wa kalam)*
38. The Religio-legal knowledge *(Hikmat-e Shari'yaah)*
39. The Science of Sufism (Prose) *(I'lm-e Tasawwuf* in Prose)
40. The Science of Sufism (Poetry) *(I'lm-e Tasawwuf* in Poetry)
41. The Science of Sufism (Epistles) *(I'lm-e Tasawwuf-Maktubaat)*
42. The Science of Sufism (Ana) *(I'lm-e Tasawwuf-Malufuzaat)*

43. Remembrance Formulae, Daily Offices & Theurgy (*Award, Waza'if & Amaliyaat*)
44. Sermons & Morality (*Mawa'iz wa Akhlaq*)
45. Arabic Literature (Prose)
46. Arabic Literature (Poetry)
47. Rhetoric (*'Ilm-e Maa'ni*)
48. Syntax (*I'lm al-Nahv*)
49. Conjugation (*I'lm al-Sarf*)
50. General History
51. History of Civilisation & Culture
52. History of Sciences and Religions
53. The Prophet's Biography (*Sirat al-Nabi*)
54. Biographies of the Companions
55. Biographies of Jurist-Consults, Traditions & other Ulema
56. Memories of the Ulema of Deoband
57. Biographies of Eminent Saints
58. Memories of Poets
59. Encyclopedia (*Da'irat al-Ma'arif*)
60. Travel Holy books
61. Particulars of Darul Uloom, Deoband
62. Genealogies (*Ansaab*)
63. Catalogue of Holy books (*Faihrist al-Kutub*)
64. Collective
65. Miscellaneous
66. The Science of Geology (*I'lm-e Tabaqat al-Ard*)
67. The Science of Chemistry (*I'lm al-Kimiya*)
68. The Natural Sciences
69. The Science of Phonology & Animals
70. Curriculum of holy books of Kuwaiti & Egyptian *madrasahs*
71. Politics

72. Philosophy
73. Logic
74. Astronomy
75. Economics
76. Newspaper & Journals
77. Sociology & General Knowledge
78. Geography
79. Medicine *(Tibb)*
80. Interpretation of Dreams
81. Holy books of the Abrahamic Scriptures *(Kutub-e Ahle-Kitab)*
82. Holy books of Hindu Scriptures and Religious Code
83. Principles of Polemics
84. Holy books of Different Religions
85. Refutation of Christianity
86. Holy books of Christianity
87. Refutation of Qadianism
88. Holy books of the Qadiani Sect or Religion
89. Refutation of Innovation
90. Holy books of the Innovation
91. Refutation of the Schismatic *(Radd-e Wafiz)*
92. Holy books of the Shia Sect
93. Refutation of Naturalism
94. Refutation of *Khaksarism* (Allama Mashriqi's Movement)
95. Holy books of the *Khaksarism*
96. Refutation of the *Mahdavi* Sect
97. Holy books of the *Mahdavi* Sect
98. Holy books of the *Bahai* Sect
99. Refutation of the *Bahai* Sect

Bibliography

Al Hai, Hakim Sayyid Abd (1994) *Hindustan Ka Nisab-e Dars Aur Uske Taghayyurat*. Lucknow: Tanwir Press.

Ali, Riyasat (2009) *Ezah-ai Bukhari*. Deoband. Maktaba Majlis Qasim-ul Maarif.

Bastavi, Shaukat Ali Qasmi (2015) Darul Uloom Deoband Ka Nisab-e Ta'lim). Deoband: Daftar: Darul Uloom.

Deobandi, Abdul Karim Farogh (1978) *Masnavi Farogh*. Kanpur: Nizami Press.

Deobandi, Mian Sayyid Asghar Husain (1977) *Hayat-e Sheikh al-Hind*. Idara-e Islamiyat: Lahore, Pakistan.

Deobandi, Mohammad Mian (1975) *Tehrik-e Sheikh al-Hind*. Delhi: AIJami'at Book Depot.

Gangohi, Rasheed Ahmed (1890, repr. 2003) *Fatawa Rasheedia*. Delhi: Maktaba Rahimiya.

Gilani, Manazir Ahsan (1966) *Musalmano Ka Nizam-e Ta'lim O Tarbiat*. Delhi: Nadvat ai-Musannafin.

Kandhalwi, Mohammad Zakariyah (1972) *Tarikh-e Mazahir-e Ulum, Saharanpur.* Saharanpur: KutubKhana-e Isha'at al-Ulum.

Madani, Sayyid Husain Ahmed (1953) *Naqsh-e Hayat.* Delhi: Dilli Printing Works.

Rizvi, Mahboob S (1972) *Tarikh-e Deoband.* 2nd ed. Deoband: Azad Press.

Sherkoti, Anwar al Hasan (1968, repr. 2014) *Anwar-e Qasimi.* Karachi: Maktaba Darul Uloom: Karachi.

Siddiqi, Zafeer Uddin (1962, repr. 2002) *Fatawa Darul Uloom Deoband.* Karachi, Darul Ishaat.

Sindhi, Ubaidullah (1944) *Shah Wali Ullah Aur Unki Siyasi Tehrik.* Lahore: Mercantile Press.

Sindhi, Ubaidullah *(1995) Zati Diary.* Lahore: Makki Darul Kutub.

Tayyab, Qari Mohammad (1967) *Rudad-e Darul Uloom Deoband:* A.H. 1283 to A.H. 1360 & A. H. 1371 to A. H.1390. Deoband: Daftar Darul Uloom.

Tayyab, Qari Mohammad (1967) *Rudad-e Amal-e Darul Uloom Deoband:* from A.H. 1383 to A.H.1396. Deoband: Daftar Darul Uloom.

Tayyab, Qari Mohammad (1967) *Rudad-e Darul Uloom Deoband (Tehsil-e Ghalla):* A.H. 1332 to A.H. 1374. Deoband: Daftar Darul Uloom.

Tayyab, Qari Mohammed (1966) *Dar-al-Ulum Ki Sau Sala Zindagi.* Deoband: Daftar Darul Uloom.

Glossary

Adl: Justice

Alim (plural/Ulema): Arabic word meaning learned person; these days the term is often used to describe members of Muslim clerical establishment.

Aqidah: Belief

Asma al-rijal: A collection of biographies of Hadeeth narrators within the Islamic discipline of biographical evaluation by the 12th-century Islamic scholar Abd al-Ghani al-Maqdisi

Brahin: Evidence, witness, symbol

Dar-al Ifta: Centre for Jurisprudence

Deen: Religion

Falsafa: Philosophy

Faqih: Jurist

Fatwa: A non-binding scholarly legal opinion

Fikr: Thought process

Fiqh: Islamic Law, another term used frequently is *Shariah*

Hijri: Islamic calendar based on the date of *hijrat* of Prophet Muhammad (PBUH) from Makkah to Madinah

Ihtemam: Arrangements

Ijazat a : A certificate or licence to teach

Ijtihād: Independent legal reasoning, intellectual effort

Ilm-i Kalam: Dialectical theology

Ilm: Knowledge

Imaan: Belief

Insha: Creation, origination

Ishraq: Prayers, Optional after-sunrise prayers

Istidlal: *Istidlal* is a method of juristic deduction not falling within the scope of analogy. The *Hanafi* jurists use the word more or less in the sense of inferring a thing from another thing in connection with the rules of interpretation

Jihad-fi Sabillah: Religiously sanctioned military efforts

Kanqaha: A *pir's* abode

Madaris: Plural of *madrasah*

Madhahib: Legal academies or guilds, law schools or rites lay Muslims follow

Maktab: Primary-level religious schools

Manhaj: Methodology of receiving, analysing and applying knowledge.

Mantiq: Logic

Maslak: Describes how an institutional memory of virtuous conduct is constructed, sustained, and cherished by folk who follow tradition

Muatta: Easy and soft or a well-trodden path

Mufti: An expert jurist authorised to issue scholarly opinions called fatwas

Muhaddith/Muhaddis: Transmitter or Interpreter of *Hadeeth*

Mutakallims: Speaker

Nahv: Way or manner

Nisab: Syllabus

Nizam: System
Para: One volume of the Holy *Qur`an*
Riyazi: Mathematics
Safeer: Ambassador
Sahabah: Companions of Prophet Mohammad (PBUH)
Sanad: Degree or a certificate
Sarf: Expenditure
Shariah: Often translated as Islamic law, but actually a moral discourse that proposes ethical guidelines for society
Sunnah: A precedent established by Prophet Mohammad (PBUH)
Tafseer: Exegesis, usually of the Holy *Qur`an*. An author of *Tafseer* is a *mufassir*
Taqlid: To follow
Tasawwuf: Name for the inner or esoteric dimension of Islam, which is supported and complemented by outward or exoteric practices of Islam
Tawheed: Divine unity
Tazbih: Rosary, Beads
Tehzeeb: Culture
Tibb: Medicine
Usool: Principles
Waqf: An endowment
Wasiyat/Wasiyatnaama: Will

References

Darul Uloom, Deoband

1. Bowering, Gerhard (2012) *Princeton Encyclopedia of Islamic political thought*. Princeton: Princeton University Press.

2. Metcalf, Barbara (2004) *Islamic revival in British India: Deoband, 1860-1900*. New York: Oxford University Press. pp. 87-94.

3. Spannaus, Nathan (2018) 'chapter on, Darul Uloom Deoband and south Asian Islam in the Deobandi network, in Bano Masood's (2018) *Modern Islamic authority and social change*. Edinburgh: Edinburgh University Press.

4. Bano, Masooda *The Deobandi Network: Steadfast in Taqlid: Modern Islamic Authority and Social Change*, P 195 Vol. I, Edinburgh University Press, ISBN: 978 1 4744 3322 8)

5. Baber, Mohammed (n.d.) *Role of Ulema-e Deoband in the Indian Independence movement*. [Online] Retrieved from: http://www.imws.org.uk/5-role-of-Ulema-e-deoband-in-the-independence-movement/

6. Qasmi, Khursheed Alam Dawood (n.d.) *Role of Darul Uloom Deoband in India's freedom struggle*. [Online] Retrieved from: http://hamariweb.com/articles/50210

7. Shah, Sayed Wiqar Ali. *Khan Abdul Gaffar Khan*. Quaid-i-Azam University in Islamabad. [Online] Retrieved from: www.baachakhantrust.org/abdulghaffarkhan.pdf.

8. Mahboob, Rizvi S (1972) *Tarikh-e Deoband*. 2nd ed. Deoband: Azad Press.

9. Ibid.

10. Ibid.

11 Metcalf, Barbara (2004) *Islamic revival in British India: Deoband, 1860-1900*. New York: Oxford University Press.

12. Ibid.

13. Al Hasani, Sayyid Mohammad, *Sirat-e Maulana Sayyid Mohammad Ali P 13*. Lucknow: Academy of Islamic Research & Publications.

14. Darul Uloom Deoband (n.d.) [Online] Retrieved from: http://www.darululoom-deoband.com/english/

15. Maulana Muhammad Tayyab. (1957) *Azadi-e Hind Ka Eik Khamosh Rehnuma*. Deoband: Darul Uloom. p. 9.

16. Smith, Wilfred Cantwell (2006) *Modern Islam in India A social analysis*. Minerva Book Shop, Lahore, pakistan.

History of Darul Uloom

1. Metcalf, Barbara (2004) *Islamic revival in British India: Deoband, 1860-1900*. New York: Oxford University Press.

2. Planning Commission (2021) *Profile of Saharanpur District*. New Delhi: Government of India. [Online] Retrieved from: www.planningcommission.gov.in/reports/sereport/ser/ stgpnt/stgpnt_ch2.pdf

3. Mahboob, Rizvi S (1972) *Tarikh-e Deoband*. 2nd ed. Deoband: Azad Press.

4. Moosa, Ebrahim (2015) *What is a Madrasa?* New Delhi: Dev Publishers & Distributors.

Shah Waliullah Dehlavi

1. Waliullah, Shah (n.d.) *Studying Islam.* [Online] Retrieved from: http://www.studying-islam.org/articletext.aspx?Id=642
2. Gilani, Manazir A (2005) *Hazrat Shah Waliullah.* Deoband: Hafzi Book Depot.
3. Ibid.
4. *Biography – Shah Waliullah* (n.d.) [Online] Retrieved from: http://www.darulihsan.com/index.php/downloads/articles/item/3330-biography-shah-waliullah--?Tmpl=component&print=1
5. Ikram, Sheikh M (1957) *History of the Freedom Movement. Vol.1.* Karachi: Pakistan Historical Society.
6. Gilani, Manazir A (2005) *Hazrat Shah Waliullah.* Deoband: Hafzi Book Depot.
7. Ibid.
8. Ibid.

Madrasahs in India Prior to 1896

1. Qazi, Moin (2017) *A look at 150 years of India's Deoband seminary, Darul Uloom.* [Online] Retrieved from: https://www.dailyo.in/variety/darul-uloom-deoband-islamic-teaching- Madrasahs/story/1/16545.html
2. Ibid.
3. Khan, Zafarul Islam (2010) *Origins of Madrasas in India predates Muslim period.* [Online] Retrieved from: http://www. milligazette.com/news/178-origins-of-Madrasahh-education- in-india-predates-muslim-period
4. Huda, Kashif-ul-(2010) in his article *System of Islamic Education in Kerala* https://twocircles.net/2010jan05/system_islamic_education_kerala.html

5.   Khan, Yusuf Husain (1957) *Glimpses of medieval Indian culture*. Bombay: Asia Publishing House.

6.   Ibid

7.   Nadvi, Abdul Hasanat (1971) *Hindustan ki qadeem Islami dargahain*. Azamgarh: Maktba-i-Maarif, Azamgarh. p. 15.

8.   Ibid.

9.   Ibid.

10. Khan, Yusuf Husain (1957) *Glimpses of medieval Indian culture*. Bombay: Asia Publishing House.

11. Ibid.

12. Ibid.

13. Ibid

14. Nadvi, Abdul Hasanat (1971) *Hindustan ki qadeem Islami dargahain*. Azamgarh: Maktba-i-Maarif, Azamgarh. p. 15.

15. Gilani, Maulana Manazir Ahsan (1944) *Hindustan mein Musalmanon ka Nizam-i-Talim wa Tarbiyat*. Delhi: Nadwatul Mussanefin, Delhi. pp. 13-15.

16. Ashraf, Kanwar M (1959) *Life and conditions of the people of Hindustan 1200-1500 AD*. Delhi: Jiwan Prakashan Educational Publishers. p.145.

17. Ibid.

18. Ibid.

19. Ibid.

20. Shahidullah, Mohammad (1985) *A brief history of Madrasa education in India*. Calcutta Madrasah College Bicentenary Celebration, Calcutta. p.6.

21. Ibid.

22. Ibid.

23. Gilani, Maulana Manazir Ahsan (1944) *Hindustan mein Musalmanon ka Nizam-i-Talim wa Tarbiyat*. Delhi: Nadwatul Mussanefin, Delhi. pp. 13-15.

24. Ibid.

25. Naumani, Shibli (n.d.) *Maqalat-i-Shibli*, 3/102-3, Vol. 5
    Azamgarh: Darul Musanefin Shibli Academy. [Online]
    Retrieved from: https://archive.org/details/MaqalatEShibli/
    Maqalat%20E%20Shibli%202/page/n5/mode/2up

26. Gilani (1944) *Op.cit.*

27. A f, Shams Siraj (1891) *Tarikh-i-Firuzshahi*.
    Calcutta: Asiatic Society. pp. 339-340.

Educational System in Darul Uloom

1. Rizvi S. Mahboob (1972) *Tarikh-e Deoband*. 2nd ed.
   Deoband: Azad Press.

2. Makdisi, George (1989) 'Scholasticism and humanism
   in classical Islam and the Christian West'. *Journal of The
   American Oriental Society*, Vol. 109, No. 2, pp. 175-182.

3. Makdisi, George (1970) 'Madrasa and university in the
   middle ages'. *Studia Islamica*, No. 32, pp. 255-264.

4. The system of education (2014) [Online
   Retrieved from: https://dn790001.ca.archive.org/0/items
   CurriculumDarseNizami/curriculum%20darse%20nizami.
   pdf

5. Makdisi, George (1970) 'Madrasa and university in
   the middle ages'. *Studia Islamica*, No. 32, pp. 255-264.

6. Ibid.

7. Ibid.

8. The system of education (2014) [Online
   Retrieved from: https://dn790001.ca.archive.org/0/items
   CurriculumDarseNizami/curriculum%20darse%20nizami.pdf

9. Moosa, Ebrahim (2015) *What is a Madrasa?* New Delhi:
   Dev Publishers & Distributors.

10. The system of education (2014) [Online]
    Retrieved from: https://dn790001.ca.archive.org/0/items/
    CurriculumDarseNizami/curriculum%20darse%20nizami.pdf

11. Rizvi S. Mahboob (1972) *Tarikh-e Deoband*. 2nd ed.
    Deoband: Azad Press.

12. Abd-al-Qādir Badā ūnī (1884) *Muntekhab Tawarikh-e
    Badauni*. Calcutta: J.W. Thomas, Baptist Mission Press. p. 86.

13. Bilgrami, Mir Ghulam Ali Azad (2008) *Ma'athir Al-Kalaam*.
    pp. 238, 260.

14. Rizvi S. Mahboob (1972) *Tarikh-e Deoband*. 2nd ed.
    Deoband: Azad Press.

15. The system of education (2014) [Online]
    Retrieved from: https://dn790001.ca.archive.org/0/items/
    CurriculumDarseNizami/curriculum%20darse%20nizami.pdf

16. Moosa, Ebrahim (2015) *What is a Madrasa?* New Delhi:
    Dev Publishers & Distributors.

17. The system of education (2014) [Online]
    Retrieved from: https://dn790001.ca.archive.org/0/items/
    CurriculumDarseNizami/curriculum%20darse%20nizami.pdf

18. Moosa, Ebrahim (2015) *What is a Madrasa?* New Delhi:
    Dev Publishers & Distributors.

19. Ibid.

20. Ibid.

21. Ibid.

22. Rizvi S. Mahboob (1972) *Tarikh-e Deoband*. 2nd ed.
    Deoband: Azad Press.

23. Ibid.

24. Ibid.

25. Ibid.

26. Ibid.

27. Ibid.

28. Ibid.

29. Ibid.

30. Ibid.

31. Ibid.

32. Ibid.

33. Ibid.

34. Lord Macaulay's address to the British Parliament (1834) [Online] Retrieved from: https://historum.com/threads/lord- macaulay%e2%80%99S-address-to-the-british-parliament-in- 2-february-1835.26268/

35. Rizvi S. Mahboob (1972) *Tarikh-e Deoband*. 2nd ed. Deoband: Azad Press.

36. Ibid.

37. Ibid.

38. The system of education (2014) [Online Retrieved from: https://dn790001.ca.archive.org/0/items/ CurriculumDarseNizami/curriculum%20darse%20nizami.pdf

39. Ibid.

40. Rizvi S. Mahboob (1972) *Tarikh-e Deoband*. 2nd ed. Deoband: Azad Press.

41. The system of education (2014) [Online] Retrieved from: https://dn790001.ca.archive.org/0/items/ CurriculumDarseNizami/curriculum%20darse%20nizami.pdf

42. Gangohi, Maulana Rasheed Ahmed (2023) [Online] Retrieved from: http://haqislam.org/maulana-rashid-ahmad-gangohi/

43. Ahmad, Aijaz. (2014) The Revolt of 1857 and Maulvi Fazle Haq Khairabadi. Retrieved from: https://archive.org/stream/maulvifazlehaqkhairabadi/maulvi%20FAZLE%20HAQ%20KHAIRABADI_djvu.txt

Darul Uloom's Administrative and Academic Structure

1. The Darul Uloom's system of education (2014) [Online] Retrieved from: https://dn790001.ca.archive.org/0/items/CurriculumDarseNizami/curriculum%20darse%20nizami.pdf

2. Rizvi S. Mahboob (1972) *Tarikh-e Deoband*. 2nd ed. Deoband: Azad Press.

3. Ibid.

4. Ibid.

5. Metcalf, Barbara (2004) *Islamic revival in British India: Deoband, 1860-1900*. New York: Oxford University Press.

6. Ibid.

7. Ibid.

8. The Darul Uloom's system of education (2014) [Online] Retrieved from: https://dn790001.ca.archive.org/0/items/CurriculumDarseNizami/curriculum%20darse%20nizami.pdf

Women's Education at Madrasahs

1. Aliyah, Zainab (2015) Great women in Islamic history: A forgotten legacy. [Online] Retrieved from: https://www.youngmuslimdigest.com/study/02/2015/great-women-islamic-history-forgotten-legacy/

2. Qazi, Moin (2018) Lost legacy of female scholars of Islam. [Online] Retrieved from: https://www.dailysabah.com/feature/2018/07/05/lost-legacy-of-female-scholars-of-islam

3. Khatun, Joynab (2016) 'Islamic education in India with especial reference to the women sector of India.' *International Research Journal of Interdisciplinary & Multidisciplinary Studies*, Vol. II, Issue. VIII, pp. 80-86. [Online] Retrieved from: http://oaji.net/articles/2016/1707-1475499660.pdf

4. Batawi, Tharwat Al (2017) *The doyennes of learning.* [Online] Retrieved from: https://en.qantara.de/content/women-and-arab-islamic-education-the-doyennes-of-learning

5. Aliyah, Zainab (2015) Great women in Islamic history: A forgotten legacy. [Online] Retrieved from: https://www.youngmuslimdigest.com/study/02/2015/great-women-islamic-history-forgotten-legacy/

6. Nadwi, Akram (2013) *Al Muhaddiath: The women scholars in Islam.* 2d revised edition. (s.l.): Interface Publications.

7. Wafy, Muhammed Nafih (2017) All-female Madrasas: Of women, by women and for women. [Online] Retrieved from: https://en.qantara.de/content/islamic-education-in-india-all-female-Madrasahs-of-women-by-women-and-for-women?nopaging=1

8. Khatun, Joynab (2016) 'Islamic education in India with especial reference to the women sector of India.' *International Research Journal of Interdisciplinary & Multidisciplinary Studies,* Vol. II, Issue. VIII, pp. 80-86. [Online] Retrieved from: http://oaji.net/articles/2016/1707-1475499660.pdf

10. Ibid.

11. Ibid

12. Bewley, Aisha Abdurrahman (1999) *Islam: the empowering of women.* London: Ta-Ha Publications.

13. Rahman, Shaikh Azizur (2013) Madrassas in India attract Hindu. [Online] Retrieved from: https://www.aljazeera.com/indepth/spotlight/indiaonline/2013/11/Madrasas-india- attract-hindu-students-2013111814457229891.html

Darul Uloom's Role in India's Freedom Struggle

1. Bowering, Gerhard (2012) *Princeton encyclopaedia of Islamic political thoughtI.* Princeton: Princeton University Press.

2. Goyal, D R (2004) *Maulana Ahmed Husain Madani A biographical study*. New Delhi: Anamika Publishers and Distributors.

3. Madani, Maulana Husain Ahmad (2005) *Muttahida qaumiyyat aur Islam*. New Delhi: Manohar Publishers & Distributors.

4. Ibid.

5. Metcalfe, Barbara (2005) Preface to Maulana Husain Ahmad Madani's, *Muttahida qaumiyyat aur Islam*. New Delhi: Manohar Publishers & Distributors. pp. 23-24.

6. Fatima, Ambreen (2019) Silk letter movement: A freedom struggle woven in silk. [Online] Retrieved from: http://heritagetimes.in/silk-letter-movement-a-freedom-struggle-woven-in-silk/

7. Retrieved from: https://journals.scholarsportal.info browse/03056139/v07i0002

8. Fatima, Ambreen (2019) Silk letter movement: A freedom struggle woven in silk. [Online] Retrieved from: http://heritagetimes.in/silk-letter-movement-a-freedom-struggle-woven-in-silk/

9. Ibid.

10. Ikram S.M. (1992) *Indian Muslims in the partition of India*. New Delhi: Atlantic Publishers and Distributors. pp. 261-262.

11. Saharanpur. [Online] Retrieved from: www.britannica.com/place/saharanpur+&cd=21&hl=en&ct=clnk&gl=in

12. Engineer, Asghar Ali (2008) *Muslim minority continuity and change*. New Delhi: Gyan Publishing House. [Online] Retrieved from: http://drasgharaliengineer.csss-isla.com/wp-content/uploads/2017/09/muslim-minority-continuity-and-change.pdf

13. Tabassum, Farhat (2006). *Deoband Ulema's movement for the freedom of India.* New Delhi: Manak Publication Pvt. Ltd. p. 184.

14. Ibid.

15. Ibid.

16. Ibid.

Western Media's View of Darul Uloom

1. Moosa, Ebrahim (2015) *What is a Madrasa?* New Delhi: Dev Publishers & Distributors.

2. Ibid.

3. Ibid.

Indian Media's Portrayal of Darul Uloom

1. *List of stories done by various news channels and newspapers on Darul Uloom's fatwas*

a. Darul Uloom's new fatwa says it's not good to hug people on Eid. [Online] India Today. Retrieved from: https://www.indiatoday.in/india/story/deoband-darul-uloom-fatwa-hug-embrace-eid-saharanpur-up-clerics-1543367-2019-06-05

b. Mehendi, not nail polish during namaz: Darul Uloom Deoband's new fatwa. [Online] NDTV. Retrieved from: https://www.ndtv.com/cities/darul-uloom-deoband-issues-fatwa-which-says-Muslim-Women-Cant-Wear-Nail-Polish-When-Offering-Namaz-1943145

c. Sin for man and woman to eat together at public events: Darul Uloom Deoband fatwa. [Online] DNA. Retrieved from: https://www.dnaindia.com/india/report-sin-for-man-and-woman-to-eat-together-at-public-events-darul-uloom-deoband-fatwa-2698355

d. Islamic seminary Darul Uloom Deoband issues fatwa banning muslim women from grooming eyebrows. [Online] Firstpost. Retrieved from: https://www.firstpost.com/india/islamic-seminary-darul-uloom-deoband-issues-fatwa-banning-muslim-women-from-grooming-eyebrows-4121393.html

e. Darul-Uloom Deoband bans muslim women from cutting nails, using nail polish in new fatwa. [Online] Zeenews. Retrieved from: https://zeenews.india.com/india/darul-uloom-deoband-bans-muslim-women-from-cutting-nails-using-nail-polish-in-new-fatwa-2153157.html

f. Darul Uloom Deoband fatwa: marrying non-Muslims is haram for Muslims (2011) [Online] MEMRI India | Special Dispatch No. 3900. Retrieved from: http://www.thememriblog.org/blog_personal/en/35192.htm

g. Darul Uloom Deoband: women cannot preach or deliver sermons (2011) [Online] MEMRI India | Special Dispatch No. 3900. Retrieved from http://www.thememriblog.org/blog_personal/en/34606.htm

h. Darul Uloom Deoband fatwa: donating blood is un-Islamic (2011) [Online] MEMRI India | Special Dispatch No. 3900. Retrieved from: http://www.thememriblog.org/blog_personal/en/32486.htm

2. Engineer, Irfan (2014) 'Fatwas and Muslim Women'. *Secular Perspective*, August. [Online] Retrieved from https://csss-isla.com/secular-perspective/fatwas-and-muslim-women/

3. Qazi, Moin (2017) India's Emerging Modern Madrasahs. [Online] The Diplomat. Retrieved from: https://thediplomat.com/2017/03/indias-emerging-modern-madrasas/

4.	Sikandar, Zainab (2020) Indian media waging holy war against Muslim hyenas. [Online] The Print. Retrieved from: https://theprint.in/opinion/indian-media-waging-holy-war-against-muslims-hyenas/400407/

5.	Ibid.

6.	Chaddha, Rajender (2002) Madrasahs: A centre of education or a nursery of terrorism. [Online] Hindu Vivek Kendra. Retrieved from: http://www.hvk.org/2002/0302/16.html

7.	Bunga, Avantika; Kumaran, Gopika and Rao, Shreyasi. (2019) Situating the Madrasa in Modern India: Is Reform Around the Corner? [Online] The Bastion. Retrieved from: https://thebastion.co.in/politics-and/education/situating-the-Madrasa-in-modern-india-is-reform-around-the-corner/

Darul Uloom in the Subcontinent

1.	Barelvi Islam. [Online] Global Security.Org. Retrieved from: https://www.globalsecurity.org/military/intro/islam-Barelawi.htm

2.	Moosa, Ebrahim (2015) *What is a Madrasa?* New Delhi: Dev Publishers & Distributors.

3.	Who are the Taleban? (2022) [Online] BBC News. 20 December 2022. Retrieved from: https://www.bbc.com/news/world-south-asia-11451718

4.	Shias killed in Gilgit sectarian attack. (2012) [Online] BBC News. 16 August 2012. Retrieved from: https://www.bbc.com/news/world-asia-19280339

5.	Iran condemns terrorist attacks in Pakistan (2017) [Online] Tehran Times. 17 February 2013. Retrieved from: https://www.tehrantimes.com/news/412254/Iran-condemns-terrorist-attack-in-Pakistan

6. Abrams, Dennis (2007) *Hamid Karzai.* New York: Chelsea House, Infobase Publishing. p. 14.

7. Hayes, L. D. (1987) *The crisis of education in Pakistan.* Lahore: Vanguard Books.

9. Ahmad, Mumtaz (2004) Madrasa education in Pakistan and Bangladesh. In: Limaya S P et al. (eds) (2004) *Religious radicalism and security in south Asia,* Honolulu: Asia Pacific Centre for Security Studies. [Online] Retrieved from: http://www.apcs.org/Publications/Edited%20Volumes/ReligiousRadicalism/ReligiousRadicalismandSecurityinSouthAsia.pdf

10. Ibid.

11. Ibid.

12. Ibid.

Darul Ulooms in South Africa and the United Kingdom

1. Bano, Masooda (2018) The Deobandi network: steadfast in taqlid, modern Islamic authority and social change. In: Bano, Masooda (2018) (eds.) *Modern Islamic authority and social change,* Volume 1 Evolving debates in Muslim majority countries. Edinburgh: Edinburgh University Press. p. 195.

2. Yasien, Mohamed (2002) Islamic education in South Africa. *ISIM Newsletter* Vol. 9, Issue. 30.

3. Ibid.

4. Ibid.

5. Tayob, Abdulkader et al. (eds.) (2011) Muslim schools and education in Europe and South Africa. Münster, München, New York: Waxman. pp. 85, 101.

6. Ibid.

7. Ibid.

8. Jame' Masjid – Leicester. [Online] Retrieved from: https://www.jameah.co.uk/

9. Office for standards in education, children's services and skills, UK. [Online] Retrieved from: https://www.gov.uk/government/organisations/ofsted

10. IMWS Al-Hikmah Centre. [Online] Retrieved from: http://www.imws.org.uk/outstanding-darul-uloom-achieve-highest-ofsted-grade/

11. Jame' Masjid – Leicester. [Online] Retrieved from: https://www.jameah.co.uk/

12. Ibid.

Differences between Deobandi, Barelawi and Ahl-e Hadeeth Sects

1. Khan, Hassan S et al. (eds.) (2016) *Indentured Muslims in the diaspora: Identity and belonging of minority groups in plural societies*. New Delhi: Manohar.

2. Sanyal, Usha (2012) *Ahmad Raza Khan Barelwi: In the path of the Prophet*. (PBUH): Simon and Schuster.

3. Metcalfe, BarbaraD(2009)Islamic revival in BritishIndia, Deoband 1860-1900. Princeton: Princeton University Press.

4. Lewis, Martin W (n.d.) Deobandi Islam vs. Barelawi Islam in South Asia". [Online] Geocurrents. (n.d.) Retrieved from:https://www.geocurrents.info/blog/2010/10/07/deobandi-islam-vs-barelvi-islam-in-south-asia/

5. Misbahi, Yaseen Akhtar, (2014) Introduction of Ahle Sunnat wal Jama'at. Delhi: Darul Qalam.

6. Interview with the Author

7. Interview with the Author

8. Interview with the Author

9. Metcalfe, Barbara D (2009) *Islamic revival in British India, Deoband 1860-1900*. Princeton: Princeton University Press. p. 267.

Split in Darul Uloom

1. Reetz, Dietrich: Islam in the public sphere, *The Madrasa in Asia: Political Activism and Transnational Linkages. The Madrasa in Asia* (2008) Retrieved from: https://www.jstor.org/publisher/amsterdamup

2. Ibid.

3. Ibid.

4. Ibid.

5. Ibid.

6. Interview with the author Nov 2022

7. Ibid.

8. Ibid.

9. Ibid.

10. Reetz, Dietrich: Islam in the public sphere, *The Madrasa in Asia: Political Activism and Transnational Linkages. The Madrasa in Asia* (2008) Retrieved from: https://www.jstor.org/publisher/amsterdamup

11. Ibid.

12. Interview with the author Nov 2022

13. Reetz, Dietrich. *The Madrasa in Asia* (2008) Retrieved from: https://www.jstor.org/publisher/amsterdamup

14. Ibid.

15. Ibid.

16. Ibid.

17. Interview with the author Nov 2022

18. Ibid.

19. Reetz, Dietrich. *The Madrasa in Asia* (2008) Retrieved from: https://www.jstor.org/publisher/amsterdamup

20. Ibid.

21. Interview with the author May 2023

22. Interview with the author June 2023

23. Reetz, D (2008) Op.cit

Comments by Maulana Wahiduddin Khan (Late), Maulana Abu Qasim Nomani, Maulana Arshad Madani, Maulana Asrarul Haq Qasmi (Late), Maulana Mahmood Madani, Maulana Syed Rabey Hasani Nadwi, Maulana Saeed-ur Rehman Azmi, Prof Akhtar-ul Wasey, Maulana Rashid Kandhalwi, Maulana Kahlid Saifullah Rahmani, Ajay Upadhyay, John Butt, Prof Ebrahim Moosa, Maulana Sufiyan Qasmi, Maulana Nadeemul Wajedi, Dr Waris Mazhari and Dr Faheem Akhtar Nadvi, are based on interviews conducted by the author between 2015 to 2022.